Intestine Enemies

Intestine Enemies

Catholics in Protestant America, 1605–1791

A DOCUMENTARY HISTORY

Edited by Robert Emmett Curran

The Catholic University of America Press · Washington, D.C.

The paper used in this publication meets the minimum requirements of
American National Standards for Information Science—Permanence of
Paper for Printed Library Materials, ANSI Z39.48-1984.
∞

Library of Congress Cataloging-in-Publication Data
Names: Curran, Robert Emmett, editor.
Title: Intestine enemies : Catholics in Protestant America, 1605–1791
a documentary history / edited by Robert Emmett Curran.
Description: Washington, D.C. : The Catholic University of America
Press, 2017. | Includes bibliographical references and index.
Identifiers: LCCN 2016050350 | ISBN 9780813229348 (pbk. : alk. paper)
Subjects: LCSH: Catholic Church—North America—History. |
Catholic Church—West Indies—History.
Classification: LCC BX1403.3 .I58 2017 | DDC 282/.709032—dc23
LC record available at https://lccn.loc.gov/2016050350

Contents

Part 6. Protestant Uprisings and Triumphs, 1666–1698

Part 7. Internal Outcasts, 1704–1774

Maps

Preface

Papist Devils: Catholics in British America, 1584–1783 (Washington, D.C.: The Catholic University of America Press, 2014) told the story of a largely unwelcome minority in the colonial period of the British Atlantic world. It covered their first faltering efforts at colonization in the late sixteenth and early seventeenth centuries; traced their presence in the proprietary colonies of the mid-seventeenth century where Catholics, if not recruited, were at least tolerated up to a certain point; and noted their largely forgotten contributions to the development of the British West Indies (Barbados, Montserrat, and Jamaica). It delineated the peculiar culture that Catholics on the North American mainland fashioned to cope with the legal marginalization that Protestant society imposed upon them. And finally it pointed up the impact of the wars of the latter eighteenth century in transfiguring their place in the colonies of Britain's American Empire that through conflict gained their independence.

   Devils utilized a broad range of public and private records—from broadsides, newspapers, and legislative acts to correspondence, diaries, and reports—to portray the life of Catholics in the British Atlantic world from New York to Barbados and Nova Scotia to Jamaica over the course of the two centuries that spanned colonization to independence. The present volume, *Intestine Enemies: Catholics in Protestant America, 1605–1791*, treats the same history but by a different means: selected primary sources bridged by contextualized introductions in the place of an analytical narrative. It has culled the most representative documents from among the array of sources upon which *Papist Devils* was based. It affords readers the opportunity to have firsthand access to this history rather than the derivative experience that narratives provide. It can, of course, also serve as a complement to *Papist Devils*. Both volumes cover the Catholic experience in British America from the first quarter of the seventeenth century to the last quarter of the eighteenth.

The vast majority of Catholics who migrated into British America were subjects of the British crown, mostly from England and Ireland. France, Germany, and Africa each accounted for significant minorities among the immigrants. Many of the arrivals from Great Britain began their American lives in a bonded state, but one normally limited by contract to four or five years. Not so for those Catholics who were African-born or of African descent— nearly all of whom knew a life of endless bondage extending from generation to generation. Relatively few Catholic gentry, much less those of higher rank, immigrated to British America. Nonetheless, the Catholic minority populations in Maryland and Pennsylvania produced a disproportionate number of individuals who, as merchants and/or planters, became highly significant members of the economic elites in those provinces, despite legal barriers that prevented them from enjoying the full rights of citizenship.

During that 150-year period, even in those colonies where Catholics were the legal owners or controlled the government, Catholics were still regarded as aliens in the land because the land, as an extension of England/Great Britain, was fundamentally Protestant, inasmuch as to be truly English was to be a "liege" of the sovereign, which typically included an oath of loyalty to the king who was the head of the Church of England and another oath that amounted, for most Catholics, to a renunciation of their faith. Such oaths Catholics were not wont to take, thereby rendering themselves outsiders and more than perennial suspects, indeed "intestine enemies," which became a stock epithet for Catholics in the eighteenth century. To be Catholic was a virtual declaration of being an enemy to English institutions and tradition.

The American Revolution turned that world upside down. That Catholics played a part in winning the war and shaping the new republic that went considerably beyond what their miniscule proportion of the population would have suggested may well have contributed to the radical change that Catholics experienced in their place in American society. (The colonies' mid-war alliance with Catholic France that turned the tide in the favor of the American rebels, it should be noted, was also a major factor in changing the Catholic image in Protestant America.) Nothing illustrated the new order better than did the oath-taking that most of the newly constituted states, including Maryland, insisted that adults take in the midst of a war that was essentially a civil one. Unlike the oaths that had been employed by colonial governments to identify and restrict Catholics, these wartime ones did not impinge on one's religious faith. Maryland, the state, like the original Calvert government, regarded religion as a private matter, not a prerequisite for citizenship. A dedication to the common good now trumped any religious affiliation. Suddenly Catholics were no longer aliens in a hostile land but, as John Carroll later observed, in a land that they could at last call "our own." With their religion no longer an automatic disqualifier, the path to full citizenship had opened for Catholics. Most took it.

A cursory look at the table of contents will reveal how ethnic- and gender-centric the otherwise rich sources in this anthology are. Virtually all the voices are those of English or Irish males. To the extent that other males or females appear in these sources, it is through those British male voices. Yet, while recognizing this shortcoming in the documentary history that this volume attempts to do, in the end I think these sources, limited as they are, allow us, through their multiple perspectives, a valuable cross-view of the changing world that Catholics were part of in British America.

A word about the editing practices I have chosen to apply to the peculiarities of colonial calligraphy. In general, for maximum legibility, abbreviations have been written out in full (e.g. "wh" to "which"). Superscripts (w^h) have been replaced with normal or standard script. The colonial thorn (y) has been converted to "th," as has the "f" to "s." As for those documents written in French or Latin, unless otherwise noted, the translations are mine. For the better blending of those documents that are transcriptions with those that are translations, I have modernized the colonial spelling of the former, except in the rare instances when modernization impedes comprehension.

Among those I would like to acknowledge for providing the sources that made this volume possible are Tricia Pyne and Alison Foley at the Associated Archives of St. Mary's University and Seminary; Damon Talbot of the Maryland Historical Society; and Lynn Conway, Scott Taylor, and Elizabeth Wilkinson at the Georgetown University Library Special Collections Research Center. The revisions that the two anonymous reviewers recommended have made this volume far better by its recasting. And special nods to Trevor Lipscombe, director of the Catholic University of America Press, who once again sowed the first seed of this project; to Theresa Walker, who once more exemplified what a managing editor should be; and to Aldene Fredenburg, whom I have been thrice blessed to have as copy editor. Hard to fail with such favorable winds behind you.

Abbreviations

AAB	Archives of the Archdiocese of Baltimore
AASMUS	Associated Archives of St. Mary's University and Seminary
AM	*Archives of Maryland*
APF	Archives of the Congregation for the Propagation of the Faith (Propaganda Fide)
BT	Board of Trade
CHR	*Catholic Historical Review*
CSP	Colonial State Papers
GULBFCSC	Georgetown University Library Booth Family Center for Special Collections
HSJNA	*History of the Society of Jesus in North America*
JCP	*John Carroll Papers*
LC	Library of Congress
MG	*Maryland Gazette*
MHM	*Maryland Historical Magazine*
MHS	Maryland Historical Society
MPA	Maryland Province Archives of the Society of Jesus
PRO	Public Record Office
USCH	*United States Catholic Historian*
WL	*Woodstock Letters*

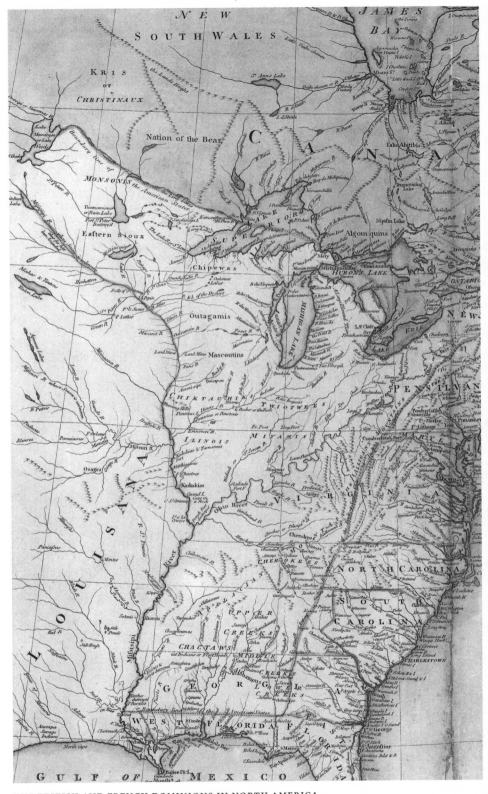

THE BRITISH AND FRENCH DOMINIONS IN NORTH AMERICA

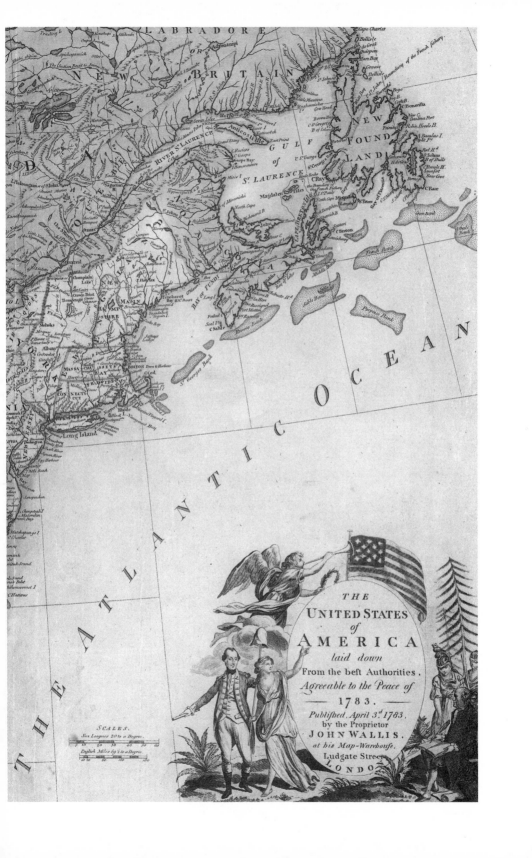

THE
UNITED STATES
of
AMERICA
laid down
From the best Authorities,
Agreeable to the Peace of
1783.
Published, April 3ᵈ 1783,
by the Proprietor
JOHN WALLIS.
at his Map-Warehouse,
Ludgate Stre
LONDO

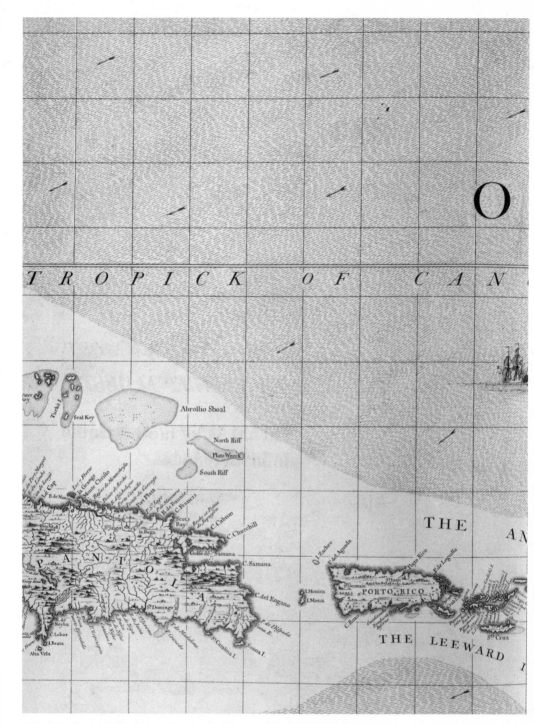

THE BRITISH EMPIRE IN AMERICA: LESSER ANTILLES ISLANDS

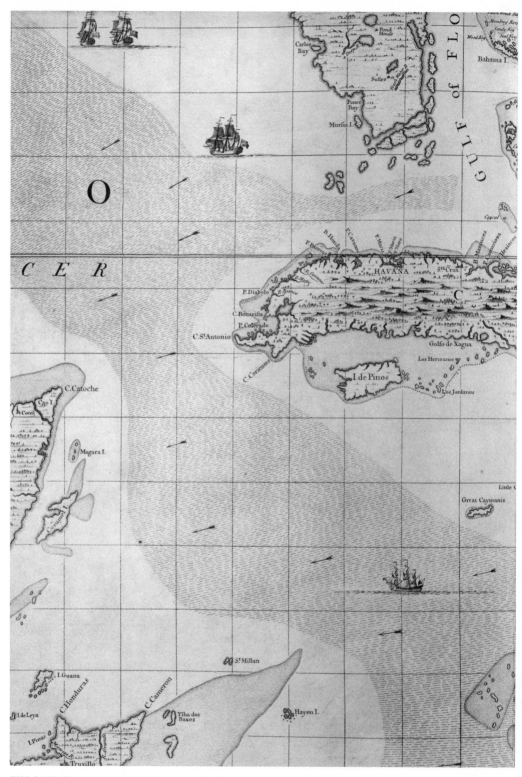

THE BRITISH EMPIRE IN AMERICA: JAMAICA

LUCAYOS OR BAHAMA ISLANDS

Mangrove Key
Man of War Key
Little Guana Key
Sotowe Key
Lucayos or
Abaco I.
Little Harbour
Hole in the Rock

Road
Rocks

North I.
Overbos I.

Biemnis I.
Keys
Prigues

Berry I.

Harbour I.
Alabaster Rocks
Æthera I.
Rocky Bank
Salt Key
Key
Long I.
Providence
Powel's Pennd

Andros Islands

Green Key

Ship Channel
Exuma
Sound

Cat I.

Little I.
Watling's I.

Juan Carcina
B.de Cadiz

Dutch Key

Lobos Key

Ragged I.

Jumentos Keys

Stocking I.

Exuma I.

Long I.

Rum Key

Atwood's Keys

French Keys

Maguana I.

Crooked I.

Heneago Key
West Caicos I.
Caicos
Bank

Verde I.
I.Mira
parvos

Ashlin's Keys

Hogshes

Heneago I.

U

B

St. Spirito

S. Covano

St. Julian

St. Cruz

Romano

C.Quibanico

Bota de
Caravelas

Mucares I.

A

Mancanilla

Caymanis
Caymanbrack

Bendrone

P.Qem

B.Parquin
B.de Sevilla
Sevilla Nueva

St.Jago

P.Perulla
Machancin

P.Palmas
P.Escondido

Bayorques

C.Mayze

P.de Jean Rond

Tortuga I.

THE WINDWARD

C. St.Nicolas
Mole St.Nicolas
C. aux Foux

C.Crux

P. de la Seringue
Cap Donna Maria

I.Gonave

P.des Irois
P.Tiberon

Navaza I.
P.des Asgruttos
P.del Chardennes
I.Anse à Vest
Pere Zabel
Pointe à Gravois

JAMAICA

Green I.
Orange Bay

Blewfields Bay

Cavallon
Aquin

Cotes de Fer

Port a Prot
St.Louis

I.de Vache

I Gonave

H I

Serranilla

Intestine Enemies

Beginnings

1605–1629

NGLISH EXPLORATION and settlement of the new world beyond the Atlantic took place amid the latter stages of the religious
revolution brought on by Henry VIII's passion-driven quest for di-
vorce, which ended in his declaration of independence from papal authority and the assumption of national ecclesiastical primacy for himself and
his successors. At Henry's death in 1547, the crown passed to his nine-year-
old son, Edward. The boy's second regent, John Dudley, Earl of Warwick,
oversaw the lightening-quick imposition of a radical Reformed template on
the church that Henry had taken over but had left basically undisturbed in
doctrine and practice. When the boy king died at fifteen in 1553, the crown
passed to Mary Tudor, Henry's first-born by Catherine of Aragon. A fervent
Catholic, Mary promptly managed through Parliament a legal restoration of
Catholicism as the religion of the land, a reversal that the public seemed to
welcome. But reestablishment of the ancient faith was not enough for the
queen, who proceeded to set in motion a bloody purge of several hundred
leaders of the recently planted Reformed Protestantism. Public opinion began to turn against her. She worsened her public standing with her marriage

to Philip II of Spain, England's ancient enemy. Disastrous military adventures on the Continent only accelerated her plummeting popularity.

Mary's vindictive reign lasted barely longer than that of her half-brother. Upon her natural death in 1558, her half-sister Elizabeth inherited the throne. The new queen gradually but relentlessly restored order to the nation and Protestantism as the Church of England—albeit not without even deadlier retribution against Catholics than Mary had inflicted upon Protestants. Executions and imprisonment were but the extreme manifestation of the penal legislation that Elizabeth initiated, which effectively outlawed the profession and practice of Catholicism in her kingdom. By Elizabeth's death in 1603, the church that she had devised as a middle ground between Catholicism and Calvinism was firmly established as the official faith of the kingdom.

During those seventy turbulent years the institutional Catholic Church had been rooted out: churches and monasteries either taken over or destroyed; priests and nuns exchanging old vows to God and pope for new oaths to a monarch, or becoming exiles on the Continent, or facing prison and the scaffold. Catholic resistance took various forms. One was the militant, epitomized by the revolt of the Catholic earls in the northern shires in 1569 and the attempted invasion of the Spanish Armada two decades later. More common was the polemical war waged by English clerical refugees on the Continent, such as Robert Persons, the Jesuit and former Oxford don who initially in his tracts proposed a military solution through Spanish bottoms and arms for the restoration of Catholicism, then, with the failure of the force option and the reluctant realization that the Catholic community in England was not a silent majority in need of being roused to revolt but a tiny, permanent minority, Persons began pushing for toleration as the official policy for Catholics.

Beginning in the 1570s, the missionary movement sent a stream of priests, both religious and secular, from their bases of exile on the Continent to England to revive and expand Catholicism's footprint there. Utilizing the scattered manors of the Catholic gentry as their center for ministry, the Jesuits, Benedictines, and other missioners stealthily served the saving Catholic remnant in preserving and spreading the faith. More than a few paid with their lives for their evangelism (it being a capital offense for a Roman priest to be in the country). By the late sixteenth century, the Catholic community in England had been reduced to certain pockets of the more traditional, less economically advanced sections, such as the seven counties along the northern tier of the country. With the coming of the Stuarts to the throne in 1603, their Catholic wives were responsible for the emergence of a "court Catholicism" around the queen's circle and the Catholic embassies in London.

Conditions for Catholics began to improve somewhat during the first years of James's rule with a relaxation of the enforcement of the penal laws, only to have the thaw in relations suddenly end in November of 1605 with the exposure of the Gunpowder Plot of some Catholic gentry hotheads to blow up king and Parliament. In its rush to impose justice, the crown made little effort to discriminate in its executions between would-be assassins and the innocent caught up in the government's sweep. On a broader level, Parliament enacted a new set of penal laws to contain and shrink the Catholic community, including oaths that, to many Catholics, forced a choice of allegiance between monarch and pope. Once again the minuscule Catholic community, perhaps numbering 40,000–50,000 in a population of four million, found itself in a state of siege.

Colonization planning by Catholics would seem to have been a natural course of action for a community living under the weight of penal laws, if not persecution. In fact, over the course of the first half century of the penal age set in motion by Elizabeth I's Act of Uniformity of 1559, there were fewer than a handful of such plans that envisioned the New World as, at least partly, a refuge for Catholics. Perhaps one reason for the scarcity was, as George Calvert discovered in the next century, the reluctance of the Catholic gentry to abandon their traditional lands, bleak as their situation might be. Catholic planning for colonization, rare as it was, tended to happen in periods when the pressure upon Catholics was particularly severe.

One such plan had its birth in the first decade of the seventeenth century when the new king, James I, with a Catholic wife and a Catholic past (having been raised in the faith), sparked Catholic hopes for toleration, if not restoration, only to dash them by reactivating Elizabeth's penal law machinery against the Catholic community. Desperate to relieve his afflicted fellow Catholics, Sir Thomas Arundell of Wardour looked to colonization. Arundell eventually involved several others in the scheme, including his Protestant brother-in-law, the Earl of Southampton. At some point Tristram Winslade, a Cornish Catholic, was brought into the undertaking. Winslade, like a good many frustrated Catholics in the British Isles in the late sixteenth century, had found an outlet in service to the Continental armies of Catholic sovereigns, most frequently the Spanish. Winslade brought to the colonization project the idea of recruiting fellow veterans to provide a defense force for the would-be plantation in the New World. They were the core of a thousand recruited Catholics of all classes who were to convene in a to-be-designated European port where they would be outfitted and supplied for the voyage to Norumbrage, evidently somewhere on the Maine coast. Besides his recruiting contacts, Winslade's Spanish military background provided him another valuable asset that apparently led the colonizers to involve him in their enterprise: his ability to secure support for the intended colony from the Hapsburgs whom he had formerly served. What we know is that in early 1605 Tristram Winslade wrote to the Jesuit émigré in Rome Robert Persons, whose connections to the top circle of the Spanish Hapsburg court were well established, to seek his assistance in securing strategic backing from the Spanish crown for the English Catholic colonial enterprise (see "Many Great Difficulties ... Scarcely to Be Superable").

Sir Thomas Arundell, as it happened, sent out a ship to explore the coast of Maine as a possible site for his colony. That was as close as the project came to becoming a reality. The anti-Catholic repression that followed the exposure of the Gunpowder Plot in 1605 effectively eliminated the possibility of Catholic colonization during King James's reign. Indeed his son, Charles, had succeeded to the throne before another Catholic nobleman, George Calvert, a relative (by marriage) of Lord Arundell, revived the prospect of colonization two decades after Arundell had given up his pursuit.

George Calvert was a secretary of state to King James in 1625 when he returned to the practice of the Catholic faith he had been pressured as a boy to disown, apparently to pursue a Trinity College education available only to members of the Church of England. Once again a Catholic, Calvert, for unrelated political reasons, resigned as secretary of state. Despite his reconversion, upon stepping down from office, he was rewarded by James with a title, "Lord Baltimore," and an enormous Irish estate. Calvert, however, had his larger sight on establishing a plantation much farther into the Atlantic world than Ireland. The year before he submitted his resignation, George Calvert had obtained a charter to erect a colony in the southeastern peninsula of Newfoundland, which he called Avalon, where he had already established a settlement. Once freed of government office, the new Lord Baltimore began to concentrate on his Newfoundland plantation. He already had taken on a Carmelite priest, Simon Stock, to assist him in London.

Very quickly Stock got caught up in Calvert's colonizing plans, becoming in effect his chief assistant in establishing and promoting Avalon. Stock's chief focus was on securing the support of the Congregation for the Propagation of the Faith in getting priests for the colony (see "To Establish Missions in All Those Lands").

George Calvert did not get to Avalon until making a brief visit in the summer of 1627. He returned the following spring with a group of around fifty Catholics, including family, relatives, and a secular priest. The previous year Lord Baltimore had secured through Stock two other secular priests to provide for the colonists' spiritual needs. But Calvert had no intention of making Avalon an exclusively Catholic settlement. Not only were the colonists a mix of Catholics and Protestants, but there was also an Anglican minister, Erasmus Stourton, in the colony. Whether Calvert had been responsible for the minister's presence in Avalon or Stourton had made his own way there, Calvert very quickly utilized his services in an ecumenical arrangement that had to have been unique in all the dominions of England. The proprietor had the Catholic and Protestant clergy conduct services in his house at the very same time. That highly irregular arrangement proved scandalous to Stourton, or so he claimed (see "Every Sunday [They] Saith Mass").

Lord Baltimore survived the Anglican informant's attempt to put an end to his Newfoundland settlement. The Privy Council was not about to condemn Calvert, who had so recently been one of them. But what Protestant intrigue failed to do, other more natural forces did. By the summer of 1629 Calvert sadly concluded that Avalon was a terrible site for the manor-centered colony that he hoped to establish. Once again he petitioned the king, now James's son, Charles, for a charter in an area more than a thousand miles south of his present colony—one that was claimed by England's oldest colony, Virginia (see "I May Yet Do the King and My Country More Service There").

Soon after dispatching his letter to the king, George Calvert, not waiting for Charles's response, boldly headed to Virginia with his family and most of the settlers at Avalon to find a new site. If Calvert had any expectation of a cooperative reception in Virginia, he should have known better. His involvement as the king's principal secretary in the rescinding of Virginia's charter five years earlier was still a very sore point with provincial officials. If the leaders of the crown's oldest colony had little reason to cordially receive a man who was responsible for their losing their independence, they had even less cause once Calvert divulged his purpose in coming into the Chesapeake region: to transfer his Newfoundland settlement there.

To prevent Baltimore from going any further to implement his plan, Virginia officials insisted that he take the customary oaths of loyalty and supremacy to the crown in order to remain within the colony (see "I Do ... Abhor, Detest and Abjure ... This Damnable Doctrine"). As they almost surely anticipated, Calvert, as a conscientious Catholic, refused to do so. For their part the Virginia officials would not consider accepting an oath that Calvert proposed as a substitute. Baltimore left for London shortly afterward to pursue the securing of a new charter that would grant him land in the region. William Claiborne, of the governor's council, followed Calvert to England to work his own high-placed connections to foil Calvert's quest. With him he carried to the Privy Council a letter from Virginia officials explaining their refusal to allow Lord Baltimore to remain in their colony (see "No Papists Have Been Suffered to Settle Their Abode Amongst Us").

1

"Many Great Difficulties ... Scarcely to Be Superable": Robert Persons on English Catholic Colonization in North America, 1605

Winslade's letter is no longer extant, but Persons's response makes clear that the Cornish Catholic was hoping that Persons could parlay his own high connections with Spanish and Italian royalty into critical, if covert, support for Arundell's undertaking. For his own part Persons found several red flags among the plans that Winslade divulged to him that allowed him to provide only scant encouragement to the potential colonizers. Even from the distance of Rome, the Jesuit knew all too well how fragile the condition of the English Catholic community was. What were Persons's particular concerns about involving the Hapsburgs in the project that led him to such negative conclusions? Do they seem legitimate reasons for the planners to cut their losses and cancel the expedition? Or is Persons merely protecting the interests of the English Catholic community and the Jesuit mission to that community?

Robert Persons (Rome) to Tristram Winslade, March 18, 1605[*]

The intention of the author and the good and godly ends proposed by him and diverse good particularities of means and helps, whereby to arrive to those ends discreetly . . . I like very well; but yet, for the execution and putting in use the enterprize itself, I find many great difficulties, which seem to me scarcely to be superable;[1] as among others these that follow.

First, for England itself, it is very likely that the King and his counsel will never allow of it, apprehending the same as not only dishonorable to them but dangerous also; . . . and out of this one head will grow many and great difficulties or rather impossibilities.

Secondly, for the Catholics to be drawn to the enterprize will be a very hard matter, for that the better and richer sort, in respect of their wealth and commodities at home and of the love of the country and fear of the state, will disdain commonly to hear of such a motion; the poor sort without the rich will be of small importance, besides that they do depend wholly of the rich and of their counsel; and the difficulty of getting out will be common to all.

Thirdly, I do persuade myself that, if this proposition should be begun or imparted to any Prince abroad without communicating the same first in England, it would be very ill taken by the Catholics generally, as a matter sounding to their discredit and contempt to have, as it were, their exportation to Barbarous people treated with Princes in their name without their knowledge and consent; the Heretics also would laugh and exprobrate[2] the same unto them, as they did when Sir George Peckham and Sir Thomas Gerrard, about xx[3] years gone, should have made the same viage[4] to Norembrage[5] by the Queen and council's consent with some evacuation of Papists as then they called them; which attempt became presently most odious to the Catholic party.

Fourthly, it may be more than probable thought that this attempt may be very prejudicial to the increase of Catholic religion in England, not only by decreasing the number of Catholics there, and thereby discouraging the rest and making them more contemptible to their adversaries, but also by

---

[*] Thomas Hughes, *History of the Society of Jesus in North America: Colonial and Federal; Documents*, vol. 1, part 1 (New York, Bombay, and Calcutta: Longmans, Green, 1908), 3–5.

1. Able to be overcome. 2. Censure.

3. Twenty. 4. Voyage.

5. Somewhere on the upper coastline of North America, most likely along that of present-day Maine.

exasperating the King and estate against them as unquiet and practicing[6] people; and so, by restraining their going out and in, the entrance of Priests and coming of scholars to the Seminaries would be more narrowly looked unto under that pretence; Priests also could not find sufficient harbour in England; and other such like things would probably follow.

Fifthly ..., wither and to what place or port shall they come that first come out of England, to wit, the first 1,000 of diverse sorts of husband men, laborers and craftsmen required by the Author; and so, supposing they might get forth freely, how shall they be maintained, and where, until their passage be ready; for no prince will easily admit 1,000 strangers into his country together without jealousy; especially if they shall offend also thereby the King and state of England.

Sixthly, I do see a mighty difficulty in behalf of the King of Spain and his counsel, who are so jealous that no strange nation take footing in any part of the Indies, as not any particular man ... though he have lived never so long in Spain, can get licence once to go thither, but by great sute and surties;[7] and then may we imagine what they will think of the going thither of a whole nation, which may in time, upon many occasions of state or otherwise, become their enemies though they be Catholics; neither is it sufficient to say that those parts are not presently occupied by the Spaniards; for they will answer, they may be in time, and that is no reason, ... the case of the Spaniards is, that no other European nation have footing in that continent besides them selves, ... and for this cause they made such haste and put them selves to such labours and charges to extinguish the Frenchmen that were in Nova Francia; and the like no doubt would they do to the English if they should go thither without their licence; the which to obtain I hold it for impossible; yet may it be attempted if any man will take it in hand.

Seventhly, it follows that we shall have very little hope to deal with his highness or with the Archduke of Flanders, or any other Prince of Italy that is friend to the King of Spain, except first the said King be dealt withall....

The collections also to be made about the world for furnishing the enterprize would have very doubtful events[8] in my opinion, and perhaps offend not only the King of England but the Catholics also, to be spoken of in pulpits for such a journey; for that the people would not so much look

6. Adhering to the Catholic religion; nonconforming to the Anglican Church.
7. Sute and surties: by petitions and pledges.
8. Outcomes.

in to the last ends of converting those Barbarous people as into the first apprehension of their flight.

Finally, what their success would be amongst those wild people, wild beasts, unexperienced air, unprovided land, God only knoweth; yet, as I said, the intention of converting those people liketh me so well and in so high a degree, as for that only I would desire my self to go in the journey, shutting my eyes to all other difficulties, if it were possible to obtain it; but yet, for that we do not dele[9] here for ourselves only but for others also, we most look to all the necessary circumstances, whereof the first and of most importance are in my opinion that the matter be broken in England and Spain, wherein for many reasons I may not be the breaker; but if those ii[10] were once obtained, I would then be willing to do in Rome what lieth in me; and this is all that I can say in this matter.

2

"To Establish Missions in All Those Lands Which the English Hold in America": Simon Stock's Correspondence with the Congregation for the Propagation of the Faith, 1625–1631[*]

When or how Simon Stock (c. 1576–1652) came into George Calvert's life is unknown. Stock, née Thomas Dougherty, was an English native who, at the rather advanced age of thirty or so, entered the Jesuits' English College in Rome, about the time its rector, Robert Persons, was being approached by Tristram Winslade. There Dougherty prepared for the priesthood and the English mission that was still taking shape. A year or two after his ordination in 1610, Dougherty entered the novitiate of the Discalced Carmelites in Brussels. Shortly af-

---

[*] Luca Codignola, *The Coldest Harbour of the Land: Simon Stock and Lord Baltimore's Colony in Newfoundland, 1621–1649*, trans. Anita Weston (Kingston and Montreal: McGill-Queen's University Press, 1988).

9. Delay.

10. Two.

ter taking his vows as a Carmelite and assuming the name of Simon Stock in honor of the thirteenth-century prior general of the English Carmelites, the order opened a mission in England. Stock was the first member sent there, in 1615. By 1620 the English Carmelite had established himself as a writer (he would publish five books between 1618 and 1623) and as a confessor at the Spanish embassy, eventually serving as the personal confessor of several Spanish ambassadors. Sometime late in 1624 Stock met Calvert, probably through the latter's work as James's liaison with the Spanish in the crown's unsuccessful attempt to forge an alliance through the marriage of his son, Charles, to the Spanish Infanta Maria Anna. The Carmelite claimed to be the catalyst for Calvert's conversion (or reconversion).

To what does Stock appeal to persuade Propaganda to commit priests to this new frontier for the church that Calvert is establishing? Why does Avalon represent, in Stock's estimation, such a vital geo-religious stake for the Catholic Church?

Simon Stock to [Propaganda Fide], London, February 8, 1625[*]

Among those others whom I have here converted to Our Holy Faith there is a lord of a land some three weeks' distance by sea from Great Britain, where our Holy Faith has never been preached. And in the spring this gentleman means to return to his land with his servants (some of whom I have converted) and desires to take with him two or three religious to sow the Holy Faith in his land. Here we are no more than three, and our two companions are ill. For this reason I conceived of writing most humbly to Your Most Illustrious and Revered Worships to beg your help in this holy undertaking. The land of this gentleman was unknown in former times[11] and has had no name until now, when we have called it Avalon [since] thus was named that land where St. Joseph of Arimathea first preached the Faith of Our Lord Jesus Christ in Britain. It lies three degrees closer to the meridian than England and is a most fertile land, of a temperate air, with an abundance of divers sorts of vessels, and most abundant fish, and most excellent sea-ports. The inhabitants are gentiles[12] and English heretics who went to live there some three or four years since. And it would now be an easy matter to plant there

[*] Archives of the Congregation for the Propagation of the Faith, vol. 347, ff. 291 rv, 298rv. B: 298r, in Codignola, *Coldest Harbour*, 77.

11. Stock reveals here how little he knows of Newfoundland, which, contrary to his assertion, was probably the best-known portion of what became British America. As Codignola observes, Stock's basic difficulty in speaking about Avalon was his failure to apprehend that Avalon was part of Newfoundland; see Codignola, *Coldest Harbour*, 176.

12. Indigenous people.

our Holy Faith since the principals are converted. And if the Holy Church offer no assistance at this time, all will become heretics, to the great detriment of the Holy Church.[13]

Simon Stock to [Propaganda Fide], London, May 31, 1625[*]

After that [letter] that I have written to Your illustrious Lordships one week ago, His Majesty of Great Britain has in a public edict announced his intention of propagating heresy in the western parts of America, of which I wrote in my last letter. For this reason it is of absolute importance that the Holy Roman Church establish missions in all those lands which the English hold in America, such as Virginia, Bermuda, New England, New Scotland, Newfoundland, etc. Since they will thus infest with heresy not only America, but also Japan, China, the Philippines and the East Indies, so near are they and of such easy journey and passage, as I wrote in my last.

Simon Stock to [Propaganda Fide], London, December 5, 1625[†]

Here there is great persecution. Many priests have been seized and thrown into prison, and the king has commanded by public edict that all anti-Catholic laws be executed with greater vigour even than the laws themselves command, without giving cause or reason other than the zeal of propagating Protestantism.

In Virginia the English heretics have founded a college to infest America with their heresy. Most humbly do I beg Your Most Illustrious Worships to remember the Avalon mission, for if the Faith be not planted there at this time, all will become pernicious heretics, to the great detriment of the Holy Church.

Simon Stock to [Propaganda Fide], London, January 1, 1631[‡]

I only received Your Most Eminent Worships' letters of June 22 in late December. And as for matters in Avalon, two fathers of the Society[14] went

---

[*] APF, vol. 347, ff. 227rv, 234rv. B: ff. 227v, 234r, in Codignola, *Coldest Harbour*, 84.

[†] APF, vol. 101, ff. 29rv, 32rv. B: ff. 29v, 32r, in ibid., 91.

[‡] APF, vol. 100, ff. 263 rv, 266 rv. B: f. 266r, in ibid., 121–22.

13. Propaganda responded in late March that, with the pope's approval, they were creating a mission to Avalon, to be staffed preferably by Carmelites, under Stock's immediate direction; see Codignola, *Coldest Harbour*, 78–79.

14. Society of Jesus (Jesuits).

thither around Easter of the year 1629 and returned here before the following feast of the Nativity of Our Lord. They brought with them to England
nearly all the Catholics who were there, leaving behind some thirty heretics
and two or three Catholic women, with no priest or minister. They say that
the winter before their arrival there was extremely cold and the earth sterile.
I have spoken with the principal gentleman of that place, and he is sorry to
be back and says that it is his intention to return thither once more, and that
the fathers of the Society have a mission or a special commission for those
places in America.[15]

3

"Every Sunday [They] Saith Mass
and Do Use All Other Ceremonies of
the Church of Rome": Erasmus Stourton
before the Justices at Plymouth,
October 1628*

Whatever his motives, upon returning to England in September of 1628, Stourton testified
before two justices of the peace at Plymouth about Calvert's flagrant disregard for the penal
laws, not only by having priests saying Mass but, worse, allowing a Catholic priest to baptize a Protestant child against the will of the child's father. Surely the Anglican priest must

---

*Erasmus Stourton examination at Plymouth, October 9, 1628, PRO, CSP 1, no. 4, at Colo-
ny of Avalon website; http://www/colonyofavalon.ca/index.

15. The "principal gentleman" is Lord Baltimore. By 1631 Calvert had no intention of returning to Avalon, but was struggling to secure a charter for a new colony, more than a thousand
miles south of Newfoundland. Stock's confusion reveals how far removed he now was from Lord
Baltimore's circle. If the Carmelite is reporting Calvert faithfully here, it is difficult to discern
just what the latter could have been referring to. There is no evidence that, at this early date, any
agreement had been reached between the Society of Jesus and Calvert about the Jesuits' supplying members to work in the colony he hoped to establish in the Chesapeake region. Nor did the
Society have a special commission from pope or congregation to work in the New World. Codignola thinks he is referring to negotiations then taking place between Baltimore and the Society
that had already resulted in the departure of the two Jesuits for Newfoundland; see Codignola,
Coldest Harbour, 187n261.

have expected, if such doings were prohibited by law in England, that that same law should apply throughout the imperial realm, even in Newfoundland. Did it? What was behind the Anglican minister's recourse to the Privy Council? Does the fact that Stourton's testimony was given under oath make it of greater significance?

The examination of Erasmus Stourton, gentleman, late preacher to the Colony of Ferryland in the Newfoundland, had and taken at Plymouth, in the County of Devon, October 9, 1628, before Nicholas Sherwill, merchant, Mayor of the Borough of Plymouth and Thomas Sherwill, merchant, two of his Majesty's Justices of Peace, within the said borough.

The said examinant saith that he came out of the Newfoundland, August 28 last, in a ship of London called the VICTORY, and arrived into this harbor September 26 last and saith that about July 23 last was twelve months the Lord of Baltimore arrived in Newfoundland and brought with him two seminary priests, one of them called Longville and the other called Anthony Smith,[16] which said Longville returned again for England with the said Lord. And afterwards, in this year, 1628, my Lord of Baltimore arrived there again and brought with him one other seminary priest, whose name is Hacket, with the number of forty papists or thereabouts, where the said Hacket and Smith every Sunday saith Mass and do use all other the ceremonies of the Church of Rome, in as ample a manner as 'tis used in Spain. And this examinant hath seen them at Mass and knoweth that the child of one William Poole, a Protestant, was baptized according to the orders and customs of the Church of Rome, by the procurement of the said Lord of Baltimore, contrary to the will of the said Poole, to which child the said Lord was a witness.

This examinant is a chaplain of my Lord of Anglesey[17] and is gone towards London, with a purpose to attend the Lords of the Council,[18] as he informs us.

16. Anthony Pole.   17. Christopher Villiers.
18. Privy Council.

"I May Yet Do the King and My Country More Service There": George Calvert's Petition to the King for Land in the Chesapeake Region, 1629[*]

From his primitive Avalon settlement, Calvert in the late summer made a bold plea to King Charles. The crown, five years earlier, had revoked the charter of the bankrupt Virginia Company and taken over the governance of the colony. Calvert himself had been secretary of state to Charles's father, James, when the decision had been made, a connection that gave the Virginians even more reason subsequently to oppose Lord Baltimore's attempt to plant a colony in America at their expense. What obstacles to the creation of a successful colony does Calvert report that he has encountered during his stay in Newfoundland? On what grounds does Calvert make his plea for the king's granting him a portion of the monarch's own colony?

Small benefits and favors can speak and give thanks, but such as are high, and invaluable cause astonishment and silence. I am obliged unto your Majesty for the latter in such a measure as reflecting upon my weakness and want of merit I know not what to say. God Almighty knows who is the searcher of hearts how mine yearns to sacrifice my self for your Majesty's service, if I did but know how to employ my endeavours worthy of that great goodness and benignity which your Majesty is pleased to extend towards me upon all occasions, not only by reaching your Gracious and Royall hand to my assistance in lending me a fair ship (for which upon my knees I render your Majesty most humble thanks) but by protecting me also against calumny and malice which hath already sought to make me seem foul in your Majesty's eyes. Whereas I am so much the more confident of God's blessing upon my labours in these plantations (notwithstanding the many crosses and disasters I have found hitherto) in that a Prince so eminently virtuous hath vouchsafed to take it into the arms of his protection, and that

---

[*] George Calvert to King Charles, August 19, 1629, PRO, CSP 5, no. 27, in *AM* 3: 15–16.

those who go about to supplant and destroy me are persons notoriously lewd and wicked. Such a one is that audacious man who being banished [from] the Colony for his misdeeds did the last winter (as I understand) raise a false and slanderous report of me at Plymouth, which coming from thence to your Majesty's knowledge, you were pleased to refer to some of my Lords of the Council, by whose honorable hands.... I have presumed to return my just and true Apologies to your Majesty.[19] But as these rubs[20] have been laid to stumble me there (which discourage me not because I am confident of your Majesty's singular judgement and justice), so have I met with greater difficulties and encumbrances here which in this place are no longer to be resisted, but enforce me presently to quit my residence, and to shift to some other warmer climate of this new world, where the winters be shorter and less rigorous. For here, your Majesty may please to understand that I have found by too dear bought experience which other men for their private interests always concealed from me, that from the midst of October to the midst of May there is a sad face of winter upon all this land, both sea and land so frozen for the greatest part of the time as they are not penetrable no plant or vegetable thing appearing out of the earth until it be about the beginning of May, nor fish in the sea besides the air so intolerable cold as it is hardly to be endured. By means whereof, and of much salt water, my house hath been an hospital all this winter, of 100 persons 50 sick at a time, my self being one and nine or ten of them died. Hereupon I have had strong temptations to leave all proceedings[21] in plantations, and being much decayed in my strength to retire my self to my former quiet; but my inclination carrying me naturally to these kind of works, and not knowing how better to employ the poor remainder of my days than with other good subjects to further the best I may the enlarging your Majesty's empire in this part of the world I am determined to commit this place to fishermen that are able to encounter storms and hard weather, and to remove my self with some 40 persons to your Majesty's dominion of Virginia, where if your Majesty will please to grant me a precinct[22] of land with such privileges as the King your father my gracious master was pleased to grant me here, I shall endeavour to the utmost of my power to deserve it.

19. Erasmus Stourton.　　　　20. Obstacles.
21. Involvement.　　　　22. Area.

5

"I Do … Abhor, Detest and Abjure … This Damnable Doctrine": The Oaths of Supremacy and Allegiance*

In a kingdom where the ruler claimed sovereignty in matters spiritual as well as temporal, allegiance could become a complicated affair, especially for the Catholics within the realm who looked to Rome and the pope as their spiritual head. As such, the loyalty of Catholics was ever suspect; at best their allegiance seemed divided between crown and pontiff; at worst, they were feared as secret agents of Rome and other Catholic powers. When the pope declared Elizabeth excommunicated for claiming headship of the Church of England and called upon his subjects in England to depose her as a heretic, all Catholics became enemies of the state in the eyes of the Tudor establishment. The oath established by the Act of Supremacy in 1558, although predating the papal excommunication by more than a decade, was clearly meant not only to flush out Catholics within the general population but to serve as a major tool within the penal apparatus to force a renunciation of Rome's spiritual/temporal rulers.

The oath of allegiance, passed in 1606, a year after the Gunpowder Plot, was obviously an effort to prevent any future violence on the part of Catholics against king and Parliament. It was modified from ruler to ruler, but remained for centuries a crucial instrument for keeping Roman Catholics from the full exercise of their rights as citizens.

Why would Lord Baltimore decline to take both oaths? What can you surmise would have been the gist of the alternate oath that he proposed taking in lieu of the customary ones?

Oath of Supremacy (1559)

I _____ do utterly testify and declare in my conscience that the Queen's Highness is the only supreme governor of this realm, and of all other her Highness's dominions and countries, as well in all spiritual or ecclesiastical things or causes, as temporal, and that no foreign prince, person, prelate, state or potentate hath or ought to have any jurisdiction, power, superiority, pre-eminence or authority ecclesiastical or spiritual within this realm, and therefore I do ut-

*William Ingoldsby, *Englands Oaths: Taken by All Men of Quality in the Church and Common-wealth of England* (London: 1642).

terly renounce and forsake all foreign jurisdictions, powers, superiorities and authorities, and do promise that from henceforth I shall bear faith and true allegiance to the Queen's Highness, her heirs and lawful successors, and to my power shall assist and defend all jurisdictions, pre-eminences, privileges and authorities granted or belonging to the Queen's Highness, her heirs or successors, or united or annexed to the imperial crown of this realm. So help me God and by the contents of this Book.[23]

Oath of Allegiance (1606)

I _____ do truly and sincerely acknowledge, profess, testify and declare in my conscience before God and the world, That our Sovereign Lord King Charles, is lawful and rightful King of this Realm, and of all other in His Majesty's Dominions and Countries; And that the Pope neither of himself, nor by any Authorities of the Church or See of Rome, or by any means with any other, hath any power or Authority to depose the King, or to dispose of any of his Majesty's Kingdoms or Dominions, or to Authorize any Foreign Prince, to invade or annoy Him or His Countries, or to discharge any of his Subjects of their Allegiance and Obedience to His Majesty, or to give Licence or leave to any of them to bear Arms, raise Tumults, or to offer any violence or hurt to His Majesty's Royal person, State or Government, or to any of His Majesty's Subjects within His Majesty's Dominions.

Also I do swear from my heart, that, notwithstanding any Declaration or Sentence of Excommunication or Deprivation made or granted, or to be made or granted, by the Pope or his Successors, or by any Authority derived, or pretended to be derived from him or his See, against the said King, His Heirs or Successors, or any Absolution of the said Subjects from their Obedience, I will bear faith and true allegiance to his Majesty, His Heirs and Successors, and Him and Them will defend to the uttermost of my power, against all Conspiracies and Attempts whatsoever, which shall be made against His or their Persons, their Crown and Dignity, by reason or color of any such Sentence or Declaration or otherwise, and will do my best endeavour to disclose and make known unto his Majesty, His Heirs and Successors, all Treasons and Traitorous Conspiracies which I shall know or hear of to be against Him, or any of them.

And I do further swear, That I do from my heart abhor, detest and abjure

23. King James Version of the Bible.

as impious and Heretical this damnable Doctrine and Position, that Princes which be Excommunicated or deprived by the Pope, may be Deposed or Murdered by their Subjects, or any other whatsoever.

And I do believe, and in conscience am resolved, that neither the Pope, nor any person whatsoever hath power to absolve me of this Oath, or any part thereof, which I acknowledge by good and full Authority to be lawfully ministered unto me, and do renounce all Pardons and Dispensations to the contrary. And all these things I do plainly and sincerely acknowledge and swear, according to these express words by me spoken, and according to the plain and common sense and understanding of the same words, without any Equivocation, or mental evasion or secret reservation whatsoever. And I do make this Recognition and acknowledgement heartily, willingly, and truly, upon the true Faith of a Christian. So help me God.

6

"No Papists Have Been Suffered to Settle Their Abode Amongst Us": Governor John Pott and Others to the Privy Council, November 1629[*]

What is the point of the Virginians' letter? Why would they be optimistic that the letter and Claiborne's personal plea would be sufficient to secure the Privy Council's support?

Right honorable,

May it please your Lordships to understand, that about the beginnings of October last there arrived in this Colony the Lord Baltimore from his plantation of Newfoundland, with an intention as we are informed, rather to plant himself to the southward, than settle here, although since he hath seemed well affected to this place, and willing to make his residence therein with his whole family. We were readily inclined to render unto his Lordship all those respects which were due unto the honor of his person,

[*] PRO, CSP 5, no. 40, in *AM* 3: 16–17.

or which might testify with how much gladness we desired to receive and entertain him, as being of that eminence and degree whose presence and affection might give great advancement to this Plantation. Whereupon according to the instructions from your Lordships and the usual course held in this place we tendered the oaths of Supremacy and Allegiance to his Lordship and some of his followers, who making profession of the Romish Religion, utterly refused to take the same, a thing which we could not have doubted in him, whose former employments under his late majestic might have endeared to us a persuasion, he would not have made denial of that in point whereof consisteth the loyalty and fidelity, which every true subject oweth unto his Sovereign. His Lordship then offered to take this oath a copy whereof is included but in true discharge of the trust imposed in us by his Majesty we could not imagine that so much latitude was left for us to decline[24] from the prescribed form, so strictly exacted and so well justified and defended by the pen of our late Sovereign Lord King James of happy memory, and among the many blessings and favors for which we are bound to bless god and which this Colony hath received, from his most gracious Majesty, there is none whereby it hath been made more happy than in the freedom of our Religion which we have enjoyed, and that no papists have been suffered to settle their abode amongst us, the Continuance whereof we most humbly implore you Lordships that by your mediations and Councils the same may be established and confirmed unto us, and we as our Duty is with the whole Colony shall always pray for his Majesty's long life and eternal security from whose royal hands this Plantation must expect her establishments and for whose honor God hath reserved so glorious a work as the perfection thereof.

> John Pott
> Samuel Mathews
> Roger Smith

Sources

Archives of Maryland. Vol. 3. http://www.aomol.msa.maryland.gov/html/index.html.

Bossy, John. *The English Catholic Community, 1570–1850.* New York and Oxford: Oxford University Press, 1976.

Codignola, Luca. *The Coldest Harbour of the Land: Simon Stock and Lord Baltimore's Colo-*

24. Deviate.

ny in Newfoundland, 1621–1649. Translated by Anita Weston. Kingston and Montreal: McGill-Queen's University Press, 1988.

Colony of Avalon Historical Documents. 1597–1726. http://www.colonyofavalon.ca/index.

Havran, Martin J. *The Catholics in Caroline England.* Stanford, Calif.: Stanford University Press, 1962.

Hughes, Thomas. *History of the Society of Jesus in North America: Colonial and Federal; Documents.* Vol. 1, part 1. New York, Bombay, and Calcutta: Longmans, Green, 1908.

Ingoldsby, William. *Englands Oaths: Taken by All Men of Quality in the Church and Common-wealth of England.* London: 1642.

Krugler, John D. *English and Catholic: The Lords Baltimore in the Seventeenth Century.* Baltimore and London: The Johns Hopkins University Press, 2004.

Mullett, Michael A. *Catholics in Britain and Ireland, 1558–1829.* New York: St. Martin's Press, 1998.

Norman, Edward. *Roman Catholicism in England from the Elizabethan Settlement to the Second Vatican Council.* Oxford and New York: Oxford University Press, 1985.

Questier, Michael. *Catholicism and Community in Early Modern England: Politics, Aristocratic Patronage and Religion, 1550–1640.* Cambridge: Cambridge University Press, 2006.

Part 2

Terra Mariae

Planning and Voyage, 1630–1634

*T*HE VIRGINIANS' campaign to scuttle Calvert's efforts to obtain land from the crown for a colony in the Chesapeake region proved an effective one, as Lord Baltimore discovered when he returned home to find a letter from King Charles counseling him to abandon his colonizing and return to government service. Calvert was undeterred, persisting in the face of royal disinterest, lack of money to finance the project, and personal tragedy (his wife went down with the ship carrying her back to England from Virginia; the following summer, bubonic plague devastated his London household). Then in the fall of 1631 a breakthrough: the king provided some financial flooring by granting Calvert an annual pension of £1,000. Months later Charles came through in a bigger way by directing his government to draw up a charter empowering Calvert to establish a colony south of Virginia.

When the Virginians got word of the king's directive, they protested strenuously that such a location would be a serious impediment to any future expansion for the oldest English colony in America. That argument plus a mounting concern about the spread of Dutch settlements southward from the mid-Atlantic area caused the crown to relocate the proposed colony to the north of Virginia to an area comprising the Delmarva Peninsula on the east to the Potomac River on the west. That designation also brought a protest from Virginia. Virginians had already made settlements on the southern portion of the peninsula, so the charter was modified to reflect that development.

The Charter of Maryland for the most part replicated its Avalon predecessor, with certain additions that reflected the peculiar circumstances in which the Calverts were making their second attempt at colonization as well as the specific plan of development that they had devised for Maryland. One new provision made clear that Maryland was entirely independent of Virginia, despite embracing territory that its southern neighbor considered part of its own domain. For the moment at least, the Calverts had the last word over their Virginia antagonists. Even more significant was a section that was repeated verbatim from the Avalon Charter. In Maryland, as in Avalon, all the king's subjects would enjoy the same "Liberties, Franchises, and Privileges" as their countrymen in England, "any Statute, Act, Ordinance, or Provision to the contrary hereof notwithstanding." When Calvert secured his earlier charter, he was not yet living as or known to be a Catholic. By 1632 both were well established. Despite this radical change in Calvert's religious allegiance, the Maryland Charter contained the same guarantee of the rights of Englishmen for its adventurers as Avalon's had for its colonists—presumably faithful adherents of the Church of England. In effect the penal laws regarding Catholics would not extend to the new province in the Chesapeake in which Catholics had such a fundamental stake (see "The Pious and Noble Purpose of the ... Barons of Baltimore").

By the time the king applied the royal seal to the charter in June 1632, George Calvert, fifty-two, had succumbed to a chronic ailment to join his wife in death. To his oldest son, Cecil, fell the task of making the colony legally empowered by the charter a reality. George Calvert had begun the planning for his new colonial venture long before he secured a charter for the enterprise. To assist him at his London office on Holborne Street in Bloomsbury, Calvert, sometime in the first half of the year 1630, had persuaded Andrew White, a Jesuit who had been teaching theology at the Liége College in Flanders, to join the planning of his new settlement in America. White, with a burning interest in carrying the gospel to the natives of the New World, jumped at the opportunity. The Jesuit, in effect, replaced Simon Stock, who had fallen out of Calvert's favor for reasons about which one can only speculate. Whatever the reasons, the religious involvement with Calvert's colonizing projects passed from the Carmelites to the Jesuits. For the rest of the colonial period, the Society of Jesus would be the public face of Catholicism in British America.

For the next three years the Calverts and White went about organizing the undertaking, including the securing of investors, settlers (both freemen and indentured servants), and vessels to transport the settlers to Maryland. To secure those able and willing to invest in the colony and/or become colonists required advertising the adventure. That responsibility fell to the scholar White. Over the next three years three tracts appeared promoting the Maryland enterprise in the most optimistic terms. The first, written by White in 1633, constituted the formal announcement of Lord Baltimore's latest colonial undertaking and the beginning of the campaign to secure the financial support and recruits to make the new plantation a reality (see "Never More Noble Enterprise Entered into English Hearts").

If advertising the incipient Maryland colony as an unexploited Eden had been counted on to attract from the nobility and gentry a large number of "adventurers," both Catholic and Protestant, it fell far short of its mark. Few gentry besides the Calverts's own relatives were willing to join the expedition to Maryland. The joint-stock company that was to generate the income to fund the development of the colony raised less than half of its needed capital. Even Catholic servants were wary of risking a dangerous Atlantic crossing and the "seasoning" that took such a terrible toll on new settlers. But if "A Declaration" got scant response from would-be backers and voyagers, it apparently generated much concern, at least in some quarters, about the prospect of an English Catholic settlement in America. That the highest-ranking official in the government to convert to Rome was behind the enterprise only heightened suspicions about the ultimate intentions of Lord Baltimore and his fellow adventurers, suspicions that earlier Catholic colonization projects had inevitably provoked. To change opinion about the significance and consequences of the undertaking, Calvert commissioned a second tract by an unknown author to present a vigorous defense of the establishment of a colony in the New World that would involve Catholic leadership and participation (see "A Matter of Toleration").

That pamphlet may have gained Baltimore some good will for his venture, but not the people of standing and capital to improve its prospects. When Baltimore's two ships, the *Ark* and the *Dove*, prepared to weigh anchor at Gravesend, the vast majority of the voyagers were servants, mostly Protestants. There were fewer than twenty gentleman adventurers, including Andrew White and two other Jesuits, a priest and a lay brother. Lord Baltimore had planned to lead his first band of settlers to the Chesapeake in early September 1633. As the *Ark* and the *Dove* lifted anchor two and a half months after their scheduled departure, Cecil Calvert was not on board. Likely the same circumstances that had delayed their departure were also responsible for Baltimore's remaining behind in London where he could better protect the interests of his new colony. In lieu of his presence, Cecil Calvert gave a list of extensive instructions to the three people he had appointed to the top three offices in the new colony: his younger brother, Leonard Calvert, as deputy governor (Cecil still intended to be governor himself, once he was free to leave England) and Thomas Cornwalys and Jerome Hawley as lord commissioners (see "Give an Account of Every Particular").

The 150 adventurers and servants made their way across the Atlantic, with several island stops, in just over three months. By April they had made their initial settlement on the eastern shore of the lower Potomac. There, in late April or early May of 1634, Andrew White sent two reports to London about their voyage and first month in Maryland: one to Lord Baltimore, the other to his religious superior (see "God's Hand Is Here").

7

"The Pious and Noble Purpose of the … Barons of Baltimore": The Charter of Maryland, 1632[*]

The new charter preserved all of the extensive powers that George Calvert had obtained in his earlier one for Avalon, plus authorizing his son and successors to institute the manor-centered feudal structure that the Calverts, following the tradition of Catholic colonizers, had adopted as the socioeconomic grid for their colony, as well as to put in place the head-right system (land granted in proportion to the number of persons brought into the prov-

---

* *AM* 549:9–31.

ince by an individual) that was intended to be the main engine of population increase for Maryland. The charter conferred "full and absolute power" upon Lord Baltimore and his heirs. Do the provisions of the charter itself confirm or throw into question the proprietor's autocratic status? What is distinctly medieval about this charter?

WHEREAS Our right Trusty and Well beloved Subject *Cecilius Calvert, Baron of Baltimore* in our Kingdom of *Ireland* Son and heir of Sir *George Calvert* Knight, late Baron of *Baltimore* In the same Kingdome of *Ireland*, pursuing his Fathers intentions, being excited with a laudable and pious zeal for the propagation of the Christian Faith, and the enlargement of our Empire and Dominion, hath humbly besought leave of Us, by his industry and charge, to transport an ample Colony of the *English* Nation unto a certain Country hereafter described, in the parts of *America*, not yet cultivated and planted, though in some parts thereof inhabited by certain barbarous people, having no knowledge of Almighty God, and hath humbly besought our Royal Majesty to give, grant, and confirm all the said Country, with certain Privileges and Jurisdictions, requisite for the good government, and state of his Colony, and Country aforesaid, to him and heirs for ever.

We ... by this our present Charter, ... do give, grant and confirm unto the said *Cecilius*, now Baron of *Baltimore*, his heirs and Assigns, all that part of a *Peninsula*, lying in the parts of *America*, between the Ocean on the East, and the Bay of Chesapeake on the West, and divided from the other part thereof, by a right line drawn from the Promontory or Cape of Land called *Watkins Point* (situate in the foresaid Bay, near the river of *Wighco*)[1] on the West, unto the main Ocean on the East; and between that bound in the South, unto that part of *Delaware* Bay on the north, which lieth under the fortieth degree of Northerly Latitude from the Equinoctial, where *New England* ends. And all that tract of land between the bounds aforesaid; that is to say, passing from the foresaid Bay, called *Delaware* Bay, in a right line by the degree aforesaid, unto the true Meridian of the first fountain of the River of *Potomac*, and from thence trending toward the South unto the farther bank of the fore-said River, and following the West and South side thereof unto a certain place called *Cinquack*, situate near the mouth of the said River, where it falls into the Bay of *Chesapeake*, and from thence by a straight line unto the foresaid Promontory, and place called *Watkins Point*....

WE DO also grant and confirm unto the said now Lord *Baltimore*, ... all

1. Wicomico.

Veins, Mines, and Quarries, as well discovered, as not discovered, of Gold, Silver, Gems, and precious stones, and all other whatsoever, be it of Stones, Metals, or of any other thing, or matter whatsoever, found, or to be found within the Country, Iles, and limits aforesaid. And Furthermore the Patronages and Advowsons of all Churches, which ... shall happen hereafter to be erected: together with licence and power, to build and found churches, Chapels, and Oratories, in convenient and fit places within the premises, and to cause them to be dedicated, and consecrated according to the ecclesiastical Laws of our Kingdom *of England*: Together *with* all and singular the like, and as ample rights, Jurisdictions, Privileges, Prerogatives, Royalties, Liberties Immunities, Royall rights, and franchises of what kind soever temporal, as well by Sea, as by land, within the Country, Iles, Iletts, and limits aforesaid; To have, exercise, use and enjoy the same, as amply as any Bishop of *Durham*, within the Bishopric, or County *Palatine* of *Durham*, in our Kingdom of *England*, hath at any time heretofore had, held, used, or enjoyed....

AND HIM the said now Lord *Baltimore*, his Heirs and Assigns, We do by these Presents ... make, create, and constitute the true and absolute Lords, and Proprietaries of the Country aforesaid, ... saving always, the faith and allegiance, and Sovereign dominion due unto Us, Our Heirs and Successors....

TO BE holden of Us, our Heirs, and Successors, Kings of England, as of our Castle of *Windsor* in our Country of *Berkshire* in free and common soccage,[2] by fealty only, for all service, ... : YIELDING and paying therefore to Us, our Heirs and Successors, two *Indian* Arrows of these parts, to be delivered at our said Castle of Windsor, every year on the Tuesday in *Easter* week; and also the fifth part of all Gold and Silver Ore within the limits aforesaid, which shall from time to time happen to be found.[3]

NOW THAT the said Country thus by Us granted, and described, may be eminent above all other parts of the said territory, and dignified with larger titles: ... We do ... erect and incorporate them into a Province, and do call it *Maryland*, and so from henceforth will have it called....

AND We ... do grant free, full, and absolute power, by virtue of these

2. The medieval system by which a vassal held land from a lord in exchange for a certain payment in goods or service.

3. In the Avalon charter, in place of the token annual payment of two arrows, was the obligation of providing "a white horse whensoever and as often as it shall happen that we, our heirs or successors, shall come into the said Territory or Region." Perhaps the arrows seemed a more practical means of showing Lord Baltimore's fealty to the monarch than the offer of a mount in a place the king was very unlikely to ever grace with his presence; for the text of the Avalon Charter, see Thomas Scharf, *The History of Maryland* (Baltimore: Piet, 1879), 1:33–40.

Presents, to him and his heirs, for the good and happy government of the said Province, to ordain, make, enact, and under his and their seals to publish any Laws whatsoever, appertaining either unto the public State of the said Province, or unto the private utility of particular Persons, according unto their best discretions, of and with the advice assent and approbation of the Freemen of the said Province, or the greater part of them, or of their delegates or deputies, whom for the enacting of the said Laws, when, and as often as need shall require, We will that the said now Lord *Baltimore*, and his heirs, shall assemble in such sort and form, as to him or them shall seem best: And the same laws duly to execute upon all people, within the said Province, and limits thereof.… And likewise to appoint and establish any judges and justices, Magistrates and Officers whatsoever, at sea and Land, for what causes soever, and with what power soever, and in such form, as to the said now Lord *Baltimore*, or his heirs, shall seem most convenient: … Our pleasure is, … that all the Liege people, and subjects of Us, Our Heirs and Successors, do observe and keep the same [laws] inviolably, in those parts, … Provided nevertheless, that the said Laws be consonant to reason, and be not repugnant or contrary, but as near as conveniently may be, agreeable to the Laws, Statutes, Customs, and Rights of this our Kingdom *of England*.…

AND WE … do straightly enjoin … that the said Province shall be of Our Allegiance, and that all … the Subjects, and Liege people of Us, Our Heirs, and Successors, transported, or to be transported into the said Province, and the children of them, and of such as shall descend from them, there already born, or hereafter to be born, be, and shall be … in all things held, treated, reputed, and esteemed as the liege faithful people of Us, Our Heirs, and Successors, … and likewise any Lands, Tenements, Revenues, Services, and other hereditaments whatsoever, within Our Kingdom of England, and other Our Dominions, may inherit, or otherwise purchase, receive, take, have, hold, buy, and possess, and them may occupy, and enjoy, give, sell, alien, and bequeath, as likewise, all Liberties, Franchises, and Privileges, of this Our Kingdom of *England*, freely, quietly, and peaceably, have and possess, occupy and enjoy, as Our liege people, … without the least molestation, vexation, trouble, or grievance of Us, Our Heirs and Successors: any Statute, Act, Ordinance, or Provision to the contrary hereof notwithstanding.…

And because in so remote a Country, and situate amongst so many barbarous nations, the incursions as well of the savages themselves, as of other enemies, pirates and robbers, may probably be feared: There fore We have given ... unto the now Lord *Baltimore*, his heirs and assigns, ... to Levy, Muster and Train, all sorts of men, of what condition, or wheresoever born, ... and to make war, and to pursue the Enemies and Robbers aforesaid, as well by sea as by land, yea, even without the limits of the said Province, and (by Gods assistance) to vanquish and take them, and being taken, to put them to death by the law of war, or to save them at their pleasure....

Also, Our Will and Pleasure is ... [to] give unto the said now Lord *Baltimore*, his heirs, and assigns, full power, liberty, and authority, in case of Rebellion, Tumult, or Sedition ... either upon the land within the Province aforesaid, or upon the main sea, ... to exercise Martial Law against mutinous and seditious persons of those parts, such as shall refuse to submit them selves to his, or their government, or shall fly to the Enemy, ... or be loiterers, or stragglers, or otherwise howsoever offending against the Law, Custom, and Discipline military....

FURTHERMORE That the way to honors and dignities, may not seem to be altogether precluded and shut up, to men well borne, and such as ... shall desire to deserve well of Us, and Our Kingdome, both in peace and war, in so far distant and remote a Country: Therefore We ... do give free, and absolute power, unto the said now Lord *Baltimore*, his heirs and assigns, to confer favours, rewards, and honours, upon such inhabitants within the Province aforesaid, as shall deserve the same; and to invest them, with what titles and dignities soever, as he shall think fit, (so as they be not such as are now used in *England*). As likewise to erect and incorporate, Towns into Boroughs, and Boroughs into cities, with convenient privileges and immunities, according to the merit of the inhabitants, and the fitness of the places....

And by these Presents, We give, and grant licence unto the said now Lord *Baltimore*, and his heirs, to erect any parcels of land within the Province aforesaid, into Manors, and in every of the said Manors, to have, and to hold a *Court Baron*, with all things whatsoever, which to a *Court Baron* do belong, ...

AND FURTHER, ... WE, Our Heirs and Successors, shall at no time hereafter, set, or make, or cause to be set, any imposition, Custom, or other taxation, Rate, or Contribution whatsoever, in or upon the dwellers and inhabitants of the foresaid Province, for their Lands, Tenements, goods or Chattels within the said Province, or in or upon any goods or merchandizes, within the said Province, or to be laden, or unladen within any the Ports or harbours of the said Province....

AND FURTHER, our pleasure is, and by these Presents for Us, our heirs and Successors, We do grant unto the said now Lord *Baltimore*, his heirs and assigns, and to the Tenants, and Inhabitants of the said Province of *Maryland*, both present, and to come, and to every of them, that the said Province, Tenants, and Inhabitants of the said *Colony* or Country, shall not from henceforth be held or reputed as a member, or a part of the land of *Virginia* or of any other Colony whatever. . . .

AND IF PERCHANCE hereafter it should happen, that any doubts or questions should arise, concerning the true sense and understanding of any word, clause, or sentence contained in this Our present Charter, We will ordain, and command, that at all times, and in all things, such Interpretation be made thereof, and allowed in any of Our Courts whatsoever, as shall be judged most advantageous, and favourable unto the said now Lord *Baltimore* his heirs and assigns, PROVIDED always, that no Interpretation be admitted thereof, by which Gods Holy and Truly Christian Religion, or the allegiance due unto Us, Our Heirs and Successors, may in any thing suffer any prejudice, or diminution.

8

"Never More Noble Enterprise Entered into English Hearts": *A Declaration of the Lord Baltimore's Plantation in Maryland, 1633* *

The first of the three tracts publicizing Maryland appeared in the late winter of 1632–33. Its *target audience* was clearly non-Catholic. While insisting that the prime objective of the new planting of the English Empire was to bring Christianity to natives desperate ("white for the harvest") to hear its saving word (an assertion that surely reflected White's priorities rather than the Calverts's), the tract mainly extolled the moderate climate and abounding

---

* Thomas Hughes, *HSJNA*, Documents, vol. 1, part I (London: Longman, Greens, 1908), 145–49; *AM* 550: 45–52.

super-sized material riches of the region that promised a more worldly harvest for those daring to commit themselves to the adventure. How does the author attempt to validate his claims about the proposed site for Lord Baltimore's colony? What perquisites, and on what basis, does the proprietor offer to those able to assist in the financing and peopling of the colony?

Declaration of the Lord Baltimore's *Plantation in Mary-land, nigh upon Virginia*; manifesting the Nature, Quality, Condition, and rich Utilities it containeth.

It pleased his most Excellent Majesty in June last, 1632, to give under the Great Seal of *England*, a Province, near unto the English Plantation in *Virginia*, to my Lord BALTIMORE and his heirs for ever calling it MARY-LAND in honour of our most gracious Queen. My Lord therefore, meaning to plant and people it, first with this express and chief intention to bring to CHRIST that and the countries adjacent, which from the beginning of the World to this day never knew GOD; and then with this end, to enlarge his Majesty's Empire and Dominions, and to make his Country-men sharers with him in the honour and benefit thereof, is preparing his Company …, both Adventurers and others, for the Voyage. And now …, having taken due prospect upon all those inconveniences, which a long time have hindered, and of the means which have helped forward other Plantations; and having fully satisfied himself, not only by the papers his noble Father, an eye-witness left him, of the Excellency of the land: but by others also, who daily come from that, and the places nigh upon it, as also by the true printed History of Captain SMITH, who first discovered it, confirmed by hundreds living in this City of *London*, who have been themselves there, and mean to return thither again.… My Lord resolves by the favour of GOD, to make Sail for the said *Country* about the middle of *September* next ensuing, and proposes many very large conditions, to such as shall for the same ends join with him in this honorable Action. Whereof the chief is this, that besides honors and place which freely he meaneth to confer upon the merits of Blood, Valour, Virtue, and larger Ventures of Gentlemen, for every hundred pounds ventur'd in Transportation of five able men (being twenty pound a man) which will transport and furnish them with Arms, Tools, Clothes, Utensils and Victuals for one twelve-Month …; shall receive of my Lord a manor of good Land, to the full quantity of 2000. Acres, for them and their heirs for ever in that Country; besides, a good share in a rich Trade hereafter mentioned, and sundry other encouragements & privileges if they go in this first Voyage.... The chief intention of my Lord is, and also the same ought to be of all others, who venture fortunes with him, to plant Christianity there. An intendment[4] so full of Christian honor, making men Angels who undertake it, as never more noble Enterprise entered into English hearts. The Regions are, *Alba ad messem*,[5] to receive the Law of CHRIST: The Indians themselves send far and nigh for Teachers, to instruct and Baptize them; and at this present, some are in Town, who as Eye-witnesses affirm, they saw Messengers sent to *James Town* in *Virginia* from their Kings to the same purpose: as also, Children sent to be baptized into *New-England* on the other side. What doubt then can be made, but many thousands of Souls may be brought to CHRIST by this most glorious Enterprise; and it may indeed be called most glorious, seeing it is the saving of Souls, which was the work of CHRIST the King of Glory. But, for that all men are not so noble-minded, as to hold their level purely at this end, so great and glorious, but commonly Pleasure, wealth and honour, are the Adamants[6] that draw them: Gods dearly-good Providence hath wrapped also all these together in this one Action, that neither higher nor lower inducements might be wanting.

The Clime of this Country is confessed the very best, lying betwixt 38. and 40. degrees Northerly latitude, about that of *Seville, Sicily, Jerusalem*, and the best parts of *Arabia Felix, China, &c.* The Air, serene and gentle, not so hot as Florida, and Old *Virginia*, nor so cold as New *England*, but between them both; having the good of each, and the ill of neither. On the East side, it hath two goodly Bays, both rich bosoms of fish. The one called Chesapeake, twelve miles over, between two Lands, running from South to North for one hundred and threescore miles, harbourable for Ships of great burthen, full of sundry large Islands good for Hay and Pasture, where is a rich fishing of Bass. The other called *Delaware*, where is fishing of Cod all the year long.... There are also sundry goodly Rivers, but the chiefest is called *Potomac*, navigable for ships of great burthen, one hundred & forty miles into the Land: upon which river is a rich trade with the *Indians* of Beavers skins, in wonderful plenty, which being newly discovered; yet did some Merchants bring from thence this last year, as many as were worth 10000. Pounds, and the return of these commodities with which they traded for these Beavers with the Natives, yielded them thirty for one. Grass there is in great plenty in the plain and open grounds, but generally the Country is

4. Design.   5. "White for the harvest."
6. Treasures.

covered with great Woods. Oakes and Walnut, both black and white are the most common Trees. Of which, the Oakes are so tall and straight, as many of them yield beams 60. foot long, and two foot and a half every way square. Cypresses there are 2. fathom about below: and fourscore foot high before they shoot any bough. Mulberry trees also there are, in great abundance, which will be useful for the making of Silk. There is also silk grasses ... to make *China* Damask. Likewise elm, Ash, and Chestnuts, which equal the best in *Spain, France, Italy*, or *Germany*, and Cedars not inferiour to those of *Lebanon*.... The use of these Trees is great for building Houses, and ships, for Wainscot, Pipe staves, Pitch, Rosin, Tar, Turpentine, Soap-Ash, Perfumes, and Salves.... There is great plenty of Grapes, whereof good wine may be made. Some of these as big as Cherries; whose juice is thick and unctuous ... Strawberries also and Raspices[7] are not wanting. As for diversities of Fish, these following are known and abound: Sturgeon, Grampus, Porpoise, Seals, Sting rays, ... Bass, White Salmons, Trouts, Soles, ... Herrings, Rock, Eels, Lampreys, Cat-fish, shad, Perch ...; Crabs, Shrimps, Cray fishes, Oysters, Cockles, and Mussels, with many more whose names are not known. Now as for beasts, there are so many Deere and Hogs, as the Country seems rather pestered therewith them filled....

Besides these, there are Muskrats, Squirrels, Beavers, Badgers, Foxes, Martins, Pole-cats, Weasels and Minks; which yet hurt not the Poultry, nor their Eggs. Among their Birds, the Eagle is the greatest devourer. Hawks there are of sundry sorts; which all prey commonly upon fish.... Infinite store of wild turkeys, nigh as big again as our tame.... In winter, is great plenty of Swans, Cranes, and Pigeons, Herons, Geese, ... Ducks ..., Dottrell[8] ..., Parrots, and much other fowl unknown in our parts.... It ... is excellent for Beans, Peas, and all manner of ... Roots: whereof Peas in ten days rise 14. inches high. The Corn is very plentiful in each of three Harvests in the same year, yielding in greatest penury two hundred for one, in ordinary years five or six hundred for one: which increase of Corn being so great, it is very easy to keep all manner of Poultry and Fowl for the Table all the year long. This Corn maketh good bread and Beer.... Of rich dyes, and drugs, there is no want; as of Tobacco, Sassafras, ... and the like.... As for Copper, the North-west Hills have that store, as the Natives themselves part the solid metal from the same without fire; and beat it into Plates from the raw ore[;]

7. Raspberries.
8. Plover.

for Gold, this only can be said, that the neighbouring nation, commonly wear bracelets of rude gobbets[9] of gold about their arms; and therefore, it is like there are mines of Gold not far off. As for Pearl, they wear large chains thereof, though deformed by burning the Oysters and boring them ill. I omit their Iron which they have already, their Glass, Hemp, and Flax, which is very excellent in this land: with many other commodities, which time, industry, and Art will discover; The fruits whereof may be easier tasted, than believed.

February, 10 anno 1633

Any man that desireth to adventure in this Plantation … [should] make known their resolution to [Lord Baltimore], at any time within Three weeks before his departure, which will be by the grace of God about, the Eight of September next, 1633.[10] For his Ship he goeth in (called the *Ark of Mary-land* being about 400. Ton) weigheth Anchor from *London* the 12. of August, and goeth about to *Portsmouth* where he intendeth himself with all his Company, to go aboard about the time aforesaid.

9

"A Matter of Toleration": *Objections Answered Touching Maryland*, 1633[*]

"Objections answered touching Maryland" appealed to logic, experience, and self-interest in making its case for Calvert's colony. By what argument(s) does the author attempt to show the futility of oaths and penal legislation regarding Catholics? On what grounds does the author defend the grant of a charter empowering a Catholic to begin a colony to which his co-religionists are particularly invited to join?

Object. 1. It may be objected that the Laws against the Roman Catholics were made in order to their conformity to the Protestant Religion, for the

---

[*] Stonyhurst College manuscripts, Anglia A, iv. ff. 206–9, no. 108g, in Hughes, *HSJNA*, Documents, vol. 1, part 1, 10–15.

9. Masses.

10. As of this date, late winter of 1633, Cecil Calvert was still intending to lead the adventurers to Maryland, setting a departure date for the feast of the Nativity of Mary in early September.

good of their souls, and by that means to free this Kingdom of Popery, rather than of their persons, but such a licence for them to depart this Kingdom, and to go into Maryland, or any country where they may have free liberty of their Religion, would take away all hopes of their conformity to the Church of England.

Answer. It is evident that reason of State (for the safety of the King and Kingdom) more than of Religion was the cause and end of those Laws, for there are no such against diverse other professions of Religion in England, although they be as different from the doctrine of the Protestant Church, established by Law in this Kingdom, as that of the Roman Catholics is. And this reason of State appears also in the nature of most of those Laws, for they express great doubts and jealousies of the said Roman Catholics affection to, and dependence on a foreign power, and tend therefore, most of them, to disenable them (by confining, disarming, etc.) from plotting or doing any mischief to the King or State, and to secure their allegiance to the King by oaths etc., and the penalties of diverse of them are abjuration of the Realm, which puts them out of the way of conformity to the Church of England. Moreover conversion in matter of Religion, if it be forced, should give little satisfaction to a wise State of the fidelity of such converts, for those who for worldly respects will break their faith with God doubtless will do it, upon a fit occasion, much sooner with men; and for voluntary conversions such Laws could be of no use. Wherefore certainly the safety of King and Kingdom was the sole aim and end of them.

Object. 2. Such a licence will seem to be a kind of toleration of (at least a connivance at) Popery which some may find a scruple of Conscience to allow of in any part of the Kings Dominions, because they esteem it a kind of idolatry, and may therefore conceive that it would scandalize their brethren and the common people here.

Answer. Such scrupulous persons may as well have a scruple to let the Roman Catholics live here, although it be under persecution, as to give way to such a licence, because banishment from a pleasant, plentiful and ones own native country, into a wilderness among savages and although it proceed (in a manner) from one's own election, yet, in this case, where it is provoked by other ways of persecution, is but an exchange rather than a freedom of punishment, and perhaps in some men's opinions from one persecution to a worse. For diverse malefactors in this Kingdom have chosen rather to be hanged, than to go into Virginia, when upon that condition they have been offered their lives, even at the place of execution, and they may with more ground have a scruple of conscience to let any of the said Roman Catholics to go from hence unto France (which few or none certainly can have in contemplation of Religion only and this Parliament hath given passes to diverse of them for that purpose), that being more properly the Kings Dominions than is all that great part of North America (wherein Maryland is included), unto which the Crown of England lays claim upon the title of discovery only, except such part thereof as is actually seated and possessed by some of his subjects; and there, in the Preamble of the Lord Baltimore's Patent of Maryland, the enlargement of the Kings Dominions is recited as a motive of the grant, which infers that it could not so properly be esteemed his Dominions before, as when by virtue of such a grant it should be planted by some of his subjects. And if it be all the Kings Dominions notwithstanding then why have not such scrupulous persons a scruple to suffer the Indians (who are undoubted idolators), as they do, to live there, which if they cannot conveniently prevent, (as without question they cannot, unless it be by granting such a licence), they may as well suffer those whom they may esteem idolators, as those whom they and other Christians whatsoever repute and know to be so, to inhabit and possess that Country. Moreover they may also (as well as in this) have a scruple to treat or make or continue a league, or to trade with any foreigners of that Religion, because in their opinions they are idolators, or to permit the public Ministers of any such foreign Prince or State to have the free exercise of their Religion while they are in England, and may fear giving scandal to others by such tolerations or connivances: all which nevertheless we see done, even in these times, and allowed of, as well by the Parliament as the King, upon reason of State, for the good and safety of this Realm. So may this licence be also thought by such persons a good expedient for the same purpose. And if any (of the weaker sort) should be scandalized at it, the scandal would be *acceptum* not *datum*,[11] and therefore not to be regarded by a wise and judicious Prince or State.

Object. 3. By it the Kings revenue will be impaired in losing the benefit which the said Laws given him, out of Recusants estates, while they continue in England of that profession of Religion.

Answer. The end of those Lawes was not the Kings profit, but (as is

11. "A matter of toleration rather than of creation."

said before) the freeing of this Kingdome of Recusants which deprives the King of any benefit by them, so as his Majesty will have no wrong done him by such a licence, because he will lose nothing by it of what was intended him by the said Laws; this is no ancient revenue of the Crown, for it had inception but in Queen Elizabeths time, and conformity or alienation to a Protestant deprives the King of this revenue. If there were no crimes at all committed in England, the King would lose many fines and confiscations, whereby his revenue would also be impaired (which in the other as well as in this branch of it is but casual), and yet without question the King and State would both desire it. The same reason holds in this, considering what opinion is had here of the Recusants,[12] wherefore it cannot with good manners be doubted that his Majesty will in this business prefer his own benefit, before that which the State shall conceive to be convenient for his safety, and the public good.

Object. 4. It would much prejudice this Kingdom by drawing considerable number of people, and transporting of a great deal of wealth, from hence.

Answer. The number of all the Recusants in England is not so great, as the departure of them all from hence would make any sensible diminution of people in it, and their profession in Religion would make them the less missed here. If the number were great, then consequently (according to the maxims of this State) they were the more dangerous, and there would be the more reason by this means to lessen it. And if it be but small (as indeed it is) then their absence from hence would little prejudice the Kingdom in the decrease of people, nor will such a licence occasion the transportation of much wealth out of England, for they shall not need to carry any considerable sums of money with them, nor is it desired that they should have leave to do so, but only useful things for a Plantation, as provisions for clothing and building and planting tools etc. which will advantage this Kingdom by increase of trade and vent[13] of its Native Commodities, and transfers the rest of their Estates by Bills of Exchange into Banks beyond the Sea, which tends also to the advantage of the trade of England, for more stock by this means will be employed in it.

Object 5. It may prove dangerous to Virginia and New England, where many English Protestants are planted, Maryland being situated between them both, because it may be suspected that the said Roman Catholics will

12. Roman Catholics or those refusing to take the oaths of allegiance and supremacy.
13. Sale.

bring in the Spaniards or some other foreign enemy to suppress the Protestants in those parts, or perhaps grow strong enough to do it of themselves, or that in time (having the Government of that Province of Maryland in their hands) they may and will shake off any dependence on the Crown of England.

Answer. The English Colonies in New England are at least 500 miles, and that of Virginia 100 miles distant from Maryland, and it will be a long time before planters can be at leisure to think of any such design, and there is little cause to doubt, that any people as long as they may live peaceably under their own Government, without oppression either in spirituals or temporals, will desire to bring in any foreigners to domineer over them, which misery they would undoubtedly fall into, if any considerable foreign Prince or State (who are only in this case to be feared) had the possession of the English Colonies in Virginia or New England. But the number of English Protestants already in Virginia and New England, together with the poverty of those parts, makes it very improbable that any foreign Prince or State will be tempted to undergo the charge and hazard of such a remote design, it being well known that the Spanish Colonies in the West Indies are farther distant than Europe is from thence. If any danger were to be suspected in that way from the said Recusants, the like suspicion of bringing in a foreign Enemy into England may (as indeed it hath often been) be had of them, while they are here, for the difference of situation may balance the difference of the power, between this Kingdom and those parts, for the accomplishing of such a design, and certainly (of the two) it were much better to throw that hazard (if it were any) upon Virginia and New England, than to have it continue here. Much less cause is there to fear that they should grow strong enough of themselves to suppress the Protestants in those parts; for there are already at least three times as many Protestants there, as there are Roman Catholics in all England. And the Protestants in Virginia and New England are like to increase much faster by new supplies of people yearly from England, etc., than are the Roman Catholics in Maryland. Moreover although they should (which God forbid and which the English Protestants in those parts will in all probability be still able to prevent) shake off any dependence on the Crown of England, yet first England would by this means be freed of so many suspected persons now in it; secondly, it would lose little by it; and lastly, even in that case, it were notwithstanding more for the honour of the English Nation, that English men, although Roman Catholics, and although not dependent on the Crown of England, should possess that country than foreigners, who otherwise are like to do it: for the Swedes and Dutch have two several Plantations already in New England, and upon the confines of Maryland (between the English Colonies in New England and Maryland), and do encroach every day more and more upon that Continent, where there is much more land than all the Kings Protestant subjects in all his Dominions (were they there) would be able to possess. But the assurance of protection from the Crown and State of England, upon all just occasions, either of danger from a foreign Enemy, or of wrongs which may be done unto them by his Majestys Protestant subjects in those parts, and the benefit of trade with England for yearly supplies, without which they will not be able to subsist, will be strong ties, if there were no other, to bind them to continue their dependence on it.

Moreover the mouth of the Bay of Chesapeake being but narrow, and at which all ships that come to Maryland must enter, is within the precincts and power of the Colony of Virginia. And the Planters of Virginia will by the access of so many neighbours be much advantaged, because their cattle and many other commodities which they abound in and have no vent[14] for, and which this new Colony will stand in need of, will by this means yield them good rates, which now are of little value to them, wherefore certainly they will fear no prejudice but will be glad of such a market for improvement of their estates; though perhaps some petty Merchants here, traders to Virginia, may conceive it prejudicial to them, and therefore may make Religion, and other vain pretences of danger to Virginia, or this State, the cloak of their avarice, to hinder this design; whereas in truth it can be nothing else, but fear of the increase of the commodities they deal in and consequently of an abatement of the prices, that may incline them to oppose it.

14. Market.

10

"Give an Account of Every Particular": Cecil Calvert's Instructions to the Governor and Commissioners of Maryland, 1633 *

Instructions to crews and passengers setting out on transatlantic voyages were common in the seventeenth century. They were largely intended as a means toward the keeping of peace among a motley assemblage forced for several months to live in the closest of quarters under conditions that ranged from bad to life-threatening. At rare times they could be much more than pleas for civility and forbearance, as was John Winthrop's discourse delivered to the Puritan passengers aboard the *Arabella* bound for Massachusetts Bay, with its majestic setting forth of their mission and the biblically based ethic that should guide it.[15] So too were the instructions that Lord Baltimore wrote out for the officials charged with establishing his second colony in the New World—his brother, Leonard Calvert, appointed deputy governor of the Province of Maryland, as well as Jerome Hawley and Thomas Cornwalys, the two lord commissioners of the incipient province. Calvert's instructions, like Winthrop's, laid out his goals for the colony and set forth the means by which they were to achieve them.

But the differences between the Puritan's manifesto and that of his Catholic counterpart far outweigh their similarities. For one, Calvert significantly had his missive read, not during their passage to Maryland but only after they had reached their destination. Moreover, in contrast to Winthrop's idealistic exhortation, Calvert's message is a much more prudential one, reflective of the precarious, embattled position that Lord Baltimore found himself in as a prominent Catholic planting a settlement for a Protestant monarch in an area claimed by Virginia; indeed, on an important island of that contested territory, William Claiborne, with the riches accrued from various offices he had held in the Virginia government since 1621, had established a base for his far-reaching, lucrative beaver trade with the various tribes in the Chesapeake region. More ominously, Claiborne was utilizing his high-placed connections in London in an attempt to nullify the Calverts's charter. That indeed was the "business of the plantation" that had kept Cecil Calvert from personally leading

---

*Clayton Colman Hall, ed., *Narratives of Early Maryland, 1633–1684* (New York: Charles Scribner's Sons, 1910), 13–23.

15. John Winthrop, *A Modell of Christian Charity* (1630).

the expedition to Maryland. Unsurprisingly, an important section of the instructions concerns the careful approach they are to take with Claiborne in ascertaining the extent of the challenge he represents to Lord Baltimore, should they fail to persuade him that his best interests will be served by recognizing Cecil Calvert's title to the entire province, including Claiborne's enclave on Kent Island.[16]

In directing that his officials as well as the rest of the settlers take an oath of allegiance to the king, is Calvert revealing that he does not share his father's conscientious objection to a formula of fealty that offends his Catholic faith? Why would the proprietor set the erection of a town as the colony's first objective rather than the development of the network of manors that had been the centerpiece of his prior planning for the colony? What particulars of Lord Baltimore's instructions reveal his economic as well as religious interests in establishing a colony in America?

1. His Lordship requires his said Governor and Commissioners that in their voyage to Mary Land they be very careful to preserve unity and peace amongst all the passengers on Shipp-board, and that they suffer no scandal nor offence to be given to any of the Protestants, whereby any just complaint may hereafter be made, by them, in Virginia or in England, and that for that end, they cause all Acts of Roman Catholic Religion to be done as privately as may be, and that they instruct all the Roman Catholics to be silent upon all occasions of discourse concerning matters of Religion; and that the said Governor and Commissioners treat the Protestants with as much mildness and favor as Justice will permit. And this to be observed at Land as well as at Sea.

2. That while they are aboard, they do their best endeavors by such instruments as they shall find fittest for it, amongst the seamen and passengers to discover what any of them do know concerning the private plots of his Lordships' adversaries in England, who endeavored to overthrow his voyage: to learn, if they can, the names of all such, their speeches, where and when they spoke them, and to whom; the places, if they had any, of their consultations, the Instruments they used and the like; to gather what proofs they can of them; and to set them down particularly and clearly in writing with all the Circumstances; together with their opinions of the truth and validity of them according to the conditions of the persons from whom they had the information; And to get if they can every such informer to set his hand to his Information. And if they find it necessary and that they have any good probable ground to discover the truth better, or that they find some

16. Off the middle portion of the Eastern Shore of Chesapeake Bay.

unwilling to reveal that which (by some speeches at random, that have fallen from them) they have reason to suspect, they do know concerning that business: that at their arrival in Mary Land they cause every such person to answer upon oath, to such questions as they shall think fit to propose unto them: And by some trusty messenger in the next ships that return to England to send his Lordship in writing all such Intelligences taken either by deposition or otherwise.

3. That as soon as it shall please god they shall arrive upon the coast of Virginia, they be not persuaded by the master or any other of the ship, in any case or for any respect whatsoever to go to James Town, or to come within the command of the fort at Point-Comfort:[17] unless they should be forced unto it by some extremity of weather, (which god forbid) for the preservation of their lives and goods, and that they find it altogether impossible otherwise to preserve themselves; But that they come to an Anchor somewhere about Accomac,[18] so as it be not under the command of any fort; and to send ashore there, to inquire if they can find any to take with them, that can give them some good information of the Bay of Chesapeake and Potomac River, and that may give them some light of a fit place in his Lordship's Country to set down on; wherein their chief care must be to make choice of a place first that is probable to be healthful and fruitful, next that it may be easily fortified, and thirdly that it may be convenient for trade both with the English and savages.

4. That by the first opportunity after their arrival in Mary Land they cause a messenger to be dispatched away to James Town such a one as is conformable to the Church of England, and ... they may ... trust; and he to carry his majesty's letter to Sir John Harvey the Governor and to the rest of the Council there, so likewise his Lordship's letter to Sir John Harvey and to give him notice of their arrival: and ... to behave himself with much respect unto the Governor, and to tell him that his Lordship had an intention to have come himself in person this year into those parts, as he may perceive by his majesty's letter to him but finding that the settling of that business of his Plantation and some other occasions, required his presence in England for some time longer than he expected, he hath deferred his own coming till the next year, when he will not fail by the grace of god to be there; and to let him understand how much his Lordship desires to hold a good cor-

17. The mouth of the York River where it meets Chesapeake Bay.
18. On the lower portion of the eastern peninsula of Chesapeake Bay.

respondency with him and that Plantation of Virginia, ... and to assure him by the best words he can, of his Lordship's particular affection to his person, in respect of the many reports he hath heard of his worth, and of the ancient acquaintance and friendship which he hath understood was between his Lordship's father and him as likewise for those kind respects he hath shown unto his Lordship by his letters since he understood of his Lordship's intention to be his neighbor in those parts....

5. That they write a letter to Cap: Claiborne as soon as conveniently ... after their arrival in the Country, to give him notice of their arrival and of the Authority and charge committed to them by his Lordship and to send the said letter together with his Lordship's to him by some trusty messenger that is likewise conformable unto the Church of England, with a message ... to invite him kindly to come unto them, and to signify that they have some business of importance to speak with him about from his Lordship which concerns his good very much; And if he come unto them then that they ... tell him, that his Lordship understanding that he hath settled a plantation there within the precincts of his Lordship's Patent, wished ... to let him know that his Lordship is willing to give him all the encouragement he can to proceed; And that his Lordship hath had some propositions made unto him by certain merchants in London who pretend to be partners with him in that plantation, ... and that they desired to have a grant from his Lordship of that Island where he is: But his Lordship understanding from some others that there was some difference in partnership between him and them, and his Lordship finding them in their discourse to him, that they made somewhat slight of Cap: Claiborne's interest, doubted lest he might prejudice him by making them any grant his Lordship being ignorant of the true state of their business and of the thing they desired, as likewise being well assured that by Cap: Claiborne his care and industry besides his charges, that plantation was first begun and so far advanced, was for these reasons unwilling to condescend unto their desires, and therefore deferred all treaty with them till his Lordship could truly understand from him, how matters stand between them, and what he would desire of his Lordship in it ...; that thereupon his Lordship may take it into farther consideration how to do justice to every one of them and to give them all reasonable satisfaction; And that they assure him in fine that his Lordship intends not to do him any wrong, but to show him all the love and favor that he can ...; in confidence that he will, like a good subject to his majesty, conform himself to his highness's gracious letters patents granted to his Lordship.... If he do refuse

to come unto them upon their invitation, that they let him alone for the first year, till upon notice given to his Lordship of his answer and behaviour they receive farther directions from his Lordship; and that they inform themselves as well as they can of his plantation and what his designs are, of what strength and what Correspondency he keeps with Virginia, and to give an Account of every particular to his Lordship.

6. That when they have made choice of the place where they intend to settle themselves and that they have brought their men ashore with all their provisions, they do assemble all the people together in a fit and decent manner and then cause his majesty's letters patents to be publicly read by his Lordship's Secretary John Bolles, and afterwards his Lordship's Commission to them, and that either the Governor or one of the Commissioners presently after make some short declaration to the people of his Lordship's intentions which he means to pursue in this his intended plantation, which are first the honor of god by endeavoring the conversion of the savages to Christianity, secondly the augmentation of his majesty's Empire and Dominions in those parts of the world by reducing them under the subjection of his Crown, and thirdly by the good of such of his Countrymen as are willing to adventure their fortunes and themselves in it, by endeavoring all he can, to assist them, that they may reap the fruits of their charges and labors according to the hopefulness of the thing, with as much freedom comfort and encouragement as they can desire; and with all to assure them, that his Lordship's affection and zeal is so great to the advancement of this Plantation and consequently of their good, that he will employ all his endeavors in it, and that he would not have failed to have come himself in person along with them this first year, to have been partaker with them in the honor of the first voyage thither, but that by reasons of some unexpected accidents, he found it more necessary for their good to stay in England some time longer, for the better establishment of his and their right …, but that by the grace of god he intends without fail, to be with them the next year: And that at this time they take occasion to minister an oath of Allegiance to his majesty unto all and every one upon the place, after having first publicly in the presence of the people taken it themselves; letting them know that his Lordship gave particular directions to have it one of the first things that were done, to testify to the world that none should enjoy the benefit of his majesty's gracious Grant unto his Lordship of that place, but such as should give a public assurance of their fidelity and allegiance to his majesty.

7. That they inform themselves what they can of the present state of the old Colony of Virginia, both for matter of government and Plantation as likewise what trades they drive both at home and abroad, who are the chief and richest men, and have the greatest power amongst them whether their clamors against his Lordship's patent continue and whether they increase or diminish, who they are of note that show themselves most in it, and to find out as near as they can, what is the true reason of their disgust against it, or whether there be really any other reason but what, being well examined proceeds rather from spleen and malice than from any other cause; And to inform his Lordship exactly what they understand in any of these particulars.

8. That they take all occasions to gain and oblige any of the Council of Virginia, that they shall ... incline to have a good correspondency with his Lordship's plantation, either by permission of trade to them in a reasonable proportion with in his Lordship's precincts, or any other way they can, so it be clearly understood that is by way of courtesy and not of right.

9. That where they intend to settle the Plantation they first make choice of a fit place, and a competent quantity of ground for a fort, within which or near unto it a convenient house, and a church or a chapel adjacent may be built, for the seat of his Lordship or his Governor or other Commissioners for the time being in his absence, both which his Lordship would have them take care should in the first place be erected, in some proportion at least, as much as is necessary for present use though not so complete in every part as in fine afterwards they may be and to send his Lordship a Plat of it, ... if it be done by that time, if not ... to send a Plat of what they intend to do in it. That they likewise make choice of a fit place near unto it to seat a town.

10. That they cause all the Planters to build their houses in as decent and uniform a manner as their abilities and the place will afford, and near adjoining one to an other, and for that purpose to cause streets to be marked out where they intend to place the town and to oblige every man to build one by an other according to that rule and that they cause divisions of Land to be made adjoining on the back sides of their houses and to be assigned unto them for gardens and such users according to the proportion of every one's building and adventure and as the convenience of the place will afford which his Lordship refers to their discretion, but is desirous to have a particular account from them what they do in it, that his Lordship may be satisfied that every man hath justice done unto him.

11. That as soon as conveniently they can they cause his Lordship's sur-

veyor Robert Simpson to survey out such a proportion of Land both in and about the intended town as likewise within the Country adjoining as will be necessary to be assigned to the present adventurers, and that they assign every adventurer his proportion of Land both in and about the intended town, as also within the Country adjoining, according to the proportion of his adventure and the conditions of plantation propounded by his Lordship to the first adventurers, which his Lordship in convenient time will confirm unto them by Patent. And herein his Lordship wills his said Governor and Commissioners to take care that in each of the aforesaid places, that is to say in and about the first intended Town and in the Country adjacent they cause in the first and most convenient places a proportion of Land to be set out for his Lordship's own proper use and inheritance according to the number of men he sends this first year upon his own account; and … he will in this first colony, content himself, for the better encouragement and accommodation of the first adventurers, unto whom his Lordship conceive himself more bound in honor …, to give more satisfaction in everything than he intends to do unto any that shall come hereafter. That they cause his Lordship's surveyor likewise to draw an exact map of as much of the country as they shall discover together with the soundings of the rivers and Bay, and to send it to his Lordship.

12. That they cause all the planters to employ their servants in planting of sufficient quantity of corn and other provision of victual and that they do not suffer them to plant any other commodity whatsoever before that be done in a sufficient proportion which they are to observe yearly.

13. That they cause all sorts of men in the plantation to be mustered and trained in military discipline and that there be days appointed for that purpose either weekly or monthly according to the convenience of other occasions; which are duly to be observed and that they cause constant watch and ward to be kept in places necessary.

14. That they inform themselves whether there be any convenient place within his Lordship's precincts for the making of Salt, whether there be proper earth for the making of saltpeter and if there be in what quantity; whether there be probability of Iron ore or any other mines and that they be careful to find out what other commodities may probably be made and that they give his Lordship notice together with their opinions of them.

15. That in fine they be very careful to do justice to every man without partiality, and that they avoid any occasion of difference with those of Vir-

ginia, and to have as little to do with them as they can this first year that they connive and suffer little injuries from them rather than to engage themselves in a public quarrel with them, which may disturb the business much in England in the Infancy of it. And that they give unto his Lordship an exact account by their letters from time to time of their proceedings both in these instructions from Article to Article and in any other accident that shall happen worthy his Lordship's notice, that thereupon his Lordship may give them farther instructions what to do and that by every conveyance by which they send any letters[,] as his Lordship would not have them to omit any[, that] they send likewise a Duplicate of the letters which they wrote by the last conveyance before that, lest, they should have failed [to] ... come to his Lordship's hands.

11

"God's Hand Is Here": Andrew White,
A Brief Relation of the Voyage unto
Maryland, 1634 *

The Jesuit Constitutions required superiors to make annual reports to Rome. White, as the superior of the new mission, was carrying out this responsibility of his office through this Latin "relation" sent to Rome to Mutius Vitelleschi, the superior general of the Society of Jesus. Apparently White was also the author of an English version of their voyage and initial settlement that the Ark carried to Lord Baltimore on its return trip. Both intrinsic and extrinsic evidence suggest that the English version antedated the Latin. For one, reporting to Cecil Calvert, for whom White had provided key assistance in the planning of the colony, would have taken precedence over submitting an annual report to the provincial or superior general of the Society of Jesus. Then there were the linguistic concerns that would be better addressed by writing out the "relation" in English first rather than in Latin. In any event the English text in the main parallels its Latin counterpart, but tailors its content for Cecil Calvert, thus skirting over religious details while expanding information that the proprietor would have welcomed, such as a candid evaluation of the tenuous relations with Virginia

* Hughes, *HSJNA*, Documents, vol. 1, part 1, 94–107; Latin.

as well as a confirmation of the abounding natural resources that had been the major selling point for joining the Maryland venture in the tracts that Lord Baltimore had published. Both versions reveal an observer who has a keen eye for natural detail as well as a deeply providential view of the history that has brought them to this new Eden with its "innocent" natives yearning, not for another tree of knowledge that had been the ruin of the first pair, but for the salvation that Christ has won through his death on a tree of life. In what ways does White's providential lens interpret their experience of the voyage and initial settlement in Maryland? What, in White's narrative, gives a Catholic cast to their "errand into the wilderness"?

On St. Cecilias day, November 22, 1633, with a gentle northern breeze we set sail from Cowes, a port on the Isle of Wight.[19] After entrusting the ship and its passengers to God's care, especially through the intercession of His most holy mother, Mary, St. Ignatius and all the angels of Maryland, a dying wind forced us to anchor at Yarmouth.... Here we were greeted with a salute of cannon. Still we were apprehensive, since we had overheard the seamen on our ship talking about a messenger from London they expected bearing letters, which information seemed to explain their apparent reluctance to get underway. But God scuttled whatever evil they had in store for us. That very night, a sudden gust of wind broke loose from her anchor a French bark docked close to us, which in turn, to avoid a collision, our pinnace, the *Dove*, was forced to sea as well, without its anchor, a dangerous condition to be in upon the open waters. Seeing that, we decided to follow. So the plotting of our sailors came to naught. It was the twenty-third of November, St. Clement's day, who was martyred by being cast into the sea tied to an anchor. Once again God showed Himself to humankind through his wondrous deeds, now in the form of an unfettered anchor.

By ten o'clock in the morning we came to Hurst Castle, at the extreme end of the Isle of Wight, whence we were greeted with rockets. This is a dangerous area of sharp rocks, aptly called the "Needles," a terror to sailors, on account of its double tide which has shipwrecked many vessels upon its rocks or sand. I forgot to mention the other close call we earlier had near Yarmouth Castle. While waiting to sail, the gale winds and raging tide

19. The voyage had actually originated at Gravesend, a port twenty miles southeast of London and more than 120 miles removed from Cowes. Only a minority of those bound for Maryland—that is, the three Jesuits and most, if not all, of the Catholics—boarded the *Ark* on the Isle of Wight, in order to escape the anti-papist oath that those departing from England were required to take.

threatened to drive our ship onto shore. Miraculously some unseen force turned the ship about and headed it out to sea. So by God's mercy we escaped the mortal danger; through the merits of St. Clement God gave us this additional pledge of His protection.

All that Saturday and the night following we had such a favorable wind that by nine a.m. the next day we had cleared the western Cape of England and the Scilly Isles.[20] We kept a moderate speed, to accommodate our slower pinnace, which we feared to leave behind, where she might become the prey of Turks or other pirates known to infest these waters.

It so happened that a fine merchant ship of six hundred tons, named the *Dragon*, on her way from London to Angola, overtook us, about three o'clock in the afternoon. And as we now, all dangers passed, had time to enjoy a little pleasure, a race between the two ships ensued. With fair weather and a favorable wind, for an entire hour we tried to outrun each other. Our ship, despite refraining from employing her topsail, would surely have prevailed in the contest, had we not been ultimately held back by our pinnace. So in the end we yielded the palm to the merchant ship, and before evening she passed out of sight.

Throughout Sunday 24 [November] and until evening of Monday ... we had fair sailing, when, the wind shifting to the north, such a terrible storm arose that the merchant ship that we had raced, being driven back on her course, had to return to England.... Those on board our pinnace, since she weighed but forty tons, began to lose confidence in her ability to withstand the storm; approaching us, they alerted us, that if they saw the prospect of her being wrecked, they would signal us by hanging lights from the masthead. All the while, our incomparable stout ship of wood and iron continued on its course. We gave our captain, a very skilled seaman, the choice of returning to England or continuing to fight the winds; if they won, the hidden rocks of the looming Irish shore awaited us, along with the ships it had claimed before us. A bold man, he relished the chance to test the strength of this new ship. He chose to continue, although he confessed that the narrow straits in which he had to maneuver made it a dangerous business.

It took little time for danger to find us. The winds increasing, and the sea growing more turbulent, we could see the pinnace in the distance, showing two lights at her masthead—the sign of distress. When she passed out

---

20. A group of small islands fifteen miles southwest from Lands End, at the tip of Cornwall.

of sight, we on the *Ark* thought it was all over for our sister ship, that she had been swallowed up in the deep whirlpools engulfing her. For the next six to seven weeks we saw nothing of her. By then we were certain she had been lost. But God had better things in store for us. Later we learned that the pinnace, finding herself no match for the violent waves, had abandoned the open sea for the Scilly Isles of England. In calm weather she resumed her voyage, along with the *Dragon*, and caught up with us … at a large bay in the Antilles. Thus God who oversees the smallest things, guided, protected, and watched over the little vessel.

We, of course, knowing nothing of these events, were filled with anxiety and grief, which the night with its recurrent terrors only made worse. When day dawned, although the wind from the southwest was against us, it was weak enough to allow us, by tacking frequently, to resume our course at a crawl. So Tuesday, Wednesday, and Thursday passed, the slight winds enabling us to make virtually no headway. Finally on Friday, [November] … 29 a south-east wind prevailing, and driving before it thick, dark clouds, so fierce a tempest broke forth towards evening, that it seemed that we would be swallowed up by the waves at any minute. Nor was the weather any more promising the next day, which was the feast of Andrew the Apostle. The clouds, accumulating in a frightful manner, were terrible to behold, before they parted, which made one think that all the demons of the storm and all the evil spirits of Maryland had come forth to battle us. Towards evening the captain saw a solitary sun fish swimming with great effort against the sun's course, a reliable sign of a powerful storm in the offing; nor did the omen prove a false one. For about ten o'clock at night a dark cloud produced a violent shower. Such was its force that, despite frantic efforts to take down the mainsail, so it would not be torn in half, part of it blew into the sea, which we managed to bring back aboard with great difficulty.

This had a terrifying effect upon both passengers and sailors, no matter how brave, who had seen ships wrecked in storms far less severe than the one we were experiencing. Prayers and vows to the Blessed Virgin Mary, as well as to St. Ignatius, the Patron Saint of Maryland, St. Michael, and all the guardian angels of Maryland, came forth spontaneously from the Catholics on board, who turned to the two priests to confess their sins. Meanwhile, the rudderless ship rolled about the teeming sea, like a discus, at the mercy of the winds and the waves, until God at last showed the way to safety. At first, I must confess, I was engrossed with the apprehension of the ship going down, myself along with it. After praying, however, in a more fervent way than was my usual style, putting forth to Christ the Lord, to the Blessed Virgin, St. Ignatius, and the angels of Maryland, the whole purpose for our watery journey: to bring salvation to savages for the glory of the Lord who had shed his blood to redeem us; to raise up, God willing, a new kingdom for the Savior, to make of it yet another oblation in honor of the Immaculate Virgin, His Mother—after such prayers, a great peace came over me, bringing with it the firm conviction that we would be delivered, not only from this storm, but from every other one we might encounter on our voyage; of that I no longer had any doubt. My prayer had begun when the storm was raging its worst. I had scarcely concluded when people began to remark that the storm was abating. I felt my state of mind transformed—filled with great joy and wonder, understanding much more clearly the greatness of God's love towards the people of Maryland.... May such a gracious Redeemer be forever praised!! Amen.

Once the sea calmed, we had delightful weather for three months....

As we made our way by indifferent winds along the Spanish Coast, we were afraid we might encounter Turks but we saw none.... After we had passed the Straits of Hercules and the Maderas, we caught a trade wind which carried us southward toward Africa. Then appeared three ships, one of which dwarfed ours, about three leagues west of us, apparently trying to overtake us, as they signaled each other back and forth. Since we suspected them to be Turks, we made ready to fight them. Some on board were urging the captain to challenge them, but he replied that he could not take that risk, for the ship owners' sake. My own feeling was that he would be taking on a very difficult fight, if he did so. As it turned out, they were merchant ships from the Canary Islands who were as apprehensive about us as we were of them....

Heading toward the Canary Islands, we entered the Great Gulf, where our paramount fear was the notorious calms which could last for two or even three weeks, reducing seafarers' provisions to starvation levels. That, fortunately, is a very rare occurrence. Normally, the lack of wind merely causes a frustrating delay in one's voyage. For our own part, the winds held steady; we hit a calm for just one hour one day around noon.

And here I cannot pass on, without praising the Divine Goodness, Who makes all things work together for good for those who love God. For, consider if we had met no delay in England and been allowed to sail at the time we had planned, namely on the twentieth of August, we would have encountered a sun still on this side of the equator. Its intense heat would not only have ruined our provisions, but would have brought disease and death upon virtually all of us. The delay saved our lives. Embarking in winter time, as we did, we escaped the sun's destructive power. And if you except the usual sea-sickness, we were spared any illness until Christmas Day, when wine was served in honor of the feast and those who overindulged came down with a fever the very next day which claimed the lives of a dozen voyagers, including two Catholics, Nicholas Fairfax and James Barefote, whose deaths greatly affected us all....

At length, sailing from St. Christopher's, we reached the cape, which they call Point Comfort, in Virginia, on February 27. We were full of apprehension that the English inhabitants, who were very unhappy about our settlement plans, would have some plot in store for us. It turned out that the letters we bore from the King, as well as from the Exchequer of England, served to allay their anger, and secure for us articles that would prove useful in Maryland. You see, the governor of Virginia was hoping that by showing us kindness he would more likely recover the large sum of money that the Crown owed him. They did pass on the vague rumor that six ships were on their way here to subdue the region for the Spanish crown, which rumor had the natives on the warpath. The Indian uprising turned out to be the truth. The original story, I suspect, originated with the English themselves.[21]

After eight or nine days of their hospitality, we left Jamestown on the third of March. Once into the Chesapeake, we headed north until we reached the *Potomac* River. The Chesapeake Bay, ten leagues (30 Italian miles) wide, flows gently between its shores; it is four, five and six fathoms deep. and is awash in fish when the season is favorable. You will with difficulty find a more beautiful body of water. Yet it yields the palm to the Potomac River, which we named after St. Gregory.

21. The English version casts the Virginians in a much darker light. It makes clear that most of the colony's officials, led by William Claiborne, were still virulently opposed to the Calverts's Maryland project and identifies Claiborne as the source of the fanciful warning about a Spanish incursion. The Virginian merchant had ample reason for his opposition, having established a very lucrative trading operation on Kent Island on the Eastern Shore of Chesapeake Bay only to have that territory included by charter in the new province of Maryland. Whatever hospitality and assistance they received at Jamestown was due to the governor's self-interest in winning their favor. During their whole stay there of more than a week, it notes, they never felt out of "imminent danger."

A more pleasing river I have never seen. The Thames seems a mere rivulet in comparison. There are no marshlands, but firm ground on which is a great variety of trees not choked by underbrush but with enough distance between them to allow a coach and four to easily get through. Just at the mouth of the river, we noticed the natives in arms. That night, fires blazed through the whole countryside. Since the natives had never seen such a large ship, messengers were sent in all directions to announce that a canoe as large as an island had come bearing as many men as there were trees in the woods. Meanwhile we pushed on to Herons' Island, so called from the immense number of those birds. The first island we came to, [we called] St. Clement's Island, the second St. Catharine, the third St. Cecilia. We went on shore first on St. Clement's, which with its high banks is impossible to reach except by wading. Here the servant women, who had headed for shore in a small boat to do our washing, nearly drowned when they upset the small craft. Much of our linen clothing was lost, a serious loss in these parts.

The island itself, at four hundred acres, was too small for our settlement. Its location at the narrowest point of the Potomac did stir us to investigate the possibility of erecting a fort there, to provide protection for river traffic and against any intrusion of foreigners.

On the feast of the Annunciation of the Most Holy Virgin Mary we celebrated Mass for the first time on this island, something that had never before been done in this part of the world. Mass being over, the governor, commissioners, and other Catholics took upon their shoulders a giant cross, which had been hewn out of a tree, and carried it in procession to a prearranged place, where we erected it as a monument to Christ our Saviour. On bended knees we recited, with great emotion, the litany of the Sacred Cross.

When our governour learned that many princes in the region were subject to the Emperor of the Piscataway, he decided to visit him, in order that, after explaining the reason for our coming, and thus gaining his good will, we might gain an easier access to his subordinates. So taking the pinnace, together with another ship we had purchased in Virginia, and leaving the *Ark* at anchor at St. Clements, by a roundabout course the governor sailed to the southern shore of the river. There he learned that the savages had fled inland, so he proceeded on by river to a town, which takes its name from the river, Potomac. Here he found Archihu, the uncle of the young king who was his guardian and regent. A sober and discreet man, Archihu patiently listened to Father Altham, who had accompanied the governor (I myself had been detained with care of the ship's cargo), as he explained as best he could through a Protestant interpreter from Virginia, all the false beliefs of the pagans. The guardian acknowledged them as his own. When informed that we had come into their country, not to make war, but in order to enlighten his people and show them the path to heaven, as well as sharing with them the goods of far-off lands, he gave the impression that this pleased him. When Altham promised to return before very long in order to continue their discussion, Archihu responded: "This is just what I wish, we will eat at the same table; my followers too shall go to hunt for you, and we will have all things in common." ...

From Potomac they went on to Piscataway, the seat of the emperor, where the whole tribe was primed for the warpath. Five hundred bowmen came with the emperor to confront them at the water's edge. When the newcomers gave signs that they came in peace, the emperor, less suspicious than his people, came aboard the pinnace, and sensing that we came with good intentions, gave his permission for us to settle wherever we liked.

While the governor had been on his way to the emperor, the local natives became bold enough to come onto St. Clement's to mingle with those families on watch. For we keep watch both day and night, to guard both our wood-cutters as well as boat-builders from sudden attacks.

It was amusing to hear them awestruck, wondering where in the world we had found the tree out of which we could have hewn such a massive ship (they supposed that, like their canoes, our ship was formed out of a single tree trunk). The sound of our cannon terrified them; they found it louder than the screaming of their arrows; equal indeed to thunder.

In his visit to the Emperor our governor had taken along Captain Henry Fleet, a Virginian who had become well-versed in the language and culture of the natives. At first he was on very good terms with us, then, under Claiborne's evil influence, he became extremely hostile, and began to poison the minds of the natives against us. Meanwhile, however, pretending still to be our friend, he showed the governor a site as fine as one could find in all of Europe. It was about nine leagues from St. Clements, on the north bank of a river which we named St. George's, which seemed an excellent spot for a harbor. That river, like the Thames, runs from south to north for about twenty miles before it loses its salty component. That harbor is made up of two bays capable of sheltering 300 very large ships. One bay we consecrated to St. George, the other to the Blessed Virgin Mary. On the left side of the river the ruler of the Yaocomacoes had his seat. So we took possession of the right side, and about a mile from the bank we laid out a town which we named St. Mary's. And to be sure that we provoked no hostility or hurt feelings by so taking the land, we purchased from the king thirty miles of his territory, in exchange for axes, hatchets, hoes, and some cloth. We gave the name August Carolinus[22] to the region.

The Susquehannas, a war-prone tribe, had a history of attacking the Yaocomacoes among others, frequently plundering their fields and forcing the inhabitants to flee to places of safety. That is the reason we were able to take over such a large part of their territory. Surely a sign of God's work in disposing things so that the way would be open for the light of his holy law to shine upon those in need of it. Many of them have gone elsewhere; everyday some leave their homes, fields, plows to us and depart. It is truly miraculous, that a tribe that a few days before had been ready to war against us, should now, lamb-like, give us their possessions. God's hand is here, intending some great good for this people. A few of them are remaining here for the duration of the year. By next year all this land will be fully ours.

The natives are tall and proper, swarthy by nature, which they exaggerate by painting themselves with a dark red oil, more for comfort than appearance; it repels gnats.... About their necks they wear twisted glass necklaces, which have recently become much less expensive, hence their commercial value has sunk.

Their customary dress is deer skins or some similar fur, which in the back hangs like a mantle, tied at their waist to an undergarment, otherwise they are nude. Children of both sexes run about without any clothing. For shoes they wear corn-like stalks with sharp thorns. Their weapons are a bow and arrows two cubits long....

Their houses are oval-shaped, nine or ten feet in height. Light is provided by a cubit-sized window in the roof. This also serves as an outlet for the smoke from the fireplace at the center of the structure around whose fire they sleep. The ruler and his court have their own chamber, with a raised bed mounted on four poles, suspended by stakes driven into the ground. I and my companions[23] have appropriated one of these huts for our quarters, until we are able to build a more spacious dwelling. You might call this Maryland's first chapel, although it is scarcely furnished better than it was

22. Literally "the Great Charles."
23. Altham and Gervase.

when the natives inhabited it. God willing, after the next ship arrives, we will have all the domestic necessities that we are accustomed to having.

This is an intelligent, quick-witted people. Their senses of taste and smell are excellent; their eyesight far superior to that of Europeans. Their main diet is a kind of porridge, which they call Pone and hominy; made from wheat; sometimes they add to it fish, or what venison or fowl they are able to get through hunting. They strictly avoid wine and hot beverages, nor are they easily led into experimenting with these vices, except for those unfortunates whom the English have corrupted. As for chastity, I can say that I have never seen any behavior in male or female which smacks even of levity; this, despite their being daily in our midst, indeed they glory in our company.... They strictly observe conjugal fidelity through plural monogamy. The women are stoical and modest in their mien. In general this is a magnanimous people, who will respond in kind to any favor you may do them....

Should this people be brought to Christianity (and to my mind the only obstacle is our unfamiliarity with their language) they would prove to be a nation renowned for their virtue.

They are keen to adopt European culture and dress; and they certainly would have already been appropriately outfitted, had it not been for the avarice of English merchants who refused to sell them cloth except in exchange for beaver, which was scarce. May we not follow their example....

Having been here but a month, I must defer saying anything more until the next ship departs. Let me close by saying ... this is a land rich in resources as well as beauty.

Sources

"A Briefe Relation of the Voyage unto Maryland" [1634]. *Archives of Maryland*. Vol. 552:5–24. http://www.aomol.msa.maryland.gov/html/index/html.

Hall, Clayton Colman, ed. *Narratives of Early Maryland, 1633–1684*. New York: Charles Scribner's Sons, 1910.

Hughes, Thomas. *The History of the Society of Jesus in North America: Colonial and Federal.* Text. Vol. 1, *From the First Colonization till 1645*. London: Longmans, Green, 1908.

Lawatsch-Boomgaarden, Barbara, trans. and ed. *Voyage to Maryland (1633): Relatio itineris in Marilandiam*. Wauconda, Ill.: Bolchazy-Carducci, 1995.

Quinn, David Beers, ed. *Maryland in a Wider World*. Detroit: Wayne State University Press, 1982.

Scharf, Thomas. *The History of Maryland*. Vol. 1. Baltimore: Piet, 1879.

Winthrop, John. *A Modell of Christian Charity*. 1630.

Part 3

A Catholic Colony
in British America

1634–1664

THE GRANTING OF A CHARTER to a Catholic high in the king's
government to plant a colony in England's New World domains
had roused fears about its subversive implications for a Protestant
nation—fears serious enough to move the Calverts to commission a tract
minimizing the significance and threat of the "Catholic colony" in the planning (see "A Rich Harvest Awaits Us"). Had the Calverts known how many
Catholics would actually be part of the initial settlement, the level of reas-
surance about the benefits that Maryland would bring to king and empire
would have been substantially higher. When the Jesuit superior of the English province in 1638 reported to Rome that "there are Protestants as well as
Catholics in the colony," he was coyly understating the actual disparity that
from its beginnings made Catholics a tiny proportion of the English community in Maryland, probably never exceeding a quarter of the population
(in the 1640s) and throughout most of the colonial era registering at less
than 10 percent.

As noted in part 2, the vast majority of the passengers on the *Ark* and *Dove* were servants who had indentured themselves for terms of four to seven years in exchange for their passage to America and support during their time of service on the plantations to be developed. The servants themselves were virtually all Protestants, in sharp contrast to the adventurers or planters, nearly all Catholics. Despite the heavily Protestant character of the newcomers, the only ministers in the colony were the two Jesuit priests, Andrew White and John Altham. Not until 1650 would the first Protestant minister arrive in Maryland; the lack of appropriate religious ministry would be a source of growing discontent among an influential portion of the colony's Protestants by the last quarter of the century. For now the Catholic clergy enjoyed a monopoly that they effectively made the most of in evangelizing the Protestants in their midst. Their outreach was made all the easier by the colonists' confinement, for their first three years in Maryland, within the walls of St. Mary's City. The Catholic chapel was the only church in the fortified village. Not surprisingly, Protestants dominated the attendance at masses and other religious rites held there. The Jesuits, for their part, despite Lord Baltimore's prudent charge that the Catholics, as a very small minority, practice their religion discreetly, were opportunistic proselytizers, particularly with those in danger of death. Over the first four years in St. Mary's, many servants became Catholics.

Maryland experienced a less harsh initial seasoning for its settlers than Virginia had three decades earlier. Still, life-threatening situations were the stuff of daily life in first-generation Maryland for planter, religious, and servant alike. Probably at least a fifth of the original colonists failed to survive the first five years. The survival rate of the planters was particularly low. Disease, accidents, and departures by 1639 claimed all but six of the original twenty gentleman adventurers. A steady influx of immigrants, both freemen and indentured servants, accounted for Maryland's annual 10 percent growth. They worked the manors that began to be developed in 1638. Once they fulfilled their terms of service, former servants easily acquired land themselves as the line of settlement in the colony pushed north and east. As the inhabitants became increasingly scattered on sprawling manors and small farms along the countless waterways that intersected the peninsula between the Potomac and the Patuxent rivers, tobacco quickly became the dominant staple crop, totally overshadowing the fur trade with nearby tribes that the Calverts had envisioned as a major source of revenue but that failed to develop as such. To meet the spiritual needs of those involved in such a centrifugal movement, the Jesuits began to expand their missions beyond St. Mary's City, even across the bay to the Eastern Shore of Maryland.

But ministering to English settlers, be they Catholic or other, had not been the magnet that drew so many Jesuits to the Maryland mission. From the first year in the colony, Andrew White and his companions had pressed Leonard Calvert to approve their going forth from St. Mary's to evangelize the Patuxent and other tribes in the general area. When Governor Calvert finally determined that the religious would find a welcome among the natives, Andrew White and John Altham, the first two priests in the colony, headed to Indian villages on the Western and Eastern shores of the Chesapeake to spread the gospel. Others followed. Despite the obstacles of nature (disease and death), Indian hostility, the lack of missioners, and language barrier, the Jesuits, through adaptation of a mobile ministry (becoming, in effect, waterborne circuit riders) and inculcation of the local culture and language of the regional Algonquian tribes, by the mid-1640s saw truly heartening results in the conversion of scores of Indian rulers, their families, and other principal figures among the Piscataway, Patuxents, and other indigenous Americans within the province. As went the leaders, so, it was expected, would their people. The annual reports of the missioners over the colony's first decade delineate the initial reaping of the abundant harvest that White had envisioned back in London in 1633 (see "A Rich Harvest Awaits Us").

Then in early 1645 Lord Baltimore's belated commitment to the royal side of the English Civil War led to an invasion of his colony by Virginia forces loyal to Parliament that brought all the Jesuit missionary progress to an abrupt halt. Richard Ingle and his mercenaries drove the Jesuits as well as the Calvert government out of the colony to begin the "plundering time" that nearly wiped out the colony (see the introduction to part 4). When the Calverts regained power nearly two years later, the Jesuits returned to find the Indians waiting for them to renew their work among them. This work never happened. At first there were too few Jesuits to take up again the all-important Indian apostolate. Then, when in the next decade there were enough Jesuits, the natives they had come to evangelize were being forced out of the province, not by the newcomer English, but by the natives' ancient foe, the Susquehannas.

Lord Baltimore's attempts to preserve peace in his colony after weathering the Ingle invasion by incorporating Protestants into his government and passing legislation that protected religious freedom (for Christians) did not succeed,[1] as civil war between Catholic royalist and Protestant parliamentarian again tore apart Maryland in 1651. Calvert had regained control within a year and a half of Ingle's invasion through a bloodless counterinvasion. The second conflict lasted much longer, six years, before the proprietor once again secured his authority in Maryland, not by force, but by shrewdly exploiting the shifting political winds in England to win the support of Oliver Cromwell.

Amid the power shifts between the Calverts and their Protestant opponents, which convulsed the colony for fifteen years, the Jesuits struggled to maintain their precarious existence in the Chesapeake. At several points, indeed, the mission seemed on the brink of dissolution, only to survive once again as the face of Roman Catholicism in British America. Even more resilient were the Calverts, who twice were driven from power but managed, through force or negotiation, to regain their colony. With the restoration of the Stuarts in 1660, Lord Baltimore and his circle of family and favorites were poised to lead the colony through a generation of unprecedented growth and prosperity.

Immigration was the engine driving population growth. Indentured males, although not as dominant among newcomers as they had been in the first decade of the province, still were a large majority. One such was George Alsop, who in 1658 left an apprenticeship in London to bind himself for service in Maryland. After completing his four-year indenture as an artisan on an estate in Baltimore County, he returned to England. There, with Lord Baltimore's financial support, he published, in 1666, a small volume on Maryland. As a promotional tract, "A Character of the Province of Maryland" extolled the abundance of economic resources and the religious equanimity that enabled indentured servants to become productive, land-owning farmers (see "The Miracle of this Age").

1. See essay 16, "The Better to Preserve Mutual Love and Amity."

12

"A Rich Harvest Awaits Us": Jesuit Correspondence relating to Maryland, 1634–1656*

As a worldwide religious body the Society of Jesus required its regional superiors to write annually to the superior general in Rome. The letters that follow were part of the correspondence between Jesuit authorities at the Roman curia and the English provincials dealing with the newly established Maryland Mission. Against the backdrop of a society in which death was virtually a constant presence, at the center of these reports is a wonder-working God who uses and transcends nature to redeem Englishmen and indigenous Americans, the first fruits of the spreading of the gospel into a virgin land, and the ultimate authentication of the Maryland Mission's errand.

The annual letters reporting on the first decade of Maryland's history focus almost exclusively on the Native American apostolate that the Jesuits were finally able to begin in 1638, four years after the Ark and Dove cast anchor off St. Clement's Island. That concentration is not surprising, seeing that the evangelization of the Indians was the driving motivation that brought most of the Jesuits to Maryland. That being said, what do the letters reveal about life for the English settlers in the first decades of the colony and about the extent of the outreach of the Jesuit ministry to Europeans in the Chesapeake region? From these annual reports, how would you characterize the moral health of the freemen and servants in Maryland? How do the Jesuits adapt in order to bring the gospel to the native tribes in the region? To what extent, if any, do the English missioners attempt to inculturate Christianity among the different tribes they encounter?

Henry More, Annual Letter of the English Province, 1634

By the gracious will of the king,[2] last year a certain Catholic baron led a large group of Catholics to the far-off shores of English America to establish a colony.[3]

---

* Thomas Hughes, HSJNA, Documents, vol. 1, part 1, 32–33, 107–31; Latin.

2. Henry was the grandson of Sir Thomas More and the superior of the English Province.

3. Actually Catholics comprised a small portion, probably fewer than thirty, of the nearly 150 persons on board.

With the voyagers went three of Ours,[4] two priests and a lay brother.[5] Since then, another priest and brother have gone there also. Their ministry will consist not only of working with the settlers, but also of evangelizing and gaining the salvation of the natives. To ensure the success of such a sacred mission many Catholics have contributed both monies and servants to the enterprise, the latter being such a vital necessity in that place. One particular servant seemed to have been providentially discovered by Ours just at the point of departure. Our lay brother had known him in Flanders to be an industrious and responsible young man. But as he was preparing for the voyage, he was constantly complaining about it. And when it seemed there was no possibility of his turning up for the sailing, as they boarded the pinnace[6] which was carrying supplies for the voyagers, unexpectedly they came upon him. He had gotten himself into a grave predicament by making a contract which he no longer wished to be bound by, to a certain Protestant merchant, who now intended to sell his indenture for service in a Protestant colony; and so he was trying to escape. Our brother bought out his contract. Thus having been snatched from such a fate, the young man with incredible joy joined our expedition.

Edward Knott, Annual Letter, 1638

Four Fathers were manning the mission, along with one lay-brother.[7] The brother, after enduring, for five years, severe hardships with the greatest patience, humility and ardent love, an epidemic finally claimed as one of its fatal victims. He happily exchanged this wretched life for that which is eternal. Brother Gervase was shortly followed by one of the Fathers, who, though young, possessed remarkable qualities of mind, which gave great promise for the future. He had scarcely spent two months in this mission, when, to the great grief of all of us, he was carried off by the sickness so general in the colony, from which none of the three remaining priests have entirely escaped, yet we have not ceased to labor to the best of our ability among the neighboring people.

Though the authorities of this colony have not yet allowed us to dwell among the savages, on account both of the prevailing sickness and of the

---

4. "Ours"—the formal Jesuit reference to fellow members of the Society of Jesus.

5. Andrew White and John Altham (Gravenor) were the priests, Thomas Gervase the lay brother or coadjutor.

6. The *Dove*.

7. Thomas Gervase.

hostile disposition shown by the savages toward the English, to the extent of murdering a man from this colony, who had gone amongst them for the sake of trade, and also of entering into a conspiracy against our whole nation; still we hope that one of us will shortly secure a station among the savages. Meanwhile, we devote ourselves more zealously to the English settlers; and since there are Protestants as well as Catholics in the colony, we have labored for both, and God has blessed our labors.

For among the Protestants, nearly all who came out from England this year (1638) and many others, have been converted to the faith, together with four servants whom we purchased in Virginia ... and five mechanics whom we hired for a month, and have in the meantime won to God. One of these died shortly after his conversion, having received all the appropriate sacraments....

A certain zealous Protestant, whom we did not know at all, was staying with a friend who was even more devoted to his religion. Having been bitten by one of the snakes that abound in these parts, the guest was in great danger of dying. One of our Fathers, hearing of his condition, went with a surgeon to the house in hope of bringing some benefit for his soul, even though he reportedly was already delirious. His host, however, suspecting the priest's intention, refused to leave him alone with his dying friend. The priest, unable to think of any other plan, said he would spend the night by the man's bed. The friend, not about to allow this to happen, stationed a guard at the door of the man's room. The priest, however, returning at midnight, when he surmised, as proved to be the case, the guard would probably be asleep, managed to slip into the room without disturbing the guard. With the dying man's consent, he received him into the church. Given the man's condition, the priest could barely give him any instructions about the faith. Remarkably, the man, contrary to all expectations, was restored to health by the surgeon. Despite the cursory nature of his catechesis, the man remained steadfast in his new faith, and for his fidelity found himself homeless. Our fathers took him in and he proved to be an excellent Catholic.

One of Ours was frustrated by the resistance of another settler to his efforts to bring him to the true faith. The man insisted that he would never embrace that religion. The poor fellow shortly afterwards fell ill and was at death's door before the priest was informed of his condition. He took himself to him as fast he could and found the man senseless but still alive. He advised those taking care of him that for the present they should provide him whatever nourishment they could and to call him, should he regain his senses. Early the next day, the priest visited the sick man and asked the bystanders whether they had noticed any recognition on his part, and whether he was capable of responding to a brief interrogation (for something as long as a sermon he could clearly not tolerate). Therefore since this was an opportunity that would hardly present itself again, the priest instructed those with him that once the man seemed to acknowledge his sins, that he wished to become a Catholic, that he was sorry for his sins, and wished to be absolved from them, he would have his sins absolved and anointed with the sacred oil. Once this was done, within a day or two the man completely regained his senses, and when they inquired what he had done, or rather what he remembered concerning what had happened, he responded with heartfelt joy that he had been admitted into the Catholic Church and that he would remain there until he drew his last breath. Everyone in his hearing was greatly moved by his words. The man later joyfully thanked the priest for what he had done, and gave convincing witness to what one needs to do in striving for perfection....

Another one, of noble birth, who by wild living had been reduced to such a pauper's state that he sold himself for service in this colony, where one of Ours was responsible for bringing him back to the faith and a fruitful life. But he was still tormented whether he was really saved. The reason: during our crossing from England he had been guilty of a small transgression in the pinnace, during that terrible storm, which he, although a very experienced sailor, had never seen the likes of, and was sure that the ship would wreck at any moment. He fervently prayed to God that he would reclaim the faith he had lately abandoned, if only he escaped this present peril. God heard his prayer, and the storm shifting its course, the calming sea brought tranquility to him. Not long after this, that same man, now gravely ill, less than an hour after receiving the last sacraments, asked the Catholic who was caring for him to pray for him. He believed that the devil was appearing to him, as the man teetered on the edge of death, and cried out in a loud voice to his nurse: Do you not see my good angel? Ah, he guards me wherever I may be carried off; he will not abandon me; and so I die in piece (as one can hope)." After his death, there was an extremely bright light shining over his grave that even the Protestants often saw....

As for the Catholics, their attendance on the sacraments is of a very impressive level, one that at least equals European practice. Every Sunday catechesis is given to the young and instructions on the faith provided for adults; on feast days a sermon is ordinarily preached. Sickness and death were very widespread this year. Despite the very scattered settlement here, not one person died without the sacraments. There were a great many funerals. We also baptized a broad variety of persons. And, although there are in this province many opportunities for dissension within the community, whenever in the last nine months one has arisen, we have quickly squelched it. Thank God, we can say that vice is not a problem among us, including the converts, and you know that settlements like Maryland do not usually attract the best class of people.

We bought the contracts of two Catholic indentured servants in Virginia. Nor was the money ill-spent, for both have proven themselves good Christians; one, in fact, is extraordinary. Some other Catholic gentlemen here have practiced the same charity of purchasing Catholics out of servitude in Virginia. And there are a great number in that condition there. Every year a great many persons contract themselves to be indentured servants in Virginia, where they typically find themselves living among the worst kind of people with no recourse to any kind of spiritual nurture. The end result is generally a shipwreck for their souls.

We have given the Spiritual Exercises[8] to several leading men of the colony. By God's incalculable grace, they have attained a really devout state. In one case, of a man bedeviled with so many worldly cares and living as a virtual pagan in Virginia, God in his mercy and providence led him to make the Exercises shortly before his death; he made such spiritual progress through them that he had resolved to live henceforth according to the purest motives. Only a fatal disease frustrated the fulfillment of this intention. He faced it with the greatest resignation, his mind fixed wholly on God, and having received all the sacraments, in a most peaceful manner that was in stark contrast to the troubles and worries of his former life, he gave back his soul to his Creator.

Death has also taken a noble lady, who as one of the first settlers of this colony, endured valiantly every kind of challenge and difficulty. Very much a woman of prayer, deeply desiring the good of her neighbors, utterly dedicated to her family as well as those in her household, in life she was greatly devoted to our Society,[9] in death she has become its benefactor. She will be

8. A manual of meditations and other instructions for the making of a retreat, an intense period, ranging from a day to a month, of prayer and reflection with the goal of transforming one's life.
9. The Society of Jesus (Jesuits).

held in benediction by all, for her outstanding virtues, especially her charity toward the sick.

Annual Letter, 1639

There are in this mission four priests and one coadjutor, all in widely scattered places, mainly to learn more quickly the local tongue while propagating more widely the sacred faith of the gospel. Father John Brocus, the superior, along with a coadjutor brother, has his residence on a plantation at Matapanny, which was given to us by the ruler of the Patuxents. This plantation is the supply center for the mission, whence many material goods are provided. Father Philip Fisher[10] is stationed in the main town of the colony which is called St. Mary's. Father John Gravenor ministers on Kent Island, about sixty miles distant. Father Andrew White is working about twenty miles from St. Mary's, at Kittamaquidi, the village of the Piscataway, having lived, from June of 1639, in the palace with the king himself, whom they call Tayac. His reason for going there was the following:

Father White had invested much time and effort in religious discussions with the Patuxent king, which seemed to hold much promise, given the benefaction we had received (the king, as we mentioned, had bequeathed territory to the Society), and the reputation he had among his people as a prudent ruler. Indeed, in treating the fundamentals of faith, it seemed that the conversion of the king would soon be a reality. Some dependents of the king, in fact, embraced Christianity and he himself seemed to thoroughly comprehend the rudiments of the faith; then the unfortunate man began to procrastinate, then gradually to lose interest, then finally to reject both internally and outwardly the call of faith. Worse still, he gave clear indications that he had become estranged from the whole colony. Governor Calvert, learning of this development, thought it wise to remove the priest from the king's quarters, to ensure that the ruler would not unexpectedly give some proof of his perfidy and cruelty at the expense of the innocent White, or at the least, that he would not have the opportunity to use White as a hostage, should the Englishmen make any aggressive move against the Patuxents.

When mentioning emperors and kings, no one imagines that they are an extraordinary human species created to rule others, such as leaders are regarded in Europe. These Indian rulers, although they hold the greatest

10. Thomas Copley's alias.

power over the life and death of others, and surpass others in the honors and prerogatives they are given, in their manner of living differ in no way from those they rule. The principal thing that distinguishes their style of living from the people is the necklace of crude gems, or the girdle, or the upper garment covered with shells. Their kingdoms are tiny, often no more than a single town and its surrounding fields; although the Tayac's realm is far larger, extending about 130 miles, to whose authority other rulers are subject.

To this particular ruler, who happened to be fearing greatly for his life at Maquacomeni,[11] Father Andrew now took himself. The Tayac gave him such a warm greeting and fell over himself in making the priest welcome. He insisted on Father White staying in his own dwelling, where his wife equaled her spouse in personally showering her hospitality upon the visitor in serving him food and other nourishment.

The cause of this remarkable affection for the priest is to be found in two dreams (unless you think them worthy of another name). The first came to Uwanno, the king's blood brother and former king, whom he had forcibly removed in the middle of his reign. In his sleep the brother seemed to see Fathers White and Gravenor and heard a voice admonishing him, "These are the men, who from their hearts loved him with all his tribe, and brought with them those blessings, which would make him happy, if he wished." Thereafter so vivid an impression of these strangers remained with him, that even at first sight, he recognized them coming toward him and embraced them warmly. He was also accustomed to call Father White his parent; to whose instruction he wants to entrust for seven years his dear son, a remarkable intention, given the tribes' intense love for their children (they will hardly let them out of their sight). The other dream happened to the Tayac, which he frequently repeats; as he slept, his dead father, whom he had venerated like a god, appeared to him, in ghostly form, beseeching him that he would not desert him. Standing there with this really hideous god was a certain Snow, an obstinate English heretic; and lastly, standing apart were the governor of the colony and Father White, also accompanied by a god, but one of great beauty, who excelled the pristine snow in whiteness and was gently calling the king to him. From that time on the king treated both the governor and the priest with the greatest affection.

Shortly after Father White's arrival, the Tayac became critically ill from

11. The Tyac had ample cause for his fear, having alienated a large portion of the tribe by forcibly displacing his brother as the tribe's chief.

a severe disease; and when forty conjurers had in vain tried every remedy, the priest, with the sick man's permission, administered medicine, that is, a certain powder of known efficacy mixed with holy water, and the next day, with the assistance of the servant boy whom he had with him, opened one of his veins for blood letting. After this treatment, the sick man began daily to grow better, and soon was completely cured. Having recuperated, he resolved to be initiated in the Christian rites as soon as possible; not only himself, but his wife also and his two daughters; for as yet he had no male offspring. Father White is now diligently engaged in their instruction; nor do they idly receive the heavenly doctrine, for by the grace poured upon them they have long since discovered the errors of their former life. The king has exchanged the skins, with which he was heretofore clothed, for a garment made in our style; he makes also some effort to learn our language. Having put away his concubines, he lives content with one wife, that he may the more freely (as he says) have leisure to pray to God. He abstains from meat on the days in which it is forbidden by the Christian laws; and thinks that those who do otherwise should be considered heretics or bad Christians. He greatly delights in spiritual conversation, and indeed seems to esteem earthly wealth as nothing, in comparison with its heavenly counterpart, as he told the Governor, who was explaining to him what great advantages he could gain from trading with the English. "Truly," he said, "I consider these trifles when compared with this one advantage, that through these preachers, I have come to the knowledge of the one God; than which there is nothing greater to me or ever ought to be."

Not long ago, when he held a council of the tribe in a crowded assembly of the chiefs and people, with Father White and some of the English present, he publicly attested that it was his recommendation, together with that of his wife and children, that they should forsake their native superstition and give themselves to Christ; for there was no other true god but that of the Christians, nor could men in any other way save their immortal souls; indeed the stones and herbs, which, through spiritual blindness, he had previously joined his people in worshiping, he now realized were merely the humblest things created by Almighty God for the use and assistance of mankind. Saying this, he cast from him a stone which he happened to have in his hand, and ground it under his foot. A murmur of applause from the people indicated well enough how these things had fallen on their ears. We have the greatest hope that once the family of the king is baptized, the conversion of his whole empire will quickly follow. In the meantime, we heartily thank God for such an encouraging start, and particularly take hope when we daily witness the contempt with which the natives now regard their idols, whom only recently they counted among the deities....

In addition to the conversion of the natives, we have real hope for a harvest among the settlers as well. On the holy days, sermons are preached to them; on Sundays, catechesis is offered. Nor is it merely Catholics who attend, but many non-Catholics as well, with some productive results. This year alone twelve persons have renounced their former erring ways and returned to grace with God and the Church. Everyday Ours are making God present here by administering the sacraments according to the needs of those they encounter. Whether it is the healthy, the sick, the afflicted, or the dying, Ours strive to assist them by our counsel, help, and in any other appropriate way.

Annual Letter, 1640

We stated in our last letter what hope we had of converting the Tayac, or the King of the Piscataway. In the meantime, such is the goodness of God, the result has not disappointed our expectations. He has indeed converted and brought to our faith some others with him. This occurred on July 5, when, sufficiently instructed in the Faith, he was solemnly baptized in the wooden chapel, which had been constructed in the native style for the occasion and for a place of worship for the Indians. On the same occasion, the king's wife, her infant son, one of the king's counselors and the counselor's young son were also baptized. The ruler, who before had been called Kittamaquund, now took the name Charles, and his wife Mary. The rest chose appropriate Christian names. The governor, along with his secretary and many other settlers, had come up for the event. Ours did everything they could possibly do to make it a magnificent affair. In the afternoon the king and queen were married according to the Christian rite; then a huge cross was erected; which the king, the governor, his secretary, and the rest took upon their shoulders and carried to the appointed spot. Ahead of the cross bearers went two of Ours reciting the Litany of the Blessed Virgin Mary. Shortly after that happy occasion, however, Fathers Andrew White and John Gravenor were given their own heavy crosses to bear. For Father White, while presiding over the baptismal ceremonies which lasted an exceedingly long time, came down with a highly dangerous chill; he was able to convalesce from that illness, only to have a relapse which lasted into the winter. Father Gravenor, far from any care, still managed to recover from his own illness, only to die, on November 5, a few days after resuming his ministry.

Last year's drought has greatly increased hunger among the Indians. Lest we appear to have no concern for their material health, in our dedication to saving their souls, we found it necessary to purchase grain, despite its dear price, in order to distribute to them the food they were lacking. Thus we passed the greater part of the winter in tending to these responsibilities, as well as administering the affairs of the mission. On the fifteenth of February we journeyed to Piscataway, a large village, where we were welcomed by the residents who seemed well disposed to becoming Christians. Indeed the king decided to send his seven-year-old daughter, whom he favored, to St. Mary's to be educated among the settlers, and, when she comprehended the Christian mysteries, to be baptized. Also his counselor, whom we referred to above, having experienced God's saving grace, wanted nothing more than to have his wife and children follow him to the baptismal font. Happily, God willing, after the appropriate instruction, he saw his wish fulfilled. Another king, of the Anacostans, whose territory is not far distant, is anxious for one of Ours to settle among them. From this it is evident that a rich harvest awaits us, one which we may work to great advantage; though we fear that we will lack the workers to realize its full fruits. There are other villages lying near, which, I doubt not, would run promptly and joyfully to the light of evangelical truth, if there was any one to bring them the word of eternal life. We should not, however, be too concerned about winning over others, lest we give the impression that we are prematurely abandoning our present flock. Nor must those who are sent here to assist us fear that they will lack the necessities of life, since he who clothes the lilies and feeds the birds of the air will not leave destitute those who are laboring to build up his kingdom.

To Father Philip Fisher, now residing at St. Mary's, the capital of the colony, nothing would have been more agreeable than to labor in the Indian harvest fields, but Superiors could not afford to dispense with his services there. Still his good will does not go unrewarded; for while many Indians are being baptized, just as many English, thanks to his industry, are being at the same time brought back into the bosom of the church from heretical depravity. The Catholic settlers are not inferior in piety to those in other countries; in urbanity of manners, according to the judgment of those who have visited other colonies, they are considered far superior to them. Everywhere the hope of an abundant harvest has dawned; and while each one of us is anxious to help even unto death as many as we can, various events are happening that deserve record. Two of the most prominent are narrated here, one manifesting the divine mercy, and the other the divine justice.

On the day on which a certain man was about to abjure heresy and expiate the sins of his past life by confession, his house caught fire, and the flames rapidly burst through the roof. He was at a little distance when this occurred, and lost no time in calling his neighbors, of whom two only would come to his help; and although all this time the fire was burning in a house that was built only of dry logs, yet it was put out before any great damage had been done. Some feared lest this unexpected calamity might deter him from converting. The consequence was just the opposite; for the marvelous preservation of his house led him to the conclusion that God was showing his approval of his intention to become a Catholic.

Another man felt some internal stirrings of the grace of God, and for a long time took steps that seemed to be leading him to conversion, but then, casting aside all such thoughts, decided to revert to all his old ways. This man, while he had been considering his spiritual health, had acquired a rosary for himself; but after his change of heart, he had the rosary ground into powder, that he mixed with tobacco for his pipe, and often joked that in a way he had swallowed his Avemaria (as he called his rosary). But divine vengeance did not let this wicked deed go long unpunished. Scarcely a year had passed, indeed it was nearly the anniversary of the day on which he had abandoned his purpose of embracing the Catholic faith, when his companions noticed he was becoming especially ribald and sacrilegious. During his daily afternoon bath in the river, he had scarcely touched the water when a huge fish suddenly seized the wretched man, and before he could reach the bank it tore away at one bite a large portion of flesh from his thigh, inflicting a mortal but merited wound which in a short time took him from the living; the divine justice thus ordained that he, who a little while before had boasted of eating his Avemarias, should see his own flesh devoured while he was still alive.

Letter from Mission Superior Ferdinand Poulton to Belgian Nuncio Charles Rosetti, 1641

A year ago I wrote to you that Almighty God seemed to be opening the way for the conversion of many thousands of souls, namely by calling to his orthodox faith the emperor or grand king of the Piscataway.... Nor is there any doubt that very many more would have followed in the footsteps of their chief and been washed as quickly as possible at the same font of baptism, had not Fathers White and Altham, who were engaged in that mission, been seized with sickness, and to regain their health had to retire to the town of St. Mary's in the English colony, where Father Altham died on the fifth of November following, and Father White, having had a relapse, was for many days after his sickness unable to return to his Mission on account of his weakness. But in February last, having partially recovered his strength, he returned and joined me at Piscataway, in order to restore, and as far as possible, solidly establish that mission, and to propagate the Christian faith, the seeds of which it had pleased God so happily to sow. However, shortly after our arrival Father White again fell sick, and has not as yet recovered his strength; and, indeed, I fear that from his age and increasing infirmities, nature will shortly put an end to his great labors. I will use my utmost endeavours to preserve his life, that this great work of God, the conversion of so many infidels, may prosperously and happily progress, because, with his grasp of their language, (which is better than the rest of us can claim) he has the greatest influence over them. Many of the Indians have received instructions preparing them for baptism. Many of the higher born give signs of being ready to embrace the Faith. Outstanding among these is the king of the Anacostians, the uncle of the king of the Potomacs.... Indeed I hope that by God's favor, if we have sufficient help, there will be great progress for the Christian faith within a very short time amid these nations of savages; and even though we are under grave economic pressures because of our substantial charitable outlays over the year's course, forced to live with growing expenses and less means, there are none in the colony who either are able or are inclined to support us, and divine providence wills that we can look to be sustained neither by our exertions nor those for whose salvation we labor, both Christians and pagans. I can, however, fear nothing. He who feeds the birds of the air that neither sow nor reap, and who supplied the apostles, whom he sent forth without staff or scrip to preach the gospel, will provide us with everything we need. He will also furnish us, His unworthy servants, with whatever His divine providence sees fit. Having set out on this mission, certainly the very thought of recalling us, or of not sending others to help us in this glorious work of the salvation of souls, would in a manner betray our faith in God's providence and His care for His servants, as if He were wanting now where He had not been wanting before. So, let no such thoughts sap the courage of any one, but rather increase and strengthen it; since God has now taken us under His protection to provide for us Himself; especially as it has pleased the divine goodness to draw some fruit from our labours. Howsoever it shall seem good to the divine Majesty to dispose of us, let His will be done; for my own part, I should prefer to work here among the Indians for their conversion, and, destitute of all human aid and reduced by hunger, to die lying on the bare ground under the open sky, than even to think of abandoning this holy work of God through any fear of privation. God grant me the grace to do him some service, and the rest I leave to His providence.[12]

The king of the Piscataway recently, that is to say on March 7, died a pious death. That death, we are confident, God will use to bring to him very soon the neighboring king of the Anacostians, who has invited me to visit and says that he has determined to become a Christian. And there are many in other places with the same desire. The hope of a great harvest is growing stronger by the day. All we lack are able-bodied ministers who are fluent in their language.

Excerpts of Letters from Missionaries in Maryland, 1642

In the mission of Maryland for the year 1642, just passed, we have had only three members and those all priests, one of whom was confined by sickness of three months' duration.... Father Andrew [White] returned to his former station at Piscataway; but Father Roger [Rigby] went to a new settlement, which the natives call Patuxent, in order to learn more easily the Indian language; also, that he might better instruct some neophytes, and scatter along the bank of that great river the seed of faith.

Father Andrew experienced a very unpleasant encounter with a troublesome New England captain, whom he had engaged to transport himself and

12. Ferdinand Poulton's selfless wish was all too soon a reality. He was killed by accidental gunfire in June of 1641 while crossing the St. Mary's River.

his baggage. He soon had cause to fear that he was in danger either of being thrown overboard or taken forcibly, along with his things, to New England, that bastion of Calvinism. After Father White silently entrusted his fate to God, the ship, without incident, pulled into Potomac, in which port they had initially docked. For seventeen days the ship was iced in and could not move. At some point the father made his way over the ice, as though on land, and went into the town. When the ship at last broke free of the ice, the force of the ice propelled it into a collision and it sank. Most of the goods on board, however, were salvaged. As a result Father White's journey was delayed for nine weeks; for it was necessary to secure another ship from St. Mary's. He made the most of that delay by evangelizing the leader of that village together with the principal residents, which resulted in their becoming Christians by being baptized.... Through the example of these leaders, the people in general were set up to embrace the Faith, when we had the first opportunity to catechize them. Shortly afterwards, the young empress (as the Piscataways themselves call her) was baptized at St. Mary's and there she was educated, so that now she is fluent in English. At about the same time, most of the inhabitants in the town of Portobacco were baptized. That town is on the river they call Pamake that is situated nearly in the middle of the Indian territory, so in that place we have decided to establish a residence from which we can conveniently make excursions into the various villages; by doing this we fear we may give the Piscataway the impression that we are deserting them because of the threat that the Susquehanna represent. That tribe is the most war-like in the region and particularly hostile to Christians; in a recent attack on one of our farms, they slew our workers, and made off with our goods, at great loss to us. Unless they be restrained by force, which we have little reason to expect the English to provide, since the latter are themselves divided among themselves, we will not be safe among the Piscataway. So we have to be content with excursions, many of which we have made this year up the river they call Patuxent. This much we can show for it: the conversion of the young queen of the town of that place, of the same name as the river there, and her mother; also of the young queen of Portobacco; of the wife and two sons of Tayac the great, as they call him—that is the king, who died last year; and of one hundred and thirty others besides.

The following is our manner of making an excursion. We, that is the priest, an interpreter ..., and a servant, travel in a pinnace or gallery, with two oars to propel the ship when there are head winds or no winds at all, and one person steers. We carry a container filled with bread, butter, cheese, dried corn, beans and some flour. Another container holds liquids, including wine used for celebrating Mass, holy water for baptisms; a small chest with prayer books; and a table we use for an altar; another chest is filled with trinkets that we give the Indians as a sign of friendship.... We also carry a small mat to lie upon ... also a larger covering to protect us from rain.... In our trips we endeavor, as much as we can, to reach by evening some English house, or Indian village, but if not, we make shore. While the priest moors the boat, collects woods, and makes a fire, the two others go off to see what game they can get; if they fail, then we make use of the food we have brought; then we retire for the night. If rain threatens, we erect our hut and cover it with a larger mat; nor, praise be to God, do we enjoy this modest fare and hard bed any less than the more luxurious provisions that Europe affords; we have this comfort: that God now imparts to us a foretaste of what he is about to give to those who labor faithfully in this life, and mitigates all hardships with a degree of pleasantness; so that his divine majesty appears to be present with us, in an extraordinary manner.

The difficulty of this language is so great, that none of us can yet converse with the Indians without an interpreter. Father Rigby has made a little progress, so that he hopes he will be able in a short while to converse with them, upon things of ordinary importance, as far as may be necessary to instruct them for baptism; for he had composed a short catechism by the aid of an interpreter. Taking all these things into consideration, it seems a miracle that we have been able to effect anything with them; especially when the only interpreter we have is a young man who has such a poor command of their language that he sometimes occasions laughter by his misconstructions. For a time our situation seemed hopeless, but by patient endurance we are slowly succeeding in approaching the goal we have hoped to achieve.

In addition, it has pleased the divine goodness, by the virtue of his cross, to effect something that transcends human power. Here is what happened: a certain Indian, an Anacostan, now a Christian, while he was making his way with others through a forest, fell behind his companions a little when some savages of the Susequehanna tribe ... ambushed him suddenly and with a strong, light spear made of locust wood ... completely pierced his body from right to left, a hand's breadth below the armpit near the heart itself. It left a wound two fingers wide across his front. The Susquehanna quickly retreated, leaving their victim on the ground. His friends, up ahead, hearing the noise and shouting, raced back and got the man into a nearby boat, and conveyed him to his home at Piscataway, where they left him disoriented and unable to speak. Father White, getting word of this (he happened to be a short distance from the village), visited him the following morning, and found the man in front of his dwelling, lying on a mat before the fire with members of his tribe in a circle about him. He was no longer speechless or delirious, as he had been the day before, but was expecting to die imminently. With mournful voice he joined the song that his friends were making, as is their custom when an important member is thought to be dying. Some of his friends, however, being Christians, sang their own sad but very different song: "may he live, oh God! if it so please thee"; and they repeated it again and again, until the priest attempted to address the dying man. The latter immediately recognized Father White, and showed him his wounds. The priest felt deeply for him, but when he saw that his condition was critical, he briefly ran through with him the principal articles of the Christian faith. White also brought him to express repentance for his sins, then heard his confession. Urging him to have full hope and confidence in God, White read the gospel for the anointing of the sick, and recited the litany of the Blessed Virgin. The priest instructed him to commend himself to Mary's intercession as well as to call upon the most sacred name of Jesus. Then White applied to his wounds, the sacred relic of the Most Holy Cross, which the priest carried in a case around his neck, but had now taken off. He himself had to leave to baptize an elderly Indian who was expected to die that very day. The father directed the bystanders, once the man had breathed his last, to convey him to the chapel for burial.

It was noon when White departed. The following day, at the same hour, the priest happened to be in his canoe when he spotted two Indians propelling a canoe with oars towards him; and when they had come along side, one of them put his foot into the priest's craft. White stared at the man, wondering how this person, whom he clearly recognized, could be the same person whom he had left on the verge of death the day before. Suddenly the man threw open his cloak revealing the scars of his wounds, or rather a red spot on each side, the only trace of the wounds. All doubt immediately vanished for the priest. The man exclaimed with great exultation that he was completely well. From the hour at which the priest had left the day before he had not ceased to invoke the most holy name of Jesus, to whom he attributed his recovered health. . . .

The priest, having instructed the man that he should be forever thankful for so great and manifest a blessing, and continue to treat that name and the most holy Cross with love and reverence, sent him on his way. The man returned to his canoe with his companion, and stoutly propelled it with his oar, something he certainly could not have done, unless he had been healthy and in full use of his powers.

Letter from Thomas Copley to the Superior General, March 1, 1648

My companion and I reached Virginia in January, after an uneventful voyage of seven weeks. Leaving him there, I took an opportunity of passing over to Maryland, where I arrived in February. There by God's unique providence I found our people, who had been so scattered three years earlier, now together as a community again. In fact they seemed happier than their enemies who had stripped them of just about everything. Joyfully they welcomed me, as though I were an angel sent by God. I stayed with them for two weeks before reluctantly parting from them. The natives, who had also suffered much from our enemies, ever since I had been dragged away in chains from them, want me to return to them. I really do not know what to do. I cannot be all things to all men. God grant that whatever I do, I do for the greater glory of His Name. There is no doubt that there is a magnificent harvest to be had here. A new route through the woods has been recently opened which reduces the travel time from Maryland to Virginia to two days. That makes it possible for one missionary to minister to both colonies. After Easter I will visit the governor of Virginia, to enter into very important negotiations. God is acting to ensure that all things work for His honor and glory.

Annual Letter, 1655–56

In Maryland this year and the previous one, Ours have been in grave danger; they have been harassed and driven from their homes. The English, who inhabit Virginia, have invaded Maryland, equally an English colony. The Maryland governor, together with many others, surrendered conditionally to the hostile forces. The latter summarily executed four of the governor's men, including three Catholics. They broke into our house, calling for the deaths of the imposters, as they termed them, bent on butchering them as soon as they caught up with them. Everything in the house that they could carry off, including books and furniture, they did. Ours, however, having been warned that the rebels were coming, managed to escape in their skiff, virtually under the nose of the invaders. Having lost their house and belongings, they made their way to Virginia where they are eking out life in the greatest want. Their home is a tiny hut half buried in the ground.... On top of all the misfortunes they have endured, the donations that friends sent them from England were seized once the ship reached Maryland. They are so impoverished that they lack even wine to celebrate Mass....

13

"The Miracle of this Age": George Alsop, *A Character of the Province of Maryland,* 1666*

A fervent Royalist, despite his low social status, Alsop looked upon the hierarchical order in society as a natural necessity. In the ideal society that Alsop envisioned, this hierarchy is not a static one, but dynamic and progressive: a society where the laws of a benign ruler ensure the order that is a precondition for economic mobility and religious tranquility; where indentured servitude is but a natural passage from one rung of society to another for those who will industriously utilize the opportunities for social mobility that a country offers. In Alsop's experience, no place held out more promise of rising from the poverty of servitude to prosperous self-reliance than did Maryland. Alsop's readers may have wondered why, if Maryland was the Eden he cast it as, he had returned to London shortly after completing his four years of indenture. We don't know. What we do know is that, for all his exaggeration and romanticizing, Maryland by the last quarter of the sixteenth century could rightly claim to be the "best poor-man's country." What, according to Alsop, are the features of Maryland that enable the colony to make that claim? What accounts, to his mind, for the lack of dissent and contention in Maryland? What does he mean by "Quakerism is the only opinion that bears the Bell away"?

* George Alsop, *A Character of the Province of Maryland* (London: Peter Dring, 1666), 33, 42–55, 59–61, 99.

Of the Situation and Plenty of the Province of Maryland

He who ... desires to see the Landskip[13] of the Creation drawn to the Life may ... view *Mary-Land* drest in her green and fragrant Mantle of the Spring. Neither do I think there is any place under the Heavenly altitude ... that can parallel this fertile and pleasant piece of ground in its multiplicity, or rather Natures extravagancy of a superabounding plenty ... had Nature made it her business, on purpose to have found out a situation for the Soul of profitable Ingenuity, she could not have fitted herself better in the traverse of the whole Universe, nor in convenienter terms have told man, *Dwell here, live plentifully and be rich.*

The Trees, Plants, Fruits, Flowers, and Roots that grow here in *Mary-Land* are the only emblems or Hieroglyphics of our Adamitical or Primitive situation ... which still bear the Effigies of Innocency according to their original Grafts; ... they need not look for any other Terrestrial Paradice, to suspend or tyre their curiosity upon, while she is extant.

Of the Government and Natural Disposition of the People

Mary-Land ... from the regularity of her well ordered Government, may ... be called *Singular*: And though she is not supported with such large Revenues as some of her Neighbours are, yet such is her wisdom in a reserved silence, and not in pomp, to shew her well-conditioned Estate, in relieving at a distance the profound poverty of those that wont be seen they want as well as those which by undeniable necessities are drove upon the Rocks of pinching wants.... I am certainly confident, there is none within the Province that would lower themselves so much below the dignity of men to beg, as long as limbs and life keep house together; so much is a vigilant industrious care esteem'd.

He that desires to see the real Platform of a quiet and sober Government extant, Superiority with a meek and yet commanding power sitting at the Helm, steering the actions of State quietly, through the multitude and diversity of Opinionous waves that diversely meet, let him look on *Mary-land* with eyes admiring, and he'll then judge her, *The Miracle of this Age.*

Here the *Roman Catholic*, and the *Protestant Episcopal*, (whom the world would persuade have proclaimed open Wars irrevocably against each other)

13. Landscape.

contrarywise concur in an unanimous parallel of friendship, and inseparable love entailed unto one another. All Inquisitions, Martyrdom, and Banishments are not so much as named, but unexpressably adhorr'd by each other.

The several Opinions and Sects that lodge within this Government, meet not together in mutinous contempts to disquiet the power that bears Rule, but with a reverent quietness obeys the legal commands of Authority. Here's never seen Five Monarchies[14] in a Zealous Rebellion, opposing the Rights and liberties of a true settled Government, or Monarchical Authority: ...

The Government of this Province doth continually, by all lawful means, strive to purge her Dominions from such base corroding humors, that would predominate upon the least smile of Liberty, did not the Laws check and bridle in those unwarranted and tumultuous Opinions. And truly, where a Kingdom, State, or Government, keeps or cuts down the weeds of destructive Opinions, there must certainly be a blessed Harmony of quietness. And I really believe this Land or Government of *Mary-Land* may boast, that she enjoys as much quietness from the disturbance of Rebellious Opinions, as most States or Kingdoms do in the world: For here every man lives quietly, and follows his labour and imployment desiredly; and by the protection of the Laws, they are supported from those molestious troubles that ever attend upon the Commons of other States and Kingdoms, ... Here's nothing to be levyed out of the Granaries of Corn; but contrarywise, by a Law every Domestic Governor of a Family is enjoined to make or cause to be made so much Corn by a just limitation, as shall be sufficient for him and his Family:[15] So that by this wise and *Janus*-like providence,[16] the thin-jawed Skeleton with his starv'd Carcass is never seen walking the Woods of *Mary-Land* to affrighten Children....

Here Suits and Trials in Law seldom hold dispute two Terms or Courts, but according as the Equity of the Cause appears is brought to a period.[17]... All villanous Outrages that are committed in other States, are not so much as known here: A man may walk in the open Woods as secure from being externally dissected, as in his own house or dwelling....

14. The Fifth Monarchy: an apocalyptic sect that arose during Cromwell's reign in the late 1650s. Adherents believed that they were living in a final age that would culminate with the establishment of a "Fifth Monarchy" under the leadership of a returning Messiah.

15. The family is a microcosm of the commonwealth. The father, as head, is responsible for supplying the necessities of life to his dependents. In this society of yeomen there is no need for the state to provide welfare.

16. A providence that rewards good and punishes evil.

17. To a close.

Here the Constable hath no need of a train of Holberteers, that carry more Armour about them, than heart to guard him.... Here's no *Newgates* for pilfering Felons, nor *Ludgates* for Debtors, nor any *Bridwels* to lash the soul of Concupiscence into a chast Repuentance.[18]

... Common Alehouses ... in this Province there are none; neither hath Youth his swing or range in such a profuse and unbridled liberty as in other Countries; for ... the Son works as well as the Servant (an excellent cure for untam'd Youth), so that before they eat their bread, they are commonly taught how to earn it....

One great part of the Inhabitants of this Province are desiredly Zealous, great pretenders to Holiness; and where any thing appears that carries on the Frontispiece of its Effigies the stamp of Religion, though fundamentally never so imperfect, they are suddenly taken with it, and out of an eager desire to any thing that's new, not weighing the sure matter in the Balance of Reason, are very apt to be catcht. *Quakerism* is the only opinion that bears the Bell away: The *Anabaptists* have little to say here ...

The Necessariness of Servitude Proved, with the Common Usage of Servants in Mary-Land, Together with Their Privileges

As there can be no Monarchy without the Supremacy of a King and Crown, nor no King without Subjects, nor any Parents without it be by the fruitful off-spring of Children; neither can there be any Masters, unless it be by the inferior Servitude of these that dwell under them by a commanding enjoynment: And since it is ordained from the original and superabounding wisdom of all things, That there should be Degrees and diversities amongst the Sons of men, in acknowledging of a Superiority from Inferiors to Superiors; the Servant with a reverent and befitting Obedience is as liable to this duty in a pleasurable performance to him whom he serves, as the loyalest of Subjects to his Prince. Why should there be such an exclusive Obstacle in the minds and unreasonable dispositions of so many people, against the limited time of convenient and necessary Servitude, when it is a thing so requisite, that the best of Kingdoms would be unhing'd from their quiet and well settled Government without it. Which levelling doctrine we here

18. Had Alsop remained in Maryland a bit longer, he may have chosen not to include this paean to the province's near-crimeless, prisonless state. In 1662 the general assembly authorized the first prison for the county. Several years later they extended the prison system throughout the province by mandating that each county establish its own.

of *England* in this latter age ... have too much experienced.... But ... those Clouds are blown over, and the Government of the Kingdom coucht under a more stable form....

Then let such, whom Providence hath ordained to live as Servants, either in *England* or beyond Sea, endure the prefixed yoke of their limited time with patience, and then in a small computation of years, by an industrious endeavour, they may become Masters and Mistresses of Families themselves ... the four years I served [in Maryland] were not to me so slavish, as a two years Servitude of a Handicraft Apprenticeship was here in *London*.

The servants here in *Mary-Land* of all Colonies, distant or remote Plantations, have the least cause to complain, either for strictness of Servitude, want of Provisions, or need of Apparel: Five days and a half in the Summer weeks is the alotted time that they work in; and for two months, when the Sun predominates in the highest pitch of his heart, they claim an ancient and customary Privilege, to repose themselves three hours in the day within the house, and this is undeniably granted to them that work in the Fields.

In the Winter Time, which lasteth three months ... they do little or no work or employment, save cutting of wood....

Now those Servants which come over into this Province, being Artificers, they never ... work in the Fields, or do any other employment save that which their Handicraft and Mechanic endeavours are capable of putting them upon....

The Women that go over into this Province as Servants, have the best luck here as in any place of the world besides; for they are no sooner on shore, but they are courted into a Copulative Matrimony....

In short, touching the Servants of this Province, they live well in the time of their Service, and by their restrainment in that time, they are made capable of living much better when they come to be free.

Sources

Alsop, George. *A Character of the Province of Maryland*. London: Peter Dring, 1666.

Carr, Lois Green, Russell R. Menard, and Lorena S. Walsh. *Robert Cole's World: Agriculture and Society in Early Maryland*. Chapel Hill: University of North Carolina Press, 1991.

Carr, Lois Green, Philip D. Morgan, and Jean B. Russo, eds. *Colonial Chesapeake Society*. Chapel Hill: University of North Carolina Press for the Institute of Early American History, 1988.

A Catholic Colony in British America, 1634–1664

Curran, Robert Emmett, ed. *American Jesuit Spirituality: The Maryland Tradition, 1634–1900*. Rahway, N.J.: Paulist Press, 1988.

Dolan, Frances E. *Whores of Babylon: Catholicism, Gender, and Seventeenth-Century Print Culture*. Ithaca and London: Cornell University Press, 1999.

Feres, Angela. "Father Andrew White, the Jesuit Order, and the Marketing of Colonial Maryland." Ph.D. diss. Claremont Graduate University, 2011.

Historic St. Mary's City. "Life in the Colony." http://www.hsmcdigshist.org/research/publications.

Riordan, Timothy B. *The Plundering Time: Maryland and the English Civil War, 1645–1646*. Baltimore: Maryland Historical Society, 2004.

Stone, Garry Wheeler. "Manorial Maryland." *MHM* 82 (Spring 1987): 3–36.

Part 4

Church and State

1639–1649

*T*HE MARYLAND CHARTER empowered Cecil Calvert to establish churches so long as they were established "according to the Ecclesiastical Laws of our Kingdom of England." If Lord Baltimore had wanted to execute this power, he would have had no choice but to establish the Church of England in Maryland. As a Catholic who had planned and inaugurated this colony so that it might, among other things, be a place where Catholics could worship freely and escape the penal laws that had so restricted and marginalized them within English society, Calvert had no intention of replicating in Maryland the repressive conditions that had weighed down the Catholic community at home.

How to achieve religious liberty without violating English law that, far from tolerating the practice of the Catholic religion, imposed so many penalties and restrictions upon those opting to live as Catholics in the hope that such draconian treatment would force Catholics to abandon the faith they had embraced, either by birth or conversion? For the Calverts the solution was the separation of church and state. What was a contradiction in terms for most of European society, which viewed uniformity in religion as an essential underpinning for an orderly state, for the Calverts was the only way to preserve and protect religious freedom. Conversely, compelling the inhabitants of any state to profess and practice a particular religion was to undermine the citizens' integrity that should constitute the moral foundation of any society.

Baltimore had the colony's General Assembly give legal footing to this policy in its spring session of 1638/39. First the delegates gave lip service to the conventional church-state structure in the English world by stating that "Holy Church shall have all her rights, liberties, and immunities" in the new colony. More relevant for Catholics and other dissenters in Maryland was another act that the assembly passed on the same day, March 19, concerning the liberties, not of the church but of the people. Echoing language in the province's charter, the act declared that all Christians in the colony were entitled to the same "rights liberties immunities [and] privileges" as any "natural born subject of England" (see "Holy Church Shall Have All Her Rights, Liberties, and Immunities"). In Maryland there was no need for oaths to determine who qualified as Christians.

&

There was no established church in the province, but there were ministers of a church that was effectively outlawed in England and whose ministers were subject to capital punishment for merely being in the country. Lord Baltimore had made clear to the Society of Jesus that its members would be treated in Maryland just as any other gentlemen adventurers. The Jesuits could expect no official support for their ministry from the state but would have to provide for themselves, working the land that they, like all adventurers, would receive for coming to Maryland and bringing others. That understanding, to the consternation of both the proprietor and the Jesuits, would be severely tested in the very first years of the colony's existence.

In establishing a colony in which religion would not be the care of the state but a private matter, Lord Baltimore had put Maryland in uncharted waters. There were no guidelines for church-state relations, as John Lewger, the secretary of the province, learned to his dismay in 1638 when a newly arrived Jesuit, Thomas Copley (alias Philip Fisher), challenged some of the laws passed in the recent assembly, arguing that several of them violated the exemptions that clergy had traditionally enjoyed in countries with Catholic leadership (paying taxes, serving in the assembly and on juries, doing military service). Lewger was clearly at sea about how to respond. To what extent did canon law, the law of the church, apply in Maryland under a Catholic proprietor? For that matter, to what extent did the laws of England apply in its "Catholic" colony? The secretary sought answers from Cecil Calvert himself in the form of a query that presented twenty hypothetical cases that Copley's protest had no doubt suggested (see John Lewger's Inquiries regarding Civil and Canon Law, 1638, in "Are Such Laws against Conscience?").

The proprietor, rather than giving Lewger directions about how to walk the line between his authority and the traditional rights of the clergy, instead negotiated an agreement with the English provincial in London in the summer of 1639 that granted most of the exemptions that Copley had initially sought. Hardly had news of that understanding reached Maryland than a new issue arose that put Calvert and the Jesuits at odds for the next five years. The issue was the Jesuit acquisition of land. Under the Conditions of Plantation, the Society had qualified for thousands of acres by bringing persons, both members of the order and servants, into the province.

When the local Jesuit superior applied for patents for some of that land in late 1639, Lord Baltimore refused to grant them, breaking his promise to treat Jesuits just as he would any secular adventurer. What Calvert could not countenance was the recognition of any Jesuit as the legal owner of land in his colony. Here the long arm of English law was his concern. The law in question, that of Mortmain, prohibited any religious order from owning land. Calvert, as a Catholic proprietor of a colony that had priests and religious brothers as a major part of the settlement from its beginning, could not risk jeopardizing his precarious standing in England, where it was a capital offense for a priest even to be in the country, by having priests as property owners in Maryland. That fear led Baltimore to issue a new set of "Conditions of Plantation" that, among other things, forbade the acquisition of land by any group or organization without the express approval of the proprietor. They also required a new oath from the colonists: that they would, under no circumstances, accept any land from the Indians. If the Calverts were going to realize their dream of a manor-centered settlement, their ownership of the land had to be absolute. To get the Jesuits' acceptance of these new "conditions" governing the acquisition of land, the proprietor drew up a statement for the English provincial to sign for his subjects in Maryland (see Cecil Calvert's Proposed Statement for English Provincial's Signature regarding Landholding, 1641).

Edward Knott, the English superior, in a long response to the proprietor, shrewdly framed Jesuit landholding within the peculiar context that
Maryland presented to show that land was the irreplaceable means by which
Maryland Jesuits were able to carry out their ministries to natives and settlers (see Edward Knott's Observations on Baltimore's Proposal, 1641).

What Calvert did not know at the time was that the Jesuits had already
received a huge gift in land from the emperor of the Piscataway. When he
eventually learned of the magnificent gift, it was the last straw. If Calvert
could not abide the Jesuits as legal owners of property, all the less could he
stand the challenge to his position as absolute lord of Maryland that the reception of land from any other source than the proprietor himself constituted. The upshot was a ban by the proprietor of any more Jesuits within
the province and a search for other priests to provide a priestly ministry in
the province. Rome in turn retaliated by refusing to allow any secular priests
permission to join Calvert's colony. The English provincial offered to assure
Calvert that the Society would accept no land in the future from anyone
other than himself. Calvert wanted more: the surrender of Indian lands they
had received in gratitude from tribes in the region, as well as all the land
they had acquired under the Conditions of Plantation.

As 1644 concluded, officials of the Society were ready to give Calvert all
he demanded, if Propaganda Fide approved. "Knowing that God is good,"
the vicar general of the order told the English Provincial, "I hope for better things."[1] Better things proved not to be in the offing for the Maryland
Jesuits over the next fifteen years. The controversy between Lord Baltimore
and the Jesuits over their respective rights and privileges petered out only
because the colony was roiled by Richard Ingle's invasion scarcely two
months after the Jesuit superior general's letter to London. That violent
Virginia-led incursion set in motion an orgy of plundering and mayhem followed by two years of virtual anarchy. The violence reduced the population
of Maryland on its main Western Shore to a remnant of 100 or so souls, a
fifth of its inhabitants before Ingle's incursion. The rest had either fled or
been killed. Few manors survived the burning and destruction of the roving
bands (mostly Ingle's) that for months terrorized the province. Desperate to
repopulate his colony, Lord Baltimore lured disgruntled Puritans from Virginia with promises of rich lands and religious liberty. So many responded

1. Vicar General Sangrius to Edward Knott, November 5, 1644, in Hughes, *History*, Documents, vol. 1, part 1, 32; Latin.

that they quickly came to form an overwhelming majority of the population. Given this dramatic demographic revolution, Cecil Calvert wanted to shore up the legal protection for religious freedom, particularly that of Catholics, now more a minority than they had ever been. The result was the Act Concerning Religion passed by the General Assembly (where Catholics still held a slim majority), the first legislation in the English-speaking world to recognize explicitly the right of Christians to worship according to their conscience, not government coercion (see "The Better to Preserve Mutual Love and Amity").

The Jesuits retained their lands, despite Lord Baltimore's determination to reclaim them and the heavy damage inflicted on them by Ingle's forces. Over the ensuing decades the Society acquired, through purchases or bequests, a good deal more property. When slaves replaced indentured servants as the labor force for the cultivation of the Chesapeake's great staple crop, tobacco, the Jesuits easily adapted to the new economy. By the end of the colonial era they would be among the largest slaveowners in Maryland, with several hundred bonded laborers on six plantations—one unseemly consequence of the separation of church and state.

14

"Holy Church Shall Have All Her Rights, Liberties, and Immunities": Maryland Assembly on Religion and Civil Rights in the Colony, 1638/39*

Given the religious situation in England, what is the significance of the assembly's declaration that all the Christians in the province would have the "rights liberties immunities privileges and free customs within this Province as any natural born subject of England?" What restrictions does the assembly impose concerning the acquisition of land by the colony's settlers?

* *AM* 1:39–42, 82–83.

An Act for the Government of the Province

Be it enacted by the Lord Proprietary of this Province by and with the Advice and approbation of the freemen of the same that Holy Church within this Province shall have all her rights liberties and immunities safe whole and inviolable in all things. This act to continue till the end of the next General Assembly and then with the Consent of the Lord Proprietary to be perpetual.

Acts of the tenth day being March 19, 1638, in the morning.

An Act for Church Liberties

Be it enacted by the Lord Proprietary of this Province by and with the Advice and approbation of the freemen of the same that Holy Church within this Province shall have all her liberties and immunities safe whole and *inviolable* in all things. This act to continue till the end of the next General Assembly and then with the Consent of the Lord Proprietary to be perpetual.

An Act for the Liberties of the People

Be it Enacted By the Lord Proprietary of this Province of and with the Advice and approbation of the freemen of the same that all the Inhabitants of this Province being Christians (Slaves excepted) Shall have and enjoy all such rights liberties immunities privileges and free customs within this Province as any natural born subject of England hath or ought to have or enjoy in the Realm of England by force or virtue of the common law or Statute Law of England (saving in such Cases as the same are or may be altered or changed by the Laws and ordinances of this Province).

An Act for Maintaining the Lord Proprietary's Title to the Lands of This Province

Be it Enacted By the Lord Proprietary of this Province of and with the advice and approbation of the freemen of the same That no Subject of his Majesties the king of England or of any other foreign Prince or State Shall obtain procure or accept of any Land within this Province from any foreign Prince or State or from any person whatsoever (the natives owners of the Land excepted) other than from the Lord Proprietary or his heirs or some person claiming under him or them

Neither Shall he obtain procure or accept of any Land within this Province from any Indian to his own or the use of any other than of the Lord Proprietary or his heirs nor shall hold or possess any land within this Province by Virtue of such Grant upon pain that every person offending to the contrary hereof Shall forfeit and lose to the Lord Proprietary and his heirs all Such Lands so accepted or held without Grant of the Lord Proprietary or under him This Act to Continue to the end of the next General Assembly

15

"Are Such Laws against Conscience?" The Baltimore-Jesuit Controversy, 1638–1644

What is the fundamental clarification that Lewger seeks from the proprietor about the interplay of civil and canonical law in Maryland? Are any of these questions that Lewger raised still relevant today?

John Lewger's Inquiries regarding Civil and Canon Law, 1638*

In a Country (as this is) newly planted, and depending wholly upon England for its subsistence, where there is not (nor cannot be, until England be reunited to the *Church*) any Ecclesiastical discipline established (by law of the province, or grant of the prince), nor provincial Synods held, nor spiritual Courts erected, nor the Canon law accepted, ... nor Catholic religion publicly allowed; and whereof three parts of the people in four (at least) are heretics, I desire to be resolved—

1. Whether a lay Catholic can with a safe conscience take charge, of government, or of an office in such a country as this, where he may not nor dare discharge all the duties, and obligations of a Catholic magistrate, nor yield and maintain to the Church all her rights and liberties, that she hath in other Catholic countries?

* Hughes, *History*, Documents, vol. 1, part 1, 1582–61.

2. Whether the lay Catholics (in such a Country as this) are bound to accept, or admit of all the Canon law, and in special of the Council of Trent (extra fidem)[2] or whether the Canon law (as such) binds in this Country....

3. Whether the exemptions of the Clergy for their persons, lands, goods, tenants, domestics, or privilege of Sanctuary to their houses, or churches, etc., are due to them of Divine right by immediate grant from Christ to his Church, so that princes becoming Christians were instantly obliged in conscience to allow, and confirm those exemptions, or at least to permit, and suffer the Church to practise, and enjoy them; or whether they hold them of the free, and voluntary gift, and devotion of pious princes, and states ... ?

4. Whether holding of Courts with external coercitive jurisdiction be a part of the powers of the Keys left by Christ to his Church, or whether it be a part of the sword put by God into the hands of princes, and from them granted unto spiritual ordinaries:[3] and when Ecclesiastical Tribunals are here to be erected with such power of external coercitive Jurisdiction, may the prince erect them by his own Charter, or must it be done by special commission and delegation of the Sea Apostolic?[4] ...

9. Whether Catholics, being members of the General Assembly in such a Country as this, may consent to a law prohibiting the bequeathing or otherwise aliening of any lay fee to spiritual persons, or religious houses, without leave of the prince, and voiding all gifts, and alienations made otherwise? ...

11. Whether may Catholics, being members in a General Assembly in such a Country as this, consent to any laws touching causes matrimonial, as to appoint the publishing of banns (for politic considerations) and to prohibit marriage without such banns published, ... or to limit the degrees of consanguinity, within which marriage shall not be contracted....

12. Whether may Catholics, being members of the General Assembly in such a Country as this, consent to a law prohibiting the marriage of Apprentices without consent or leave of their master and mistress, and imposing penalties upon the priest or minister solemnizing such marriage; and whether such a law be against the liberty of marriage?

13. Whether may Catholics, being members of the General Assembly in such a Country as this, consent to a law that for politique considerations bars the female from inheriting, or holding of Lands, unless they marry

2. On matters other than defined doctrines of the faith.
3. Bishops or religious superiors.
4. Holy See.

within a time limited (only leaving them at liberty, to sell or dispose thereof to their best advantage), and whether such a law is against conscience? ...

17. Whether, in such a Country as this, may the prince or secular Judge being Catholic summon Ecclesiastical persons to the General Assembly, or draw them into secular Court, where they are defendants in actions of debt, ... trespass, and other personal, and real actions, and may he give sentence therein as lawful Judge and execute it upon their persons, lands, or goods, without incurring the censures of Bulla Coenae?

18. Whether, in such a Country as this, may the secular Judge being Catholic proceed to the trial and punishment of Clerks[5] being in orders for any offences against the peace, and dignity of the Lord Proprietour, or for capital crime extending to the loss of life, or member, without the incurring of Bulla Coenae?

19. Whether, in such a Country as this, may Catholics being members of the General Assembly consent to laws imposing general contributions towards public charges for the necessary support of the prince, or defence of the Country, and whether are spiritual persons, their lands, or goods included within such laws (for want of exception)? ...

20. Whether the Representative body, met in General Assembly, may make laws to dispose of the Interest and Rights of particular persons, as namely of Clergy men, not being present, nor having proxies in such Parliament, or Assembly (though lawfully summoned thereunto), nor otherwise holding synods provincial, wherein their consents to such might be expected; and whether are such laws against conscience?

Cecil Calvert's Proposed Statement for English Provincial's Signature regarding Landholding, 1641[*]

1. Notwithstanding any former pretences whatsoever, I will not that any of our Body or Society within the Province of Maryland shall by themselves, their agents or servants, directly or indirectly trade or traffic with any Indian or Savage without the special licence of the Lord Baltimore, Lord of the Province, or his Lieutenant General, or other Governor of the same for the time being hereafter, to be signified in writing under his or their hand and seal....

---

[*] Hughes, *History*, Documents, vol. 1, part 1, 166–68; Latin.
5. Priests.

2. That no person whatsoever within the said Province, whether spiritual or lay, may or ought to purchase or accept or make use of any land within the said Province from any Indian or Savage or any other person whatsoever, directly or indirectly, but such as shall derive a legal right thereunto by some grant under the great seal of the Province from the Lord Baltimore or his heirs.... And I do hereby disavow and disannull all purchase or acceptance whatsoever of any such land made or to be made by any of our community or Society there....

3. And that, considering the dependency which the Government of Maryland hath upon the State of England, unto which it must be (as near as may be) conformable, no ecclesiastical person whatsoever, inhabiting or being within the said Province, ought to pretend or expect, nor is the Lord Baltimore or any of his officers (although they be Roman Catholics) obliged in conscience to allow unto the said ecclesiastical persons, inhabiting or being within the said Province, any more or other privileges, exemptions or immunities for their persons, lands or goods within the said Province, than what is allowed by his Majesty or any of his officers or magistrates to the like persons in England: and that any magistrate or officer of him the said Lord Baltimore or his heirs, lords and proprietaries of the said Province, may proceed against any such ecclesiastical person, or for the maintaining & preservation of all the rights, prerogatives and jurisdictions granted to the said Lord Baltimore & his heirs within and over the said Province & people, inhabiting and being therein, by his Majesties gracious letters patents under the great seal of England, as well as in the like cases the said officers may do against the person, lands or goods of any lay person, inhabiting or being within the said Province, without committing any sine or incurring the censure of Bulla Coenae for so doing.

4. That all causes testamentary, probate of wills, granting of letters of administration, &c, and granting of licences for marriage (where banns are not asked) and also all other mixt causes, which in other countries bel[ong] unto ecclesiastical courts to hear, determine & punish, as adultery, fornication, &c, until some ecclesiastical court be established within the said Province with the Lord Baltimore's consent, may be heard, determined & punished within the Province of Maryland by such officer or officers (although they be Roman Catholics) as shall be authorized thereunto by the said Lord Baltimore or his heirs, lords & proprietaries of the said Province, or by Act of General Assembly made or to be made within the same, with the assent of the said Lord Baltimore or his heirs.

Edward Knott's Observations on Baltimore's Proposal, 1641[*]

Certain observations meant to shed light on the points proposed by Lord Baltimore....

OBSERVATION 1: When the Maryland colony was in its initial planning stage, Lord Baltimore repeatedly petitioned that as many priests of the Society who volunteered, be sent to Maryland to minister to Catholics and to evangelize the infidels, about whom there was much hope for a grand harvest. For their part, the fathers had a burning desire for such a mission, but did not want to decide upon anything without the superior general's permission. Subsequently, having secured the necessary faculties from Rome, they took up Lord Baltimore's insistent invitation and decided to join his adventure. In their negotiations with the proprietor, they touched on many challenges that they faced in becoming part of his undertaking. The most pressing question was how they were going to be able to support their work in the colony. There was no hope of living off of benefactors or donations. On the other hand, they had no desire to invest their energies in supplying their material needs, so as to severely limit their ability to provide for others' spiritual ones. They went back and forth with Lord Baltimore over the matter but were never able to persuade him to provide for them out of his own resources or some other source. Finally after much deliberation, the proprietor proposed, as the most sensible resolution of the problem, that the Jesuits would enjoy the same terms and benefits as the rest of the adventurers had agreed to, and would participate in the appropriate distribution of land according to the conditions established for the settling of the colony. Having land to cultivate would provide the means not only to support themselves but to increase the number of Jesuits to spread the faith and gospel among the unbelievers. This plan was a hard one for the Jesuits to accept, not only because it violated the spirit of their Institute,[6] but also because it was rife with many other potential difficulties, for which remedies would not easily be found. In the end, for God's glory and their neighbor's good, they felt they had to accept Lord Baltimore's terms.

[*] Hughes, *History*, Documents, vol. 1, part 1, 166–68; Latin.
6. The Institute of the Society of Jesus was the core of the order's Constitutions.

OBSERVATION 2: There is no currency in use in Maryland, but they live by a barter economy, by which they manage to secure food, clothing and other necessities of life by having merchants ship their crops to England where they are sold for cash, which is used to buy goods which are in turn transported to Maryland. This cycle of exchange is unavoidable but works well. Given this economic environment, the universal prohibition against the clergy's involvement in financial transactions does not apply, and clergy have as much right as the laity to participate. It is really the only way they can secure the means to live by. Besides it is more a matter of exchange rather than some financial transaction done, not for the sake of earning money, but of securing the necessities of life. And it should be pointed out that such is the practice in the Indies and New France.

OBSERVATION 3: The natives, possessing absolute dominion over their lands and goods, can not nor ought not be deprived of this right on the grounds that they are non-believers, nor by the laws of justice can anyone prohibit them from exchanging, selling, or granting land to anyone they choose.

OBSERVATION 4: If any ruler attempts to declare his subject incapable of either legitimately buying or receiving as a gift anything from the infidels (as is the apparent position of Lord Baltimore), this opinion seems to defy the principles of justice and equality, by insisting that the items sold or given are the property of the ruler, no matter the intentions of the natives, who are the real owners.

OBSERVATION 7: The Fathers, after discernment, have refused to sign the propositions put forward by Lord Baltimore, because they contradict certain principles of ecclesiastical immunity. They are well aware that Dr. Lewger, formerly a Protestant minister before his conversion, and secretary to Lord Baltimore, has been his key agent in the general assembly or parliament; and lacking knowledge of theology, and poorly educated, tends to hold opinions and openly espouses dogmas which are repugnant to Catholics, such as to deny much of the authority held by the Vicar of Christ. Some examples: the pope holds no temporal jurisdiction from God, but solely spiritual, that in the realm of conscience; that there is no immunity for him or other clergy regarding the person or property, except to the extent that it pleases secular rulers to grant it to them; and other similar heresies. Nor is he less heterodox in mere political tenets, as when he holds that it is a capital crime for anyone to exercise authority of any sort, even granting absolution from sins, unless one has the permission of the proprietor, the seat of all legal jurisdiction. Or if any young woman makes a vow of virginity and chooses not to marry, after she reaches the age of twenty-five, she automatically loses the right to any land she has inherited from her parents, and must sell them, by force, should she refuse. To the general assembly or parliament he holds they have total authority, including stripping someone of all his worldly goods, as is done in republics. These examples should suffice.

OBSERVATION 8: The assembly (which has unlimited power to do just about whatever it pleases), is composed overwhelmingly of non-Catholics; many of them former servants, who after completing their specified years of indenture, become free men with all the rights of citizens. The Secretary along with a few other allies controls these people and their votes, so that they enact whatever he directs them to, laws which bind everyone; this a way of governing that no one in good conscience could approve.

OBSERVATION 9: Since in England, as is well known, many of the laws in effect are directed against Catholics because of revulsion for their religion as well as the repudiation of the authority of the Vicar of Christ on Earth ... by what rationale can Catholics living in Maryland be obliged by Lord Baltimore to fall subject to the said laws of Parliament and give up their Catholic privileges, immunities, and exemptions regarding persons, lands, and goods, which the laws of England require? ...

OBSERVATION 10: The missionary fathers of the Society, even though grievously delinquent (which God forbid) should be punished by their religious superiors, and not by the secular authorities; nor can we renounce this exemption without incurring mortal sin. And since whatever possessions they may come into acquire the character of ecclesiastical goods, it follows that they cannot be given up without doing injury to the Church.

Having given due discernment to these matters, although they are fully prepared to endure patiently any burdens, and to endeavor with Christian humility and courage to turn evil to good, as they have often indicated to Lord Baltimore, nevertheless they have determined that they will not be pressured into affirming such statements that are damaging not only to themselves but to the dignity and authority of the Supreme Pontiff, and judge that such an act would do universal harm to the interests of the Church. Still, if prudent and disinterested individuals, most notably the Supreme Pontiff, who is the ultimate judge in such matters, would determine that the Fathers may licitly and with a good conscience affix their signatures to what the baron exacts, they will willingly do so. If, on the other hand, they find the demands unwarranted, and uphold the Father's refusal to sign them and thus give their approbation, then let them humbly say as much, as well as make clear that it would be illicit for anyone to sign them....

All the while the missionaries of the Society have been the sole workers in this vineyard of the Lord. With God's grace, they have produced some fruit, and have their sights on an even greater harvest in the future, especially among the indigenous people.... Whatever shall come to pass, may the Society see its goals realized.

16

"The Better to Preserve Mutual Love and Amity": An Act concerning Religion, 1649*

What is new about this measure? Does it add anything to the legislature passed in 1638/9? Some commentators have judged this act a regressive measure when measured against the earlier legislation. Do you agree? If so, in what respects does the act represent a narrowing of the boundaries of religious freedom?

Forasmuch as in a well Governed and Christian Commonwealth matters Concerning Religion & the honor of God ought in the first place to be taken into serious Consideration and endeavoured to be settled.

Be it therefore Ordered and Enacted by the right honorable Cecilius

*AM 1:244–47.

Lord Baron of Baltimore absolute Lord and Proprietary of this Province with the advice and Consent of the General Assembly that whatsoever Person or Persons within this province and the Islands thereunto Belonging shall from henceforth Blaspheme God that is Curse him or deny our Saviour Jesus Christ to be the Son of God or shall deny the holy Trinity the Father Son & Holy Ghost or the Godhead of any of the said three Persons of the Trinity or the unity of the Godhead or shall use or utter any reproachful speeches words or Language Concerning the said holy Trinity or any of the said three Persons thereof shall be punished with death & Confiscation or forfeiture of all his or her lands and Goods to the Lord Proprietary and his heirs and be it also Enacted by the Authority and with the advice and assent aforesaid that whatsoever Person or Persons shall from henceforth use or utter any Reproachful Word or speech concerning the blessed Virgin Mary the Mother of Our Saviour the holy Apostles and Evangelists or any of them shall in such Case for the first offence forfeit to the said Lord Proprietary and his heirs Lords and Proprietaries of this Province the sum of five Pounds Sterling or the Value thereof to be levied upon the Goods and Chattels sufficient for the satisfying of such forfeiture or that the same be not speedily satisfied that then such Offender or Offenders shall be publicly whipt and be imprisoned during the Pleasure of the Lord Proprietary or the Lieutenant or chief Governor of the Province for the time being and that every such Offender or Offenders for every Second Offence shall forfeit ten pounds Sterling or the Value thereof to be levied as aforesaid or in Case such Offender or Offenders shall not then have Goods and Chattels Sufficient for the Satisfying of such forfeiture then to be publicly and severely whipt and imprisoned as before is Expressed and that every Person or Persons before mentioned offending herein the third time shall for such third offence forfeit all his lands and Goods and be forever Banished and expelled out of this Province and be it also further enacted by the same authority advise and Consent that whatsoever Person or Persons shall from henceforth upon any occasion of offence or other wise in a reproachful manner or way declare call or denominate any person or persons whatsoever ... within this Province ... an heretic, Schismatic, Idolater, Puritan, Independent, Presbyterian, Popish Priest, Jesuit, Jesuited Papist, Lutheran, Calvinist, Anabaptist, Brownist, Antinomian, Barrowist, Roundhead, Separatist, or any other name or term in a reproachful manner relating to matters of Religion shall for every such Offence forfeit and Lose the sum of ten shillings Sterling or the Value thereof to be levied on the Goods and Chattels of every such Offender and Offenders the One half thereof to be forfeited and paid unto the person and persons of whom such reproachful words are and shall be spoken or uttered and the other half thereof to the Lord Proprietary and his heirs Lords and Proprietaries of this Province but if such person or persons who shall at any time utter or speak any such reproachful words or language shall not have Goods & Chattels sufficient and overt within this Province to be taken to satisfy the Penalty aforesaid or that the same be not otherwise speedily satisfied that then the Person or Persons so Offending shall be publicly whipt and shall suffer imprisonment without bail or main prize until he she or they respectively shall satisfy the Party so Offended or Grieved by such reproachful language by asking him or her respectively forgiveness publicly for such his Offences before the Magistrate or chief Officer or Officers of the Town or Place where the Offence shall be Given and be it further likewise enacted by the Authority and consent aforesaid that every Person and Persons within this Province that shall at any time hereafter profane the Sabbath or Lords day Called Sunday by frequent swearing drunkenness or by any uncivil or disorderly recreation, or by working on that day when absolute necessity doth not require it shall for every such first Offence forfeit 2s 6d sterling or the value thereof and for the second Offence, 5s sterling or the Value thereof and for the third Offence and so for every time he shall Offend in like manner afterwards 10s sterling, or the value thereof … and whereas the enforcing of the Conscience in matters of Religion hath frequently fallen out to be of dangerous Consequence in those Commonwealths where it hath been practiced and for the more quiet and peaceable government of this Province and the better to preserve mutual Love and Amity amongst the Inhabitants thereof Be it therefore … enacted … that no Person or Persons whatsoever within this Province … [professing] to believe in Jesus Christ shall from henceforth be in any ways troubled molested or discountenanced for or in respect of his or her Religion nor in the free exercise thereof within this Province … nor any way Compelled to the Belief or exercise of any other Religion against his or her consent so [long] as they be not unfaithful to the Lord Proprietary or molest or Conspire against the civil Government … in this Province.

Sources

Carr, Lois Green, Russell R. Menard, and Lorena S. Walsh. *Robert Coles's World: Agriculture and Society in Early Maryland.* Chapel Hill: University of North Carolina Press, 1991.

Carr, Lois Green, Philip D. Morgan, and Jean B. Russo, eds. *Colonial Chesapeake Society.* Chapel Hill: University of North Carolina Press, 1991.

Carragielo, Michael L. "Runnymeade or Rome? Thomas Copley, Magna Carta, and *In Coena Domini.*" *Maryland Historian* (Fall and Winter 1985): 59–69.

Krugler, John B. "Lord Baltimore, Roman Catholics, and Toleration: Religious Policy in Maryland during the Early Catholic Years, 1634–1649." *CHR* 65 (January 1979): 492–75.

Lahey, Raymond J. "The Role of Religion in Lord Baltimore's Colonial Enterprise." *MHM* 72 (Winter 1977): 492–511.

Maloney, Eric John. "Papists and Puritans in Early Maryland: Religion in the Forging of a Provincial Society, 1632–1665." Ph.D. diss. State University of New York, Stonybook, 1996.

Menard, Russell R. "Maryland's 'Time of Troubles': Sources of Political Disorder in Early St. Mary's." *MHM* 76 (June 1981): 1242–40.

Riordan, Timothy B. *The Plundering Time: Maryland and the English Civil War, 1645–1646.* Baltimore: Maryland Historical Society, 2004.

Spalding, Thomas W. *The Premier See: A History of the Archdiocese of Baltimore.* Baltimore: Johns Hopkins University Press, 1989.

Terrar, Edward. "Was There a Separation between Church and State in Mid-Seventeenth-Century England and Colonial Maryland?" *Journal of Church and State* (Winter 1993): 61–82.

Part 5

The West Indies

1634–1675

S INCE THE THIRD QUARTER of the sixteenth century, the English had coveted the West Indies, that archipelago of islands ranging westward from Barbados in the Atlantic to Jamaica in the Caribbean, for their strategic value in the imperial struggle among European powers, as sites for trading centers and settlements, as well as bases for privateering. Nearly a half century elapsed before they were able to establish a presence in the northern islands of the Lesser Antilles, beginning with St. Christopher (later St. Kitts) in 1624 when the English allied with the French to claim the island from the Spanish and the local Carib Indians. Three years later the English made a settlement on Barbados, the easternmost of the islands. Sometime between 1629 and 1631 (the exact date is unknown) they expanded to Montserrat, the tiny (thirty-nine and a half square miles) ham-shaped island below St. Kitts in the Leeward Islands.

A quarter of a century later Jamaica became the largest island in England's Atlantic empire as the first prize of Oliver Cromwell's "Western Design" to extend the English empire through the Caribbean and Central America to Peru. Cromwell's motivator was Thomas Gage (1603–56), the son of Catholic gentry and a Dominican apostate, whose book *A New Survey of the West Indies* had persuaded Cromwell that Spain's New World empire was low-hanging fruit, ripe for the taking. Just as the Catholic convert George Calvert had altered the course of colonization within the British Empire by introducing a Catholic element into its North American domains, so Thomas Gage, the Dominican friar turned Puritan clergyman, had a major impact on expanding England's Protestant footprint in the New World (see "Why Should My Country-men … Be Debarred?"). Gage's cry for a Protestant crusade to liberate Central and South America from the "Romish" Spaniards moved Cromwell, with his imperial ambitions and need of money, to plan, with Gage as an adviser, a grand naval/army campaign intended to sweep through the Greater Antilles of the Caribbean and to culminate in the conquest of that Shangri-La of precious metals, Peru.

That campaign, in which Gage himself participated as chaplain, precipitated the migration of British settlers, mostly servants, including many Irish, from Barbados and the Lesser Antilles to Jamaica. Indeed servants, inducted by force or self-choice, comprised the majority of the 9,000 military force that in 1655 struck first at Santo Domingo. This initial target of the English armada proved to be anything but the pushover Gage had predicted, as the Spanish defenders decimated the English invasion force. Jamaica, with its great potential for producing sugar, was another matter, as the local authorities made no attempt to defend the island against the thirty-ship invasion fleet. The Spanish residents carried on a disruptive guerrilla campaign for nearly three years, but that little affected the stream of immigrants from the other English holdings in the Indies, which quickly swelled the island's population. In addition there were the thousands of emigrants each year from England and Ireland, Catholics here and there among the former, dominating the latter.

From their first decade of settlement, England's West Indies had become a magnet for emigrants from the British Isles. For the remainder of the seventeenth century West Indian immigrants accounted for a majority of those going to the New World. Equally remarkable was the high minority of settlers who were Catholic, a demographic due largely to the more than 30,000 Irish who, as victims of the land revolution being carried out by the British crown, were forcibly transported to or chose the West Indies. As the Antilles and the Leeward Islands counted the largest concentration of emigrés from the British Isles in the seventeenth century, so did they have more Catholics than did all the English colonies on the North American mainland. Their significant presence in the West Indies went largely unnoted due to the virtual absence of any institutional church in the main areas of Catholic settlement to afford visibility.

As indentured servants for terms ranging from five to seven years, these emigrants initially were the major labor force on the plantations, whose staple crop evolved from tobacco to cotton and finally sugar as chief engine of the economy on the islands. For the vast majority, life was harsh, violent, and short. That was especially so once sugar became the staple crop. And nowhere in the English Isles was life worse for the agrarian laborers than in Barbados. Andrew White and the travelers to Maryland got a taste of the desperate lengths to which such barbaric treatment could lead when they chanced upon an aborted uprising of servants, this barely seven years after the English had opened the land for colonization (see "Inhabitants Who Have Been Expelled by the English").

Life for the Irish in Barbados only got worse in the last thirty years of the century. Slave labor became cheaper to acquire and maintain than that of bonded servants. After mid-century any kind of economic mobility became less and less feasible. Irish ex-servants found themselves in the same landless, jobless, underfed condition that many of them had fled Ireland to escape. A good number resumed their westward journey, some to other islands, more to North America. Many hung on without hope, a living parable of failure.

As English colonies, the British islands in the West Indies were theoretically under the same penal legislation that so constricted the lives of Catholics in England. In practice local governments in Barbados, Montserrat, and elsewhere tolerated the practice of Roman Catholicism, if done discreetly. For much of the seventeenth century there was seldom the opportunity to do so. Catholic authorities in the British Isles as well as the expatriate communities on the Continent sent out missioners to the Indies very rarely. The initial attempt to do so, in the late 1630s, stemmed from the pleas of island Catholics themselves (see "So That the Proselytizers of Heresy Will Not Prevail"). What sporadic ministry there was for Catholics in the British holdings came, for the most part, from the nearby islands under French control—Martinique, Guadeloupe, and St. Christopher. One random missioner in the mid-1650s was the French Jesuit Antoine Biet, who discovered by chance the considerable number of Irish and English Catholics in Barbados when he arrived there, in disguise, with a group of French Catholics. The local Catholics had managed, despite the church's institutional absence, to form a functioning community within which to keep alive their faith. Still, as they made all too clear to Biet, they badly missed the sacraments and instruction that a priest provided them. Unfortunately, after serving them for a few months, the French cleric had to move on with his sojourn-ers (see "Freedom of Belief . . . Provided They Do Nothing in Public").

The longest of the missions was that of John Stritch, who for nearly four years in the early fifties deftly played the dissembling game that British of-ficials preferred as their way of tolerating recusants. In 1650 the Irish Jesuit, like his two diocesan predecessors, made his base on St. Christopher. This was the safest location for a Catholic mission inasmuch as control over the island was split between England and the Catholic power France. Indeed, when Stritch built a chapel on St. Christopher as the initial manifestation of an institutional presence of Catholicism in the British West Indies, it was built within the French sector, beyond the reach of English authority (see "To the Last Degree of Poverty").

As John Stritch and Antoine Biet had discovered in Montserrat and Bar-bados respectively, government would abide the practice of Catholicism as long as it was done out of the public eye. Catholicism might not have enjoyed formal toleration, but there was no significant body of penal laws that identi-fied Catholics as internal enemies who had to be controlled and made to pay a stiff price for their religious allegiance. That began to change by the mid-1650s when the effects of Parliament's consolidation of power after its triumph in the English Civil War began to assert itself in the colonies, nowhere more so than in Barbados. That colony for a long while had attempted to remain neu-tral in the struggle between crown and Parliament, but finally cast its lot in the royalist camp. It paid dearly for the choice, as a fleet sent by Parliament took control of the island in 1651. The new administration in time enacted a range of anti-Catholic or penal laws (see "A Business of Great Importancy").

Six years after the return of the Stuarts to power, a priest from the British Isles was once again serving Catholics in the West Indies. Given the more favorable climate, one might have expected the impetus for restoring the mis-sion to have come from Rome or from an Irish prelate, as had been the origin of John Stritch's going to the islands. But the initiative came not from the top, in Rome or Galway, but from a faculty member at the Irish seminary in Par-is (St. Barbara's College) responding to the horrific reports regarding Irish indentured servants in the Indies that had been circulating in the seminary. With partial support from Propaganda Fide and his bishop in Cashel (Ireland), John Grace set out to make a difference in the spiritual lives of the Irish Catholics in the Antilles. During Grace's two years in the region, although his selfless service fell short of his heroic intentions, he nonetheless brought spiritual and material relief to hundreds of Catholics on the several islands and was responsible for an unprecedented number of conversions. When he returned to Ireland in 1669 with the intention of recruiting enough priests to enable the Irish mission to have an effective institutional presence at last throughout the islands, the prospects seemed better than promising (see "The Irish Had Suffered There So Unspeakably in Body and Spirit").

Among the Irish Catholics who migrated to the West Indies in the seventeenth century were a tiny minority who had sufficient means to avoid indentured servitude as their ticket out of Ireland. In the islands these self-sufficient emigrants went as sojourners, with the intent of securing enough riches as planters or merchants to retire to a gentleman's life back in Ireland. This was evidently the mindset of the three Blake brothers who settled in Barbados and Montserrat in the late 1660s (see "Trading Groweth Daily Here Worse and Worse").

17

"Why Should My Country-men … Be Debarred from … That Which God … Did Ordain for the Benefit of Mankind?": Thomas Gage's View of the Georeligious Stakes, 1648*

Thomas Gage (1603–56) had been born into a family that was a pillar of the gentry-centered Catholicism struggling to survive amid the oppression and persecution that had plagued the Catholic community since Elizabeth's accession. His parents had been prisoners in the Tower of London for two years, the consequence of providing sanctuary for the Jesuit Henry

---

* Thomas Gage, *The English-American His Travail by Sea and Land; or A New Survey of the West India's* (London: R. Cotes, 1648), 1–3, 9, 55–57, 66–68, 82, 118, 127–30, 212.

Garnet in 1692. No fewer than five of their offspring became priests, including Thomas, who, after a continental education at the Jesuit schools in St. Omers and Valladolid, joined the Dominicans in 1621. As Gage notes in A New Survey, the order had assigned him to a part of Spain's New World empire (Guatemala) where he had worked for a dozen years before disillusionment drove him in 1637, without permission, back to England. Five years later he converted to Anglicanism but shortly afterward moved leftward on the Reform spectrum to Puritanism. When he wrote New Survey, he held a pulpit at Acris in Kent County.

In his dedicatory remarks, Gage asserts that God in his providence had placed him in New Spain to garner the knowledge that would empower him to call England to the destiny it should have fulfilled a century and a half earlier, when a Tudor king failed to sponsor Christopher Columbus's initial voyage to the New World. As God used spies in Jericho to open up the Promised Land for the Israelites, so God is channeling Gates to give a new Elect Nation, England, a second chance to expand its empire throughout the Americas. Although in the genre of A Pilgrim's Progress from the superstition and depravity of Rome to the "godly Reformation" that English Puritanism constituted, Gage's New Survey had another objective: to reveal a New Spain groaning with natural wealth and practically inviting invasion by the feeble state of its defenses. His account of his twelve years in Guatemala plays on most of the excesses of Spain's New World experience associated with the "Black Legend"—the extravagance, exploitation, and sexual transgressions of religious and laity. What is his purpose, beyond titillating his readers, in so dwelling on the opulent and salacious details? Gage dedicated the volume to Sir Thomas Fairfax, "Captain-General of the Parliaments Army," signaling the primary audience he was writing for. By the time his book appeared in 1848, Oliver Cromwell held that official position, a fortuitous change, as subsequent events validated. How so? What are the principal arguments Gage makes in justifying England's right to the Spanish possessions in the New World?

The Divine Providence hath hitherto so ordered my life, that for the greatest part thereof, I have lived ... in exile from my native country ... partly by reason of my education in the Romish Religion, and that in foreign Universities; and partly by my entrance into Monastical orders. For twelve years space of which time, I was wholly disposed of in that part of America called New-Spain, and the parts adjacent ... my returning home, not only to my Country, but to the true knowledge and free profession of the Gospels purity, gave me reason to conceive, That these great mercies were ... appointed me by the heavenly Powers, ... that I should impart what I there saw and knew to the use and benefit of my English Country-men.... To your Excellency therefore I offer a New-World, to be the subject of your future pains, valour, and piety, beseeching your acceptance of this plain but faithful relation of mine, wherein your Excellency, and by you the English Nation shall see what wealth and honor they have lost by one of their narrow hearted Princes, who living in peace and abounding in riches, did notwithstanding reject the offer of being first discoverer of America; and left it unto Ferdinando of Aragon ... to set forth Columbus upon so glorious an expedition. And yet, if time were closely followed at the heels, we are not so far behind, but we might yet take him by the fore-top. To which purpose, our Plantations of the Barbados, St. Christophes, Mems,[1] and the rest of the Caribe-Islands, have not only advanced our journey the better part of the way; but so inured our people to the Clime of the Indies, as they are the more enabled thereby to undertake any enterprise upon the firm Land with great facility. Neither is the difficulty of the attempt so great, as some may imagine; for I dare to be bold to affirm it knowingly, That with the same pains and charge which they have been at in planting one of those petty Islands, they might have conquer'd so many great Cities, and large Territories on the main Continent, as might very well merit the title of a Kingdom.... And to meet with that objection ... That the Spaniard being entitled to those Countries, it were both unlawful and against all conscience to dispossess him thereof. I answer, that (the Popes donation[2] excepted) I know no title he hath but force, which by the same title, and by a greater force may be repelled. And to bring in the title of First-discovery, to me it seems as little reason, that the sailing of a Spanish ship upon the coast of India, should entitle the King of Spain to that Country, as the sailing of an Indian or English ship upon the coast of Spain should entitle either the Indians or English unto the Dominion thereof. No question but the just right or title to those Countries appertains to the Natives themselves; who, if they shall willingly and freely invite the English to their protection, what title soever they have in them, no doubt but they may legally transfer it or communicate it to others. And to say, That the inhumane butchery which the Indians did formerly commit in sacrificing of so many reasonable Creatures to their wicked Idols, was a sufficient warrant for the Spaniards to divest them of their Country; The same argument may by much better reason be enforced against the Spaniards themselves, who have sacrificed so many millions of Indians to the Idol of their barbarous cruelty, that many populous Islands and large territo-

1. Montserrat.

2. In the bull *Inter Caetera* (1493), Pope Alexander VI recognized Spain's claim to all the lands discovered by Columbus and granted the Spanish monarchs Ferdinand and Isabella full title to them; hence the "pope's donation."

ries upon the main Continent, are thereby at this day utterly uninhabited, as Bartholomeo de las Casas,[3] the Spanish Bishop of Guaxaca in New-Spain, hath by his Writing in Print sufficiently testified. But to end all disputes of this nature; since that God hath given the earth to the sons of Men to inhabit; and that there are many vast Countries in those parts, not yet inhabited either by Spaniard or Indian, why should my Country-men the English be debarred from making use of that, which God from all beginning no question did ordain for the benefit of mankind?

Chap. I. How Rome Doth Yearly Visit the American and Asian Kingdoms

It would be a long story to insert here how the Popes Policy sucks out of England our gold and silver for the authorizing of our Papists private Chambers and Altars for the gaining of Indulgences in them, and delivering of souls out of purgatory, when Masses are said and heard at them. Thus hath *Rome's* policy blinded and Deceived many of the *European* Kingdoms; and with the same greediness gapes at *Asia* and *America*. Who would not admire to see that at this day in *America* only, the Popes authority and usurped power is extended to as many Countries as all *Europe* contains, wherein no Religion but mere blind Obedience and subjection to that Man of Sin is known? … But the pity is, that what power these Princes have, they must acknowledge it from Rome, having given their own power and strength unto the Beast…. Which, Policy since the first Conquest of the West Indies … hath granted to the Kings of *Spain* by a special title, naming those Kingdoms, *El Patrimonio Real* The Royall Patrimony, upon this Condition, that the King of *Spain* must maintain there the preaching of the Gospel, Friars, Priests and Jesuits to preach it with all the erroneous Popish doctrines, which tend to the advancement of the Popes glory, power, and authority….

Chap. II. Showing That the Indians Wealth under a Pretence of Their Conversion Hath Corrupted the Hearts of Poor Begging Fryers, with Strife, Hatred, and Ambition

O that this … discovery … of those dissembling and false Priests, would make us wise to know and discover under the ashes of their pretended Reli-

---

3. Bartolomé de Las Casas (1484–1556), Dominican friar and bishop of Chiapas, who in his writings exposed and castigated the Spaniards' subhuman treatment of the indigenous peoples.

gion, the fire of strife and contention which they kindle in Kingdoms, and to rake up that covetousness, which we may easily find in them; tending to the ruin of many fair estates, and to the temporal and spiritual danger of this our flourishing Kingdome!

Chap. III. Shewing the Manner of the Missions of Friars and Jesuits to the Indies

Such are the fruits of the zeal of those wretches, who upbraid our Church and Ministers for want of zeal to labour in the Conversion of Infidels. Who when they arrive to those parts, are entertained with ringing of Bells, with sounding of Trumpets most part of the way as they travail, and as Apostles are received by the *Indians*, though soon like *Judas* they fall from their calling, and for pleasure and covetousness sell away Christ from their Souls. *England* may here learn to beware of such Converters, who are daily by name of Missionaries sent hither by the Pope to preach among us Popery; but … come to feed and cherish their wanton lusts, as I could give many instances, might I not be censured for long digressions in mingling English Histories with my *American* Travels.

Chap. XII. Shewing Some Particulars of the Great and Famous City of Mexico in Former Times, with a True Description of It Now; and of the State and Condition of It the Year 1625

In the year 1625, when I went to those parts, this Suburb [of Mexico City] was judged to contain five thousand Inhabitants; But since most of them have been consumed by the *Spaniards* hard usage.… So that now there may not be above two thousand Inhabitants of mere *Indians*, and a thousand of such as they call there *Mestizos*, who are of a mixt nature of *Spaniards* and *Indians*, for many poor *Spaniards* marry with *Indian* woman, and others that marry them not but hate their husbands, find many tricks to convey away an innocent *Uriah* to enjoy his Bathsheba.… Most of these [women] are or have been slaves, though love have set them loose at liberty, to enslave souls to sin and Satan. And there are so many of this kind both men and women grown to a height of pride and vanity, that many times the *Spaniards* have feared they would rise up and mutiny against them. And for the looseness of their lives, and public scandals committed by them and the better sort of the

Spaniards, I have heard them say often who have possessed more religion and fear of God, [that] they verily thought God would destroy the City, and give up the Country into the power of some other nation.

Certainly God is offended with that second *Sodom*, whose inhabitants though now they be like the green bay-tree flourishing with jewels, pearls, gold, silver, and all worldly pleasures, *They shall soon be cut down like the grass and wither as the green herb. Ps.* 37.2 ... and I doubt not but the flourishing of *Mexico* in coaches, horses, streets, women, and apparel is very slippery, and will make those proud inhabitants slip and fall into the power and dominion of some other Prince of this world, and hereafter in the world to come, into the powerful hands of an angry Judge, who is the King of Kings and Lord of Lords....

Chap. XIII. Showing My Journey from Mexico to Chiapa Southward, and the Most Remarkable Places in the Way

Let the Lord's great goodness and wonderful providence be observed who suffered not an *English* stranger in all these dangers to miscarry, but was a guide unto him there in all his travels, discovered unto him as to the spies in *Canaan*, and as to *Joseph* in *Egypt* the provision, wealth and riches of that world, and safely guided him back to relate to *England*, the truth of what no other *English* eye did ever yet behold....

Chap. XVIII. Describing the Dominions, Government, Riches, and Greatness of the City of Guatemala, and the Country Belonging unto It

The Churches though they be not so fair and rich as those of *Mexico*, yet they are for that place wealthy enough.... The Dominicans, Franciscans, and Mercenarians are stately Cloisters, containing near a hundred Friars a piece, but above all is the Cloister where I lived, of the Dominicans.... The yearly revenues which come into this Cloister ... are judged to be ... at least thirty thousand ducats, wherewith those fat Friars feast themselves, and have to spare to build, and enrich their Church and Altars....

This hot, but rich Country ... is a haven for ships from *Panama*, *Peru*, and *Mexico*; It serves to enrich *Mexico* but not to strengthen it, so it hath neither Fort, nor Bulwark, nor Castle, nor any Ammunition to defend it self....

In *July* or at furthest in the beginning of *August* come into that Gulf three ships, or two, and frigate, and unlade what they have brought from *Spain*. They presently make hast to lade again from *Guatemala* those Merchants' commodities of return, which peradventure have lien[4] waiting for them … two or three months before the ships arrival. So that these three months of *July August and September,* there is sure to be found a great treasure. And O the simplicity or security of the *Spaniards*, who appoint no other watch over these their riches, save only one or two *Indians* and as many *Mulatto's*.… Such is this Gulf, whose entrance is strained with two rocks or mountains on each side (which would well become two great Pieces,[5] and scorn a whole fleet, and secure a Kingdome of *Guatemala*, nay most of all *America*).…

Chap. XXII. Shewing How, and for What Causes, after I Had Arrived in England, I Took Yet Another Journey to Rome, and Other Parts of Italy, and Returned Again to Settle My Self in This My Country

At the beginning of the [civil] wars I confess I was … as a Neophyte and new plant of the Church of *England* concerning the lawfulness of the war; and so continued above a year in *London* … till at last I was fully satisfied, and much troubled to see that the Papists and most of my kindred were entertained at *Oxford*, and in other places of the Kings Dominions; whereupon I resolved upon a choice for the Parliament cause.… From their hands and by their order I received a Benefice, in the which I have continued almost four years preaching constantly for a through and godly Reformation, intended by them, which I am ready to witness with the best drops of blood in my veins.… [I] offer up my daily prayers unto him, who … miraculously brought me from *America* to *England* and hath made use of me as a Joseph to discover the treasures of *Egypt*, or as the spies to search into the land of *Canaan*.… *Amen.*

4. Been lying.
5. Cannon.

18

"Inhabitants Who Have Been Expelled by the English": Andrew White's Report on Catholics in the Lesser Antilles, 1634[*]

Among the first to report the Irish presence in the islands was Andrew White, Lord Baltimore's Jesuit publicist. The trade winds had carried the Ark with its Maryland-bound passengers westward toward the Lesser Antilles, eventually bringing them to Barbados in the beginning of 1634. It was the second stop on their crossing, the first at an English port. They arrived to find hundreds of men in arms, patrolling the streets and roads, in the immediate aftermath of an aborted revolt of indentured servants. In a colony much less than a decade old, the crushing work conditions had driven the labor force, or a large portion of it, to rebel. Would that circumstance possibly explain the reception that White and his fellow Catholic travelers got on the island?

When we had cleared the Canaries, Lord Leonard Calvert, who was leading the expedition, began to worry about securing merchandise for the return trip to England which would defray some of the costs Lord Baltimore had incurred in getting up the voyage. We had no hope of getting any in Virginia, which very much opposed our starting a new plantation. So we headed for St. Christopher's; but a general discussion raised the fear that a late season's storm might prevent us from reaching there. Instead we headed south toward Buenavista, an island off the Angolan coast of Africa, 14 degrees from the equator.... We had not gone two hundred miles, when further reflection produced a new suggestion, that we should not lengthen our journey by going so off-course, but head west for Barbados.[6]

This is the most remote of the Caribee or Antilles Islands, 13 degrees above the equator. It serves as a granary for the rest, which extend in a long line in the shape of a bow, all the way to the Gulf of Mexico. When we reached

---

* Hughes, *History of the Society of Jesus in North America*, Documents, vol. 1, part 1, 99–102; Latin.

6. The English version of White's account has the two commissioners pleading with Leonard Calvert to change course, in order to avoid the risk of exhausting their food supplies by lengthening their voyage. Calvert does so, after learning from the steward that they will certainly run out of food if they stay on their present route.

Barbados, on the third of January, we had hope of securing many articles of trade from the English inhabitants, as well as from the governor, who was our fellow countryman;[7] but they all conspired not to sell us any wheat (which had been selling on the island for half a Belgic florin a bushel), for less than five times that price, that is two florins and a half. Chickens were twenty-five Indies. Other similar fowl were no less than three florins. They had no beef nor sheep. The inhabitants' common fare is corn bread and potatoes. The latter is so plentiful that one can cart away as much as one wills.[8]

But God's Providence provided consolation for us amid this cruel treatment. For we learned that a Spanish fleet was stationed off the island of Buenavista to prevent any foreigners from engaging in the salt trade. Had we gone there, as we had intended, we would have walked into their trap and our ships and persons would have become their prizes. Closer at hand, we were delivered from a greater danger. The servants throughout the whole island of Barbados had formed a conspiracy to kill their masters. Once having gained their freedom, they intended to seize the first ship to land there and make their escape. Fortunately, the plot was exposed by a servant horrified by the prospect of the murderous mayhem his fellows were poised to commit.... Our ship, as the first one to dock, was their intended target. But, by the time we actually arrived, we found eight hundred men in arms and the uprising put down....

On January 24 we weighed anchor at night and around noon of the following day we passed St. Lucia on our left and before evening reached Martinique....

The next day, we reached ... around mid-day Montserrat, where there is a colony of Irish Catholics whom the English drove out of Virginia because of their religion.[9] Then the next morning we made it to Nevis, an island notorious for its pestilent air and fevers. After a day's stay there we were on to St. Christopher's where we remained for ten days enjoying the hospitality of the English governor and two Catholic officers; I myself was the guest of the French governor of the island.[10]

7. In fact, the governor was the brother of the Maryland commissioner, Jerome Hawley.
8. This, however, had little appeal to those bound for Maryland; potatoes were not part of their diet.
9. The Irish presence on Montserrat had multiple origins, including Virginia. Other Irish had come there, forcibly or freely, by way of Brazil, St. Christopher, and Ireland itself.
10. The island had been divided between the English and the French for a decade, the result of an alliance between the two nations in order to jointly secure St. Christopher from both the dominant tribe in the region (the Caribs) and the Spanish.

19

"So That the Proselytizers of Heresy Will Not Prevail": Early Efforts to Evangelize the Islands, 1638–1643*

As the English Carmelite Simon Stock had turned in the 1620s to the Sacred Congregation for the Propagation of the Faith to make priests available for an American mission, so too did an Irish prelate turn to the Roman congregation a decade later for priestly aid to another part of England's Atlantic Empire, the West Indies. Stock was acting on behalf of the Catholic founder of a colony on Newfoundland. Malachy O'Queely,[11] archbishop of Tuam, made this later appeal in response to the pleas of some of the emigrant Catholics themselves, presumably former subjects of the archbishop in Connacht Province in western Ireland. When the congregation deferred acting on the petition, the archbishop took the initiative himself and created a mission by assigning two of his priests to work in the islands. This marked the beginning of an institutional presence for British Catholics in the islands, a presence that proved to be, at best, a sporadic, covert one over the next several decades, the consequence of the penal laws, a shortage of priests, and the physical toll upon those who became missionaries. On what does the archbishop place his hope that conversions on a large scale can be the near future of St. Christopher? How successful is the archbishop in securing the clergy necessary not only to maintain the Catholic community but also to evangelize on a broad scale?

Archbishop of Tuam to Members of the Congregation for the Propagation of the Faith, 1638†

There are English, Scottish, and Irish inhabitants on the island of St. Christopher, together with the adjacent islands in the West Indies, whose econo-

---

*Memoriali del 1638, Scritture Originali riferite nelle S. Congregazione Generale, Prop. Fide, vol. 399, fol. 84, in Aubrey Gwynn, "Documents Relating to the Irish in the West Indies," *Analecta Hibernica* 4 (1932): 186–91.

† *Scritture riferite nelle Congregazioni Generali*, vol. 399 (*Memoriali del 1638*), Fol. 257; Latin.

11. Archbishop of Tuam from 1631 to 1645, O'Queely became heavily involved in the Irish uprising in 1642. He was among the founders of the Kilkenny Confederation and was named president of Connacht Province by the Confederation. In 1645 he took command of the Irish forces attempting to recover Sligo from Parliament's control, only to be killed in October in an ambush.

my has lately generated a steady commerce between Ireland and those parts. Indeed there are a large number of Irish, both male and female, daily migrating there, where they intermingle with English and Scotch heretics.

The Archbishop of Tuam has learned that Irish Catholics in these territories lack any spiritual assistance whatever, and are exposed to the proximate danger of falling away from the faith due to the proselytizing of heretical ministers. In these circumstances it seems appropriate to send immediately two zealous and deeply religious priests to the large group of Catholics there, priests who are well trained in how they should conduct themselves, until the Holy See is able to commit others to assist them, as well as the faculties, and other necessities which the Sacred Congregation deem fitting.

And so the said archbishop humbly petitions your eminences that you will designate the said archbishop or some other prelate in Ireland to appoint a prefect of this mission, whose power will consist of granting the usual apostolic faculties to missionary priests, either secular or religious, for ministry in the Indies, and to charge the same prefect with their close supervision so that the said missionaries will not be wanting in any means needed to promote the spiritual good of souls, such as holy oils, vestments, books, etc. and that he will make frequent reports to the Sacred Congregation about the state of affairs.

Archbishop of Tuam to Propaganda, 1638[*]

In this past March 600 Irish of both genders, all Catholics, departed for the islands.... The Archbishop of Tuam, moved by charity and the petition of the said Catholics there, and aware that all the Catholics living there are permanently wanting for the consolation of spiritual ministry because of a lack of priests, deemed it imperative that two priests of his diocese (Ferdinand Fareissy and David Onellus), both deeply religious and zealous, be sent along with that mass of Catholic emigrants, and provided, as far as our sparse means allowed, with all the appropriate necessities. So, properly prepared in how to conduct themselves, he sent them off with his blessing. He has promised to send others, as well.

In these circumstances we humbly petition that you would see fit to appoint a prefect of the mission in those parts of Virginia, so that in the island of St. Christopher and in the other places in which are found English, Scots,

---

[*] *Scritture riferite nelle Congregazioni Generali*, vol. 399 (*Memoriali del 1638*), Fol. 257; Latin.

and Irish, he would have full power to grant apostolic faculties to the diocesan and religious[12] Irish who have gone to that place, and have the authority to make available the sacred oil, vestments, and the other necessities for saying Mass and conferring the other Sacraments. The prefect would have the responsibility of making frequent reports about the spiritual state of the region. Until now the only ministers that the English and Scotch heretics in the islands have are ignorant or uneducated. Zealous, hard-working missionaries could easily bring them to the Catholic faith, or at the very least bring it about that the Catholic part would dominate the religious landscape, no inconsiderable achievement, and in time could lead to the entire region pledging its obedience to the Holy See; otherwise, it will be a den of Calvinists.

However it should be pointed out that the said archbishop who by his title alone has no benefice or income, is unable to supply what the above-named missionaries have need of, the expenses of their long journey, vestments, books, spiritual aids, and other necessities which can not be found in those parts. So it is necessary that the Sacred Congregation take appropriate measures by which these needs can be met.

Acta S. Cong. de Prop. Fide. Anno 1638–39. fol. 441 v

Decembris 19, 1639. num. 60

Concerning the mission of Irish priests to the Irish settlers on the islands of St. Christopher and the adjacent ones, which mission the Archbishop of Tuam proposes as a necessity, the Sacred Congregation instructs by letter that the archbishop should choose some religious who have their superior's permission and possess the character and knowledge needed, and forward their names, especially the person made prefect of the mission, so that they can expedite the faculties and other permission the missionaries will have need of.

Malachy, Archbishop of Tuam, to Cardinal Prefect of Propaganda Fide, December 8, 1639

The priests who were sent to the island of St. Christopher to work in the vineyard of the Lord, I am sorry to report have gone the way of all flesh, such

12. Priests of a religious order.

is the punishing climate and savagery of the inhabitants, that newcomers often do not long survive. Still this does not deter us from assigning others to replace them, and so we earnestly ask your eminence and the Sacred Congregation that you will kindly conclude that such a mission is worthy of the support you will see fit to provide in due time by issuing the necessary faculties.

20

"Freedom of Belief ... Provided They Do Nothing in Public": Antoine Biet's Account of His Ministry in Barbados, 1654[*]

The French Jesuit came to the West Indies as a chaplain for a group of his countrymen intent on establishing a colony there. After one failure, they relocated in Barbados, where the Catholic community quickly discovered the Jesuit's identity (Biet had been attempting to pass as a layman). Adopting the discreet modus operandi that Stritch had effectively employed on Montserrat and elsewhere, Biet provided very welcome ministry for several months before obligations to his patrons forced him to move on.

Chapter 31: Our Arrival in the Island of Barbados Where We Were Very Well Received by the English

I went for a walk in a secluded spot, between the orange and lemon trees, in order to say my prayers and to communicate with God, when I was surprised by a large man who came up to me. He was of the Irish nation, and a good looking man. He spoke to me in a corrupt language intermixed with Italian, Portuguese, and Provençal, or to say it better, a corrupt language which those who sail on the Mediterranean understand very well. "*Seignor Padre*," he said, "I am a servant of your Lady." I gave him an angry look, and replied in this same language: "What do you mean, I am not a priest."

* Jerome S. Handler, "Father Antoine Biet's Visit to Barbados in 1654," *Journal of the Barbados Museum and Historical Society* (1967): 58–62.

He then started to show me a great deal of tenderness, making the sign of the cross to let me know that he was Catholic, but I rebuffed him because I feared that he was someone who came to expose me and reveal me as a priest in court. He almost fell to his knees in front of me, once again making the sign of the cross, and recited the Lord's Prayer in Latin, the Hail Mary, the *Credo* and the *De Profundis* to certify that he believed in the prayer for the dead, and he told me he was Catholic, Apostolic, and Roman; that I had nothing to fear, that he clearly saw that I was a priest; that in having met me he considered himself happy, not only for his solace, but also for the solace of many other good Catholics whom he would have me meet in this island, who were in great distress without any spiritual comfort. I was unable not to make myself known, and I could only confess to him that I was what he believed, and that I considered myself happy to be able to serve him and all good Catholics. . . . He did not fail to come to see me every day for the eight or ten days that we lived in the town. What vexed me was that I could not express my thoughts to him in a suitable manner, which compelled me to force myself to learn the English language so as to be capable of rendering a service to more than two thousand Catholics who were in this island. . . .

Our gentlemen had our baggage taken to the plantation which they had bought, where we lived peacefully in the practice of our Holy Religion. I did the prayers daily, evening and morning. I only said mass on holidays and Sundays, above all Sundays, when each one is free to do as he wants on the plantation, and to live with whatever religion he wants. Provided that one does not carry out religious exercises in public, no one bothers with what one is doing. . . .

Toward Holy Week I went to the Bridge.[13] The first person I met as I entered town was Captain Halay, who was delighted to see me. After having embraced me, he took me to a large dwelling, and led me into a very large room which was decorated with a great number of palm leaves; which led me to believe that this was the house of some Catholics who were observing the solemnity of Easter as much as they could. . . . Immediately I saw about ten or twelve persons coming towards me, both men and women, who kissed my hands and threw themselves at my feet, crying with joy to find themselves so close to a priest. I was confused to see myself so honored, and by the fact that I was unable to console them,—for I could neither address them nor understand what they were asking me through the intermediary

13. Bridgetown.

of Captain Halay who acted as my interpreter. I took my leave of these good Catholics, telling them that I was only returning to our plantation, to use the island term, to apply myself entirely to learning their language in order to render them assistance; and that since God had not permitted I work in the conversion of the savage Indians, I would stay here with them for their solace and to care for the health of their souls. They displayed a great deal of happiness at my promise which I was unable to carry out, God having ordained otherwise....[14]

As for religion, Calvinism is the only one that is professed in public....There are Catholics, who are not in small numbers, and even Jews. All are given freedom of belief, provided that they do nothing to be conspicuous in public, to such an extent that on Sunday one is free to do what one wants in his house, no one bothers to see what he is doing. That is why I carried on all of my religious functions with great freedom.

21

"To the Last Degree of Poverty": John Stritch's Clandestine Mission to Montserrat, 1650–1653[*]

During his first few years in the Lesser Antilles, Stritch, from his base on St. Christopher, sailed a circuit to other islands where there were Catholic communities. Usually in disguise, in keeping with the tacit agreement between priest and local officials that the latter would tolerate the former's presence so long as he practiced his ministry discreetly, Stritch said Mass and administered sacraments in the deep woods.

This détente unraveled when the English authorities on St. Christopher set the French section off-limits for residents in the English portion of the island. In the face of Catholic defiance of the order, the English government there seized the elite males within the Catho-

---

[*] Pierre Pelleprat, *Relation des Mission des PP. de la Compagnie de Iésus dans les Isles, et dans la terre ferme de l'Amérique Meridionale* (Paris: 1655), 36–46; reprinted in Gwynn, "Documents," 208–13.

14. Dispatched by his patrons to go to Martinique to attend to some business they had there, Biet never had the opportunity to return to Barbados.

lic community and shipped them off to the dreaded Isle of Crabs, where the hapless exiles experienced even more than "the last degree of poverty" that the English governor of St. Christopher had promised. Father Stritch finally gave up the hopeless effort to maintain a Catholic witness there and accepted the hospitality of the French on Guadeloupe as a refuge for himself and some of his Irish congregants. He did keep up as best he could his old island-hopping circuit until superiors called him home in 1660.

Pierre Pelleprat's Account of the Irish Mission

The number of Irish in America being considerable, a number increasing every year, we sought and secured a priest from that nation to go to their assistance. It was an opportune time to do so, for inasmuch as the English, in whose service many of the Irish were indentured for seven years, would not allow them to practice their religion; on the contrary, they treated them in such an abysmal manner that many of the poor folk, in an attempt to avoid the cruel treatment and the violence inflicted on them, fell away from the church and almost without knowing it gradually lost their faith.

Father John Stritch, who was assigned to minister to them, arrived at St. Christopher in 1650. He at once built a chapel on Sable Point, in the French section but close by English territory where the great majority of the Irish had their quarters. The Irish were overjoyed that one of their own had come to be their priest. Their delight at the opportunity to practice their religion that his coming gave them made them forget the dangers to which they were exposing themselves, for they went in a crowd, in broad daylight, to greet the priest whom they looked upon as an envoy sent by God to come to their aid. Some grasped his hand in order to kiss it; others threw themselves at his feet to receive his blessing; the scene produced in the priest an indescribable happiness. The missionary told them that his sole reason for coming to the islands was to be their spiritual minister. The first thing he did was to arrange with them the most appropriate times and ways in which he could provide them with his ministry, in order to avoid giving their masters any excuse to abuse and inflict violence on them; but most of the Irish had such a religious fervor, that they had no fear at all in exposing their bodies in order to save their souls.

The priest spent all his days at the chapel administering the sacraments; during the entire three months he spent there, he was always busy, from dawn to one in the afternoon, hearing confessions and giving communion, baptizing their infants and giving catechesis. God so blessed his work that many who had fallen into heresy found again the right road. Even though the priest was there but a very brief time, he so reclaimed his flock that he estimated his congregation grew to nearly three thousand persons.[15]

After he had taken care of the most pressing spiritual needs of the Irish on St. Christopher, he went on to the island of Montserrat, where the Irish had originally been their own masters. The English, however, had confiscated their land, and they were now servants. The priest, realizing that the authorities would not allow a priest on the island, disguised himself as a merchant, and went there on the pretext of wishing to buy some timber. As soon as he arrived, he revealed his identity to certain Irishmen, who spread the news to their fellow countrymen. They chose a spot in the woods where the priest spent his days saying Mass and administering the other sacraments. Every morning he devoted himself to nourishing souls; afterwards he would chop wood provided to him by the good Catholics there, to satisfy the English that he had indeed come to the island to obtain wood.

One day while the priest was in the woods, administering the sacraments, two thousand Caribs, who had been in a long-running war with the English, staged a raid on the island. The invaders burned a number of houses, massacred many people, looted storehouses, carried off cattle and people, and left behind a trail of chaos....

The priest having met the spiritual needs of the Irish on that isle, returned to St. Christopher, where ... those who wished ill to the Catholics determined not to allow the Catholic faith to make any progress there and intensified their efforts to destroy that nascent church. With their backs up, the English prohibited the Irish Catholics in the future from going into the French section, on the pretext that they were seeking work there while their real intention was to congregate for Mass.

15. The Dominican Jean Baptiste du Tertre, who had worked in the Antilles for eight years (1639–47) and subsequently wrote a history of the region, judged this claim to be a gross exaggeration. "I can," he maintained, "without any aspersions on the pious ministry of the Jesuit fathers, say with certainty that that congregation never counted a thousand people, at the very most there were five hundred, that is counting Father Stritch's years there, plus the twelve years preceding the sending of the Jesuits to Saint-Christopher when the Capuchins realized great results through their work there, ... and by us Dominicans, such as Fathers Pelican and Nicholas of St. Dominic, and in brief the many Irish priests who with great edification produced a fine harvest among the heretics"; Jean Baptiste du Tertre, *Histoire Generale Des Isles Des Christophe, de la Guadeloupe, de la Martinique et autres Dans L'Amerique* (Paris: 1654), 195–96). In other words, despite the valiant efforts of many, including Stritch, the Catholic congregation on St. Christopher's never approached a thousand members, much less three times that number.

Not content with preventing them from any religious practice, they resorted to maltreating them in the worst ways imaginable. Their hatred reached such a fury that they rounded up at night one hundred and twenty-five Irish Catholics, whom the English considered the most devoted and most important, loaded them aboard a vessel and abandoned them on the Isle of Crabs, about two hundred leagues distant from St. Christopher,[16] which is uninhabited and totally lacking all necessities.

While the exiles were reduced to the worst possible state, those who remained among the English on St. Christopher were themselves subjected to all sorts of hardship. For after they had stripped them of arms, they were threatened with the most severe punishment, if they disobeyed the order to stay away from the chapel. When a young girl refused to abide by such a command, she was dragged along by her hair and treated so cruelly that a number of persons, frightened by the excesses that had been inflicted on that noble Christian, heeded the order, at least externally, and resumed attending the heretical services.

Some of those occasionally came to Mass, but they came stealthily, to avoid detection. There were some so steadfast and fervent, who, seeing that the English had stationed a band of soldiers on the main road that leads to the chapel, stole away from their cabins on the eves of holydays and Sundays, and walked the whole night through the woods covered with underbrush and by mountain passes, in order to attend Mass....

For many days those exiled were in the direst of situations on the Isle of Crabs. The only living matter on the island were a few herbs and some shells that they would search for at the sea's edge. They thought their death an inevitable one, when they spied a boat passing near their island. They signaled the craft which thereupon headed for shore When they arrived, they entreated them to take them to Santo Domingo; but the boat was too small to take them all aboard; they could only add as many as would not endanger the ship. And so a portion of those unhappy people, brought to the very depths of wanting, had to remain on that isle with no hope of rescue. Those who managed to get aboard the vessel made it to Santo Domingo; but the Spanish, who control the island, once they learned that they came from St. Christopher, refused to let them land, for fear of some sneak attack. And as to drive home the impression that the whole world was conspiring against them, shortly after they got there, a horrific storm broke upon them which

16. About six hundred nautical miles.

carried them out to sea, four leagues from land. They passed four days at sea without food or water. They were so depressed and so feeble that they more resembled cadavers than living men. For they were not only without anything they needed; they had absolutely no hope of getting any. One of them actually proposed casting lots to see who would be first to be slain in order to provide food for the others. His thought was that it was better for one of them to hasten his death so that the rest might be spared from dying a wretched death. One of the most eminent members of the band would simply not entertain such a proposition, finding it unworthy of a Christian and offensive to God's providence. With a great deal of zeal and candor, he rebuked those who had given voice to that opinion; that done, he encouraged his companions to have more confidence in God, who often allows bad things to happen as a test of faith and to provide occasions for his creatures to gain merit for themselves.

He had barely finished his exhortation when there appeared close to the boat a gargantuan fish; but since they had no line nor any other instrument with which to catch it, they tried to seize it with their hands; and they managed to do so with such incredible dexterity, that they managed to hold him motionless at the water's surface. Now, I have no doubt that He who multiplied two fish to nourish the people who were following him, would not send similar aid to those poor people who had suffered so much out of love for Him. They could not have surpassed that catch they had made, for the fish was so huge that all those in the boat, who had not lost their appetites, lived off that fish for many days. Just about that time they came upon a warship which took them to Tort, where they were well received by the French....

As for those who had been left on the Isle of Crabs, for lack of room upon the boat, the general belief is that they perished at sea in some manner. For, seeing that they were fated to die of famine on that island, they bound together their chests with cords to fashion a kind of raft, on which they cast out to sea, in the hope that the winds and the tides would carry them to some coast, where they might find some means of subsistence; but it might well be that a storm sank them, or their craft was becalmed; whichever, they had a miserable ending at sea....

Since that time, Father Stritch has made his residence [at Guadeloupe] where he provides the ministry of a good pastor. From time to time he visits the other islands, where there are Irish; but he never goes to any controlled by the English except in disguise. He comforts them, strengthens them in the faith, and secretly administers the sacraments. And in working among the Catholics, he always gains many converts, among both the English and the Irish. In one instance, not long since, he had seventy people foreswear in his presence their erring ways. Even though he spent only five years working in the islands, he brought back to the church more than four hundred heretics.

22

"A Business of Great Importancy": Reining in Catholics in Barbados, 1654–1660[*]

A major precipitant of the anti-Catholic measures was war with a Catholic power, or at least the looming likelihood of it. That danger always intensified the inherent distrust of English society, whether home or abroad, for the Catholics in their midst. In many of the following documents, there is a presupposition that freedom for Catholics involves a threat to public security that the law urgently needs to address. In what ways does the penal legislation of the provincial council and the proclamations/orders of other officials attempt to rein in the Catholics among them? What parallels do you see between the public treatment of the indentured Irish of Barbados in the seventeenth century and that of either the slave or freedmen communities in the South of the nineteenth century? And the differences? Why do the governor and his council in August of 1660 suddenly call for repeal of the acts disarming the Irish in the colony?

Extracts from the Minutes of the Council of Barbados

Dec. 6, 1654

Ordered that the three [sic] Irishmen, by name, Garrett Plunkeet, Finian Martin, Owen Carthy, Deniel Oge O'Mehegan, which came over free

[*] Aubrey Gwynn, "Documents Relating to the Irish in the West Indies," *Analecta Hibernica* 4 (1932): 233–39.

with Mr. Barrow, in the Ship called The Two Brothers, do put themselves into some employment with some freeholder of the English Nation; and that they do bring with them before the Governor on Monday next, their Masters with whom they do agree to put in security for their good demeanour, for the time they stay on the Land.

Jan. 2 1654/5

Complaints being this day made to the Governor and Council, that three Irish Priests were landed on this Island out of a ship that arrived lately to Spikes Bay, notwithstanding the Governor's order to Col. Yeamans to examine said persons, and an account thereof to be returned unto him....

Nov. 6, 1655

Upon Information given by Cap: Richard Goodall, and Mr. John Jones, as also by a Letter from Lieut: Coll: John Higgenbotham, that there are several Irish Servants and negroes out in Rebellion in the Thicketts and thereabouts, It is ordered, that Lieut: Coll John Higginbotham have power to raise any of the Companies of Coll: Henry Hawley's Regiment, to follow the said Servants, and Runaway Negroes; and if he shall meet with any of them, to cause them forthwith to be secured, and to send them before the Governor, or some Justice of the Peace, to be dealt with according to Justice; but if the said Servants and Runaway Negroes shall make any opposition, and resist his forces, and refuse to come in peaceably, and submit themselves, then to use his utmost Endeavour to suppress or destroy them, Provided, they do stand out in Rebellion, and cannot be otherwise taken.

Jan. 15 1656

In Pursuance of a Statute of this Island, ... empowering the Governor and Council to inflict Corporal Punishment, on such persons as give out Mutinous Language, It appearing to the Governor and Council, by the Depositions of Jonn Bowler and Dennis Powell, that Cornelius Bryan, an Irishman, did say as he was eating Meat in a Tray, that if there was so much English Blood in the Tray as there was Meat, he would eat it, it is therefore ordered, that he have One and Twenty lashes on the bare back, by the Common Hangman, before the Cage, at the Indian Bridge town.

Ordered, that Cornelius Bryan, an Irishman, the Piper, for great suspicion of raising a Mutiny, to the disturbance of the peace and quiet of this Island, stand Committed to the P.M. (Provost Marshall), till he hath put in security for his good behaviour, for one Month's time to Depart the Island:

but if after the aforesaid Limited Time, he be found on the Land, then is to be proceeded against as a Mutineer.

PROCLAMATION (Sept. 22, 1657)

Whereas it hath been taken notice that several of the Irish Nation, free men and women, who have no certain place of residence, and others of them do wander up and down from Plantation to Plantation, as vagabonds, refusing to labour, or to put themselves into any service, but continuing in a dissolute, lewd, and slothful kind of life, put themselves on evil practices, as pilfering, thefts, robberies, and other felonious acts, for their subsistency, and endeavouring by their examples and persuasion to draw servants unto them of said Nation to the same kind of idle, wicked courses, as complaints to that purpose hath daily made to appear; and information having been given, and oath made before myself and council, that divers of, as well Freemen as Servants, have of late uttered threatening words, and menacing Language, to several the inhabitants of this Place, and demeaned themselves in a very Peremptory and Insolent way of carriage and behaviour; and that some of them have endeavoured to secure themselves with Arms; and others now forth in Rebellion, and refuse to come in; by all which it appears, that could they be in a condition of power, or had opportunity, they would soon put some wicked and malicious design in execution.

Myself and Council having taken the premises into consideration, for avoiding those evil effects that might ensue, if such exorbitant courses be not timely suppressed, and the idle and wandering life of said persons, prevented, do therefore order, and, in Highness's name, will and require, all Masters and Mistresses of Families, Overseers of Plantations, and others that, if any person of the Irish Nation, Man or Woman shall, at any time come into their Houses or Plantations and cannot give a ready and good account the reason of their coming be upon some business or message to the Master, Mistress or Overseer of such Plantation—if it be a servant, and have not a Ticket under the hand of his or her Master, Mistress, or Overseer, that they cause to be given to him or her reasonable correction; and, after wards, that he be conveyed to the next Constable, and so from constable to constable, until he or she be returned to his or her Master, Mistress or Overseer.

But, if it be a Freeman Free Woman, and out of service, and have no constant or settled place of abode; that then he, or she so taken, be conveyed to the next Justice of the Peace, who is required to cause him, or her, to be whipt, according to the Law, as a Vagabond and Wanderer; and, after such correction given, to command him or her to labour for one whole year in some Plantation, or House, be willing to receive him, or her, so appointed to serve.

And, if such person or persons so ordered to serve shall not accomplish the order appointed by the Justices, but absent and run away; in that case, as often as they shall absent and run away, being found, to be again whipt, and ordered to service, as before is mentioned.

And, whereas information hath been given, that some of the Irish Nation that are in Rebellion do pass up and down from Plantation to Plantation with counterfeit and forged Testimonials, that they are freemen; ... all persons are desired to be very circumspect in their inquiries into such Tickets and Testimonials, as shall be produced unto them; and, if they shall appear to be counterfeit or forged, that they cause such persons having the same to be conveyed before the next Justice of the Peace, to be proceeded against according to law.

And further, myself and Council, on good grounds and consideration, having given order for the discovering all persons of the Irish Nation, inhabiting or abiding within this Island, these are, therefore, in the name of His Highness, the Lord Protector,[17] to prohibit all and every person whatsoever, that for the future they do not sell any kind of Arms or Ammunition whatever to any one of the said Nation; and if, from and after publication thereof, any Arms or Ammunition shall be found in the Custody, or in any of the houses or habitations of the Irish; or, that they shall at any time travel, or go armed; upon information or complaint thereof, made to any of his Highness's officers within this Island, Military or Civil, it shall and may be lawful to any of them to seize on any such Arms or Ammunition, and them cause to be delivered to the next Field Officer, within the Precincts where such Arms or Ammunition shall be found; ...

Order of Governor and Council, Sept. 22, 1657

Myself and council having taken into consideration ... the considerable number of Irish, freemen and Servants, within this Island, and the Dangerous consequences in this Juncture of time, of Wars betwixt the Commonwealth of England and Spain, both in Europe and here in America, that may

17. Oliver Cromwell.

ensue to this Place upon the appearance of an Enemy, if the Irish and such others as are of the Romish Religion, should be permitted to have any sort of Arms or Ammunition within their Houses or Custody, or at any time to wear or go Armed: have thought it necessary for the better security of this Place, and continuance of Peace thereof, to order, that all such as are of the Irish Nation, or known or reputed to be Recusants be forthwith Disarmed. These are therefore in the name of His Highness Oliver, Lord Protector of the Commonwealth of England etc. to Will and require you Coll. Lewis Morris on Saturday next the 26th Day of this Instant September, to make or cause to be made, by the respective Officers of your Regiment (not being Irish), a strict search, and Diligent enquiry within the Limits of your Regiment, in all and every the house or out-house of such persons above mentioned, what arms or ammunition they have in their Custody, as fire arms for horse or foot, of what nature so ever they be, Swords, Rapiers, Cutlasses, Daggers, Sheaves, Pikes, half-pikes, Lances, Powder, Bullet, Shot or Match, and what thereof they shall so find, that you forthwith seize and secure the same.

Journal of the Proceedings of the Governor and Council of Barbados from May 29, 1660, to November 30, 1686

At a meeting of the Rt honorable Daniel Searle Esq. Governor of Barbados and the Right Worshipful. His Council June 11, 1660.

It is ordered the field officers of every Regiment do take an Exact list of what Irish so ever are in their particular precincts and to give an account of the Number of them, at the next day of Exercise, as also of their abode.

It is ordered that no Irish be commander or sharer of any shallop; or boat belonging to or in this Island.[18]

June 26–27, 1660

It is ordered that upon the approach of an Enemy, ten horses be drawn out of each troop with some discreet person to command them to secure through the several Quarters and parts of this Island to take up Irish or other stragglers &c ... and it is further ordered, that none but freeholders ride in the said party, and a discreet person appointed to Command them.

18. On page two of the Minute Book of the Provincial Council it is noted that Governor Searle had received a message from Col. Middleton who warned him that the King of Spain "had appointed a fleet of Dutch ships to transport ten thousand English, Irish, and Scots to what place he pleaseth."

It is ordered that the Trustees, and church wardens of the Respective Parishes in this Island, do meet on Monday next, in their several Parishes, and take an account and exact list of all the Irish that live or be in their Parishes, and such amongst them, as are of turbulent, seditious, troublesome, or dangerous Spirits, that they return the names of such to the Governor and council upon Friday next, … of which they are not to fail, it being a business of great importancy and concernment to the Peace and Security of this Island.

August 1, 1660

The Governor and council presents it to the Assembly as their opinion that all acts which related to the disarming of the Irish, ought to be repealed, and desire the concurrence of the Gen. of the Assembly therein.…

The Assembly concurs the repealing of the said Acts.

23

"The Irish Had Suffered There So Unspeakably in Body and Spirit": John Grace's Mission, 1667–1669[*]

John Grace set off for the islands at the close of 1666 but found himself a virtual exile on the French island of Martinique, as war between the French and the English effectively kept Grace from widely ministering to the Irish in the islands where they had the heaviest concentration. When the political and military conditions began to signal an opportunity for him at last to begin an island-hopping ministry, he barnstormed through British islands with Catholic populations, bringing the sacramental church once more to hundreds and stirring conversions to the faith among others. Then his health turned bad, expediting a decision he had been pondering: to return home to raise the financial support he had lacked so far and to recruit other priests to join him in an enlarged mission in the islands. More frustration awaited him in France and Ireland. His two-year-plus mission proved to be the last one of the century involving priests from the British Isles in the West Indies. What does the origin of Grace's mission say about the importance that the official church gave to the

* Propaganda Archives, *Scritture riferite nelle Congregazioni Generali*, vol. 257, fol. 96, 117; Propaganda Archives, *Scriture riferite nei Congressi Irelanda*, vol. 2, fol. 146, in Gwynn, 253–58; Latin.

English-speaking Catholic diaspora in the West Indies? Reflecting on the first half century of English settlement in the islands, what factors seem to best account for the minimal sporadic presence of the institutional church?

Annual Report of John Grace, March 11, 1667

It is already three months since we arrived at Martinique. I have seen here two small ships crowded with our countrymen, who were living on St. Christopher in the English section before the French drove the English off the island. The Irish had suffered there so unspeakably in body and spirit that one has to think and believe that God will not forsake us but rather crush those who have been guilty of such inhumanity. The English blamed the Irish for the loss of the island. The French did not appreciate the service the Irish had rendered them. You see those wretched beings, who were living there comfortably enough, now driven out and robbed of any consolation, left to collapse on the journey and give up the ghost. Among the refugees there was a woman with five children, the oldest of whom was merely six. She was but one of a mass of people at death's door. Her name was Margaret Riordan. Three days earlier I had heard her confession and given her Communion. I saw many such sights and was powerless to do anything to help.... While we were stuck in Martinique, I dared not try to make it to St. Christopher, so long as the English were infesting the waters. Still I did what I could for those long-suffering individuals. Indeed in my circuit through Martinique, Guadeloupe, and Antigua, I heard more than three hundred general confessions; about fifty of those penitents died. When I did finally get here, I fell ill, but kept up my ministry wherever I spotted a rich harvest, of which I alone could make the most modest beginning in gathering. When my health allows, I intend to get to the tiny island of St. Bartholomew, where there were forty Irish who in the entire time in which they had been laboring there, have never seen a priest.... But unless some fellow priests are sent here to labor with me, the burdens are going to be too much for me and I will have to return home. Still, for all of that, I remain, through God's grace, devoted to this ministry, and I challenge others to follow me. Be sure to have apostolic faculties sent, should any of our companions feel the call to work zealously in the Lord's vineyard.

Note: I have faithfully translated this from the French. William Burgat, Vicar Apostolic of Limerick.

Letter of John Grace to Rome, July 5, 1669

Directed by my ordinary, the Rev. Archbishop of Cashel, that I provide you an account of the mission that I undertook in the islands of western America, I humbly obey:

My dedicated love of the Faith, which your Reverence's charity and concern inspires in me to hold dear and to work to deepen, moves me to point out the many islands in western America claimed by various nations, especially the French and the English. In those islands which are subject to the English, there are a very large number of Catholics, who recently under the tyrannical government of Cromwell and other fierce enemies of the Catholic faith, were deported from Ireland to work the fields of the English. There they are living miserable lives, starved both materially and spiritually. They are forbidden any access to the Sacraments or Catholic instruction. They can have no contact with the Church's ministers. Wherever the English hold power, priests risk their lives to assist people, and none were found who were willing to court this danger, even though it was vitally necessary. Made aware of this terrible situation by some pious Irishmen then living in Paris, in the year 1666, lacking virtually all that I clearly needed for the demanding, dangerous journey, I set out for the islands together with some French merchants. When I got there, I found that the state of the Catholics toiling there was every bit as terrible as I had heard.

I began immediately to instruct, hear confessions, administer the Eucharist and Extreme Unction, to bury the dead, in which ministry, with God's grace, I happily spent more than two years. And I should add that I converted about thirty of the English, as the accounts of the notable men which I have brought back with me make clear. Among them was one statement given me by the Jesuit Fathers as I was leaving St. Christopher, which I send your eminence as an example of the rest. They show that I have used to good effect the too generous stipend which the Sacred Congregation in its charity provided me; for that and for all that you have done for me, I extend my most sincere gratitude....

So I head back to Ireland, with the intention of returning to the poor suffering people in those islands, however my ordinary deems best, provided suitable co-workers are found for undertaking such a demanding mission. Indeed one or two are not sufficient to man a mission that involves covering so many widely scattered places and no fewer than 12,000 Catholics (Barbados has 8,000, the other five together that I have visited, namely Antigue, Martinique, Guadeloupe, St. Christopher, and St. Eustace … have as many).

On my last mission there, I had gone through all the funds I had raised, when the peace treaty between the kings restored the islands to the English which the French had captured during the war. That made it impossible for me to remain there, indeed to settle on any of the English islands, so I deemed it best, on the advice of friends, to return home for a while.

24

"Trading Groweth Daily Here Worse and Worse": The Blake Family in Barbados and Montserrat, 1675[*]

Henry, John, and Nicholas were younger sons of John Blake Fitz Nicholas, one of the most powerful of the Old English "Tribes" or oligarchy of merchant families that had ruled Galway for centuries. The father had been mayor of Galway City during the war between the Kilkenny Confederation and the English Parliamentarian forces in the Irish theater of the Civil War. Having belatedly cast their lot with the Confederation, the Blakes were among the Catholics expelled from Galway City and stripped of their ancient estates for their treason. The three sons went to the West Indies on their own mission: to regain in the islands the wealth they had lost in the previous decade. Nicholas, for unknown reasons, stayed but a short time there before returning to Ireland. The other two, John and Henry, bought a substantial plantation on Montserrat, where Irish immigrants, including many relatives of the Blakes, were rapidly becoming a majority among the couple thousand whites on the island. Henry ran the plantation; John headed east to Bridgetown in Barbados to establish a business. Their fortunes in the planting and mercantile worlds took very different turns, as evidenced by John's wife joining him in Barbados seven years after her husband arrived there. John still hoped to make his fortune in the islands and return home, but it would be in planting, not business; in Montserrat where the Irish dominated the society, not Barbados.

*Kerby A. Miller et al., eds., *Irish Immigrants in the Land of Canaan: Letters and Memoirs from Colonial and Revolutionary America, 1675–1815* (New York: Oxford University Press, 2003), 124–28.

On the other hand, as John was determining to move from Barbados to Montserrat, Henry was returning home to his wife in Galway, having fulfilled his goal of making enough money to put the family in the position of reclaiming its place in the homeland. Why would John Blake's family in Galway oppose his son joining him in Barbados? What does the experience of the Blakes in the islands say about the opportunities for economic mobility that the Irish could expect to find there in the seventeenth century?

John Blake, Bridgetown, Barbados, to Thomas Blake, County Galway, Nov. 1, 1675

Yours of Aug. 26 last I have on Aug. 28 the ultimo received.[19] I am glad you received the monies mentioned in your said letter; Seeing that yourself and nearest relations are against the sending hither of my son I do willingly submit to your better judgements wherefore let him remain there of whom I most earnestly entreat you to be most careful and to see him decently provided with all necessaries for which purpose I will not from time to time fail to remit you moneys by the way of London. Mr. Nicholas Lynod the school master at Mace hath written me that he would be very kind to him for which cause if you & my father in law will think it convenient let him remain under his tuition; for whom is one of the enclosed to whom pay plentifully what you will think fit, that he may be the more encouraged to take pains about the child: … I am very glad of my brother Nicholas and nephew Martin's safe arrival.… The wench came over along with my wife; I am most sensible what my brother Henry hath written me heretofore of her as likewise what you intimated per your said letter, to which I say that though I find her as yet most vicious less here perhaps deterred through the most severe correction I keep her under yet because of said bad reports I would not at all abide her under my roof but I thereunto am as yet inevitably compelled by reason my wife being as I find her of a very weak constitution cannot discharge all herself; for washing starching making of drink and keeping the house in good order is no small task to undergo here; if I would dismiss her another I must have which may prove ten times worse than her; for until a negro wench I have be brought to knowledge I cannot considering my present charge be without a white maid.[20] I hope all will do well for I have as much peace and tranquility in my house as any one in the world can desire for which the

---

19. Thomas Blake was the older brother of John.
20. "Brought to knowledge": taught to do the work involved in housekeeping.

Lord of heaven be for ever praised. Trading growth daily here worse and worse, only that provisions now and then, as now it is [are] very scarce and dear; viz beef sold at 35 shillings per barrel: and some new beef lately come in at 40 shillings per barrel: which prices I am sure will long continue because provisions do now begin to come in from New England and some few from Bermuda. If you could at any time send hither 10 or 20 barrels or more of good beef and finding freight at a moderate rate you may expect thereby reasonable profit. The last Hurricane we had here was on the last day of August last hath at least by a third part made this Island worse than it was, God Almighty grant us patience.

John Blake, Bridgetown, to Thomas Blake, County Galway, July 28, 1676

My last unto you was on the 14th of xbr[21] last by the way of London since which I did till now forbear to trouble you with any unnecessary lines; yours of Feb. 17 last with its enclosed account I have received. For your great care and pains taken about my children I am to you infinitely beholden for which I render you all possible thanks: I hope God Almighty will reward your great charity extended towards me and mine the continuance whereof I most earnestly beg. I have per this convenience ordered my correspondent at London … to remit you £25 sterling towards the relief of my children which is little enough; but this our present crop proving so extreme bad as it doth and my purchasing of my brother Henrys share of the plantation that was in halves between us at Montserrat, hindered me from sending a larger relief according to my ardent desire, for which I am exceedingly grieved; however by sending any more than the said sum I cannot otherwise help myself at present. I hope God Almighty will for the future enable me to provide more plentifully for them, which to bring to pass, my utmost industry will never be wanting: … To my Father I would have written but that I am loathe to trouble him with the perusal of frivolous lines, whose sight I most vehemently long for, which if I had competent means to remove from hence I would quickly attempt to enjoy; in the meantime I must have patience: … the enclosed for my brother Henry who is homeward bound I leave open that you may understand of part of my grievances. If further employment will not come upon me more than now I have, I am resolved as soon as I can discharge myself from hence, to remove for Montserrat and there to settle

21. The Roman "ten" signifying the tenth month, or October.

myself for some years to the end I may in time gain something for to bring me at last home.[22]

Sources

Akenson, Donald H. *If the Irish Ran the World: Montserrat, 1630–1730*. Montreal and Kingston: McGill-Queen's University Press, 1997.

Beckles, Hilary. *White Servitude and Black Slavery in Barbados, 1627–1715*. Knoxville: University of Tennessee Press, 1989.

Dunn, Richard S. *Sugar and Slaves: The Rise of the Planter Class in the English West Indies, 1624–1713*. Chapel Hill: University of North Carolina Press for the Institute of Early American History and Culture, 1972.

du Tertre, Jean Baptiste. *Histoire Generale Des Isles Des Christophe, de la Guadeloupe, de la Martinique et autres Dans L'Amerique*. Paris: 1654.

Fergus, Howard A. *Montserrat: History of a Caribbean Colony*. London: Macmillan Caribbean, 1994.

Gage, Thomas. *The English-American His Travail by Sea and Land; or A New Survey of the West India's*. London: R. Cotes, 1648.

Gragg, Larry Dale. *Englishmen Transplanted: The English Colonization of Barbados, 1627–1660*. New York: Oxford University Press, 2003.

Gwynn, Aubrey. "Documents Relating to the Irish in the West Indies." *Analecta Hibernica* 4 (1932): 186–91, 233–39.

Hamshere, Cyril. *The British in the Caribbean*. Cambridge, Mass.: Harvard University Press, 1972.

Handler, Jerome S. "Father Antoine Biet's Visit to Barbados in 1654." *Journal of the Barbados Museum and Historical Society* (1967): 58–62.

Johnston, Shona Helen. "Papists in a Protestant World: The Catholic Anglo-Atlantic in the Seventeenth Century." Ph.D. diss., Georgetown University, 2011.

Miller, Kerby A., et al., eds. *Irish Immigrants in the Land of Canaan: Letters and Memoirs from Colonial and Revolutionary America, 1675–1815*. New York: Oxford University Press, 2003.

Osborne, Francis J. *The History of the Catholic Church in Jamaica*. Chicago: Loyola University Press, 1988.

Pelleprat, Pierre. *Relation des Mission des PP. de la Compagnie de Iésus dans les Isles, et dans la terre ferme de l'Amérique Meridionale*. Paris: 1655. Reprinted in Gwynn, "Documents," 208–13.

Shaw, Jenny. "Island Purgatory: Irish Catholics and the Reconfiguring of the English Caribbean, 1650–1700." Ph.D. diss., New York University, 2009.

22. John Blake's decision to make the move from Barbados to Montserrat may have involved several factors, including the devastation caused by the hurricane in the summer of 1675, the failure of his business in Bridgetown, and the more supportive society that Montserrat held out for a Catholic Irishman.

Part 6

Protestant Uprisings and Triumphs

1666–1698

*M*ARYLAND EXPERIENCED a period of phenomenal growth in the three decades that encompassed the Stuart restoration (1660–89). The population increased twelvefold, thanks largely to a robust immigration that deepened the religious pluralism that increasingly characterized Maryland in the late seventeenth century. Anglicans, Presbyterians, Independents, Anabaptists, Quakers—all flowed into Maryland, most of them attracted by both the economic opportunity and religious toleration that the province offered. These Protestant groups, for the first time, began to build an institutional presence by erecting churches and appointing ministers to lead their congregations. No group was more active in organizing and evangelizing than the Quakers, who began to establish meeting houses, particularly on the Eastern Shore where their proselytizing won many converts. By the 1680s the Quakers were the largest Protestant group in Maryland. Nor was it only in the religious realm that they knew success. No religious body, either Catholic or Protestant, took better advantage of the favorable economic climate of Maryland during the period than did the Quakers. Their economic progress tended to lead to political power, as well. As the Calverts continued their policy of ecumenical governance in the 1660s and 1670s, Quakers came to dominate the Protestant appointments to the Provincial Council and other government positions.

This Catholic-Quaker alliance at the top of Maryland's political structure epitomized the affinity between these two groups of English dissenters. Whatever the reason for it—the close-knit nature of their communities, the elevated position that women tended to hold within them, their outlier status within the larger English society, their commitment to church-state separation—Catholics and Quakers seemed to be natural partners in ruling the unique province that Maryland was under the Calverts.

That reality did not sit well with the Anglican minority in the province, a minority that was, by the 1670s, made up of immigrants of substance, practicing Anglicans who appreciated the economic gains they made in their new home but felt deeply frustrated by the barriers that prevented them from achieving the political power that would match their economic status. They also expected government to provide for their religious needs. As members of the established Church of England, they could not see why the ecclesiastical order in the colony of Maryland should differ in any way from the one they had left in England. The laissez-faire policy that the Calverts had adopted regarding ecclesiastical support had created a severe shortage of Anglican clergy that unordained want-to-bes, especially Quakers, were exploiting by forming congregations whose theology and liturgical practice were very much to the left on the spectrum of English Reformed Christianity.

When Cecil Calvert, an absentee proprietor who had ruled the province with a strong hand for more than forty years, died in 1775, John Yeo, one of only three Anglican priests in Maryland, sensed an opportunity to change the colony's policy. In the spring of 1676, Yeo appealed to the archbishop of Canterbury, the leading prelate in the Church of England, to use his influence to get the crown to order the new Lord Baltimore, Charles Calvert, to provide the same support for the Anglican Church in Maryland that the king provided in England (see "The Deplorable ... Condition of ... Maryland for Want of an Established Ministry"). In the end John Yeo failed to get any satisfaction from London.

A more serious challenge to the new proprietor came that same year from a group of Protestant planters in the same county as Yeo's parish, ironically named for the Calvert family. Exploiting Charles Calvert's absence from the province (he had found it necessary to go to London to defend his northern boundary against New York's claims) and encouraged by Roger Bacon's successful rebellion in neighboring Virginia, these planters took up arms to march on St. Mary's City and seize power. The Provincial Council, as the acting head of government, twice failed to persuade the rebels to lay down their arms and reverse their course. Finally, the provincial militia accomplished by force what the council had attempted to do peacefully. Most of the insurgents retreated pell-mell across the Patuxent back into Calvert County. Their principal leader, William Davis, was not so fortunate. Davis was captured, tried for treason, and executed.

Davis's hanging did not put an end to the Calvert County uprising. The remaining leaders, following Yeo's effort, appealed in a letter to the king's government for redress against the corrupt "papist" government filled with relatives and cronies of the Calverts, a government that was tyrannizing "the King's freeborn Subjects of England" (see "A Complaint to Heaven with a Huy and Crye"). Like the earlier appeal that year, the planters' "hue and cry" brought no action from London, as Charles Calvert again effectively rebutted their complaints.

The center of dissent shifted from the Calverts's eponymous county to its neighbor, Charles County. There two wealthy Protestant planters, John Coode and Josias Fendall, began hosting meetings to discuss political grievances and spread rumors of Catholic conspiracies, often involving native tribes allied with the Catholics. When "Indians" murdered several persons in St. Mary's County in 1681, government officials, suspecting that Coode and Fendall were behind the atrocities, peremptorily arrested the pair and charged them with promoting false rumors in order to provoke an insurrection. A sympathetic militia leader attempted to lead an armed band on a rescue mission from Charles County to the St. Mary's City jail; once again, the Provincial Council thwarted the rebels by cutting off their march with a larger force. In subsequent trials the military leader and Fendall were both banished from Maryland. Coode was acquitted of any treasonous behavior, a verdict Maryland authorities would bitterly regret before the decade's end.

When Charles II in 1664 granted the immense tract of land between the Connecticut and the Delaware rivers to his brother James, the Duke of York, it became the second proprietary colony in British America. With James's conversion to Roman Catholicism a decade later, New York became the second province to be headed by a Catholic. Few of the Duke's subjects, whether the Dutch in the Hudson River Valley or the English in the peripheral islands, shared his new religion. Under Dutch rule the Reformed Church had been the established religion for the northern territory where the majority of the 10,000 settlers resided. Without government support half the Reformed ministers returned to the Netherlands. James's attempt to replace the departed clergy with anglicized Dutch ministers only deepened the residents' resentment of the new order under the English. In 1683 the duke appointed Irish-born Thomas Dongan, a career military officer as were so many of the governors in colonies controlled by the crown or royal family members in the late seventeenth century; he was also, like the duke, a Roman Catholic. Dongan, in turn, put fellow Catholics in the major military and political positions within his administration. When a band of Jesuits arrived in New York City, in response to the governor's insistent invitation, anti-Catholic sentiment spiked throughout the province. Protestants, both Dutch and English, saw a pattern of events that pointed to a Catholic conspiracy under the duke to impose "popery" upon the province.

To dispel such suspicions as well as to attract immigrants from Europe or other American colonies, James, under pressure from his New York subjects, consented to the establishment of representative government with the creation of a general assembly elected by freeholders. At its first meeting the assembly approved a "Charter of Liberties and Privileges" (see "All Christian Churches ... Shall Have the Same Privileges"). The New York charter, enlightened as it was, never went into effect. In 1685 James succeeded Charles II as king and New York found itself a royal colony.

James's reign barely spanned three years. His undoing was the reckless manner in which he attempted not merely to annul the penal legislation that had pressed down the Catholic community for more than a century, but to restore Catholics to a prominent place within government. When Parliament refused to cooperate in the king's campaign to abolish the penal laws, James dismissed the body and attempted to achieve by executive action what Parliament had refused to do. For failing to promulgate his orders he put nearly a score of Anglican bishops in the Tower of London. From justices of the peace to the Privy Council, the monarch stocked his government with a vastly disproportionate number of Catholics (who still made up but 1 percent of the English population). James's Catholic favoritism and autocratic governance fed deeply rooted fears of a conspiracy to restore Catholicism as the religion of the land.

The birth of a son in the late spring of 1688, guaranteeing a Catholic successor to James, was the final straw that drove the English Protestant nobility to seek redemption in the person of William of Orange, husband of James's oldest child, Mary, a Protestant. William obliged, and, on November 5, the anniversary of the most egregious attempt to restore Catholicism in England, his expeditionary force landed on the southwestern coast and began a march on London. Any opposition quickly dissolved as James's military defected to the Protestant invaders. James fled to France, and "The Glorious Revolution" was completed with the crowning of William and Mary as Protestant monarchs.

The bloodless revolution in England proved the springboard for a series of uprisings in British America, beginning in Boston in April of 1689 and rapidly spreading southward to New York and then to Maryland, all fed by rampant fears of a cabal composed of French, Indians, and local Catholics. In Maryland, men on the political make exploited this fear and prejudice to call for overturning the "Catholic government" of the Calverts. The key leader of the Protestant Association, as the insurgents styled themselves, was John Coode, who had been one of the chief instigators of an abortive uprising in Charles County eight years earlier (see "The Yoke of Arbitrary Government of Tyranny and Popery"). The Protestant Association's revolution against the proprietary proved as bloodless as the "glorious" one in England that had provided a convenient opportunity to carry it out. But if there was scant physical resistance on the part of Lord Baltimore's loyalists, once the insurgents had taken power there followed a war of petitions in which each side tried to get the new sovereigns' sanction. Nine formal appeals went to London from county contingents, six in favor of the association and three calling for a restoration of Charles Calvert. Meanwhile, Lord Baltimore's representatives and former office holders kept him abreast of the fast-moving events in Maryland and did their best to bolster his spirits about recovering his province (see "The Strange Rebellion of Your Ungrateful People").

The Calverts's long success in keeping Maryland under their control came to a sudden end in early 1690 when King William, in deference to the charter, upheld Lord Baltimore's extensive property rights in Maryland, but denied him any power to govern. Even had the monarch been willing to condemn Coode's revolution, which had so closely paralleled his own, restoring the Calverts to their ante-revolution position would have gone against the policy of colonial centralization that the new regime had inherited from James's reign. Like Massachusetts, Maryland effectively lost its charter as it, like its New England counterpart, became a royal colony. In 1692 the now Protestant Maryland Assembly very willingly made the Church of England the established religion in the colony. That did not mean, however, that Maryland Catholics were now bound by the penal laws that so constricted the lives of their English counterparts. King William, in fact, for whatever reasons, had adopted an unofficial policy of allowing Catholics in Maryland to continue to live more or less as they had under the Calverts, with public worship, bearing arms and serving in the militia, practicing law in certain provincial courts, voting, and holding proprietary offices (but now barred from provincial ones).

The initial royal governor, Thomas Copley, the first of a series of military officers appointed by the crown to govern Maryland, carried with him explicit directions about respecting the religious liberty that Catholics had traditionally enjoyed in the colony. During his two years as governor, Copley, whose ear the Associationists quickly won, basically left Catholics wondering where they stood in the new Maryland. Matters became clearer under Copley's successor, Francis Nicholson.

Nicholson conscientiously, if reluctantly, implemented William's policy. He restored to Catholics the arms that the association had confiscated. He reopened the Great Brick Chapel in St. Mary's City. He allowed Catholic lawyers to practice in certain courts of the province. What he was not about to tolerate was the persistent bold efforts of Catholics, both clergy and laity, to convert Protestants, especially servants in Catholic households. Such proselytizing became so aggressive (in Nicholson's eyes) during an epidemic in 1697 that the governor issued a proclamation warning Catholics that such "scandalous and offensive actions" could cost them the generous toleration that they enjoyed in Maryland. More worrisome for Nicholson than the convert-seeking by individual Catholics was the refusal by the Catholic gentry and their former Protestant partners in power to accept the new order. That attitude constituted an ongoing threat to royal rule in Maryland. At the lower end of the social scale, the rapid increase in the Irish servant population, together with the great number of Africans being brought into the colony as slaves, was creating a dangerous demographic revolution that the governor intended to spur the legislature to enact legislation to counter (see "They Might Make Great Disturbances, If Not a Rebellion"). The assembly complied by imposing a tax of twenty shillings on every servant imported, the first of five such taxes over the next twenty years to curb the size of the Catholic community.

25

"The Deplorable … Condition of … Maryland for Want of an Established Ministry": John Yeo's Letter to the Archbishop of Canterbury regarding Proprietary Favoritism toward Catholics and Lord Baltimore's Reply, 1676

John Yeo, pastor of Christ Church on the Patuxent River in Calvert County, had been one of the first Anglican ministers in Maryland. From the experience of a quarter century in the proprietary colony he appealed for the formal establishment of the Church of England so that its clergy would no longer lack state support. The archbishop found Yeo's appeal so "laudable" that he urged the Privy Council to find its way "to obtain some settled revenue for the Ministry of that place."[1] Once that support was provided, the prelate assured them that he could find suitable priests for the mission. Unfortunately for Yeo and the archbishop, neither the Privy Council nor the Board of Trade and Plantations urged any change in church-state relations. Based on your reading of the letters of Yeo and Calvert, did the imperial bodies make the proper decision?

Letter from John Yeo, Minister in Maryland, to the Archbishop of Canterbury, May 25, 1676*

There are in this Province ten or twelve Counties & in them at least twenty thousand Souls & but three Protestant ministers of us that are Conformable

---

* PRO, CSP, vol. 52, in *AM* 5:130–32.
1. Archbishop of Canterbury to Lord London, Croyden, August 2, 1676, in *AM* 5:132.

to the Doctrine & Discipline of the Church of England others there are ...
that Run before they are Sent & Pretend they are Ministers of the Gospel
that never have a Legal call or Ordination to such an holy office, ... & no law
Provided for the Suppression of such in this Province so that here is a great
Necessity of able & learned men to confute the gainsayer especially having
so many Professed enemies as the Popish Priests & Jesuits are, who are encouraged & Provided for & the Quaker takes care & provides for those that
are Speakers in their conventicles, but no care is taken or Provision made
for the building up Christians in the Protestant Religion by means whereof
not only many Daily fall away either to Popery, Quakerism or fanaticism
but also the lords day is profaned, Religion despised, & all notorious vices
committed so that it is become a Sodom of uncleanness & a Pest house of
iniquity. I doubt not but Your Grace may be an instrument of a universal
reformation amongst us with greatest facility Cecilius Lord Baron Baltimore, & absolute Proprietor of Maryland being dead & Charles Lord Baron
of Baltimore & our Governour being bound for England this Year (as I am
informed) to Receive a farther confirmation of that Province from his Majesty at which time I Doubt [not] but Your Grace may so prevail with him as
that a maintenance for a Protestant ministry may be established as well in
this Province as in Virginia, Barbados & all other his Majestys Plantations
in west indies & then there will be encouragement for able men to come
amongst us, ... as yet I think the Generality of the people may be brought by
Degrees to a uniformity, Provided we have more ministers that were truly
Conformable to our mother the Church & none but such Suffer to preach
amongst us.

Lord Baltimore on the Present State of Religion in Maryland 1676*

For the encouragement of all such persons as were desirous and willing to
adventure and transport themselves & families into the Province of Maryland a law [was] ... made by the advice and consent of the Delegates of the
Freemen concerning Religion, wherein a toleration is given to all persons
believing in Jesus Christ freely to exercise their Religion & that no person of
what judgement soever, believing as aforesaid should at any time be molested or discountenanced for or in respect of his Religion or in the free exercise
thereof and that no one should be compelled to the belief or exercise of any

* PRO, CSP, vol. 52, in *AM* 5:133–34.

other against his consent. Upon this Act the greatest part of the people and Inhabitants now in Maryland have settled themselves & families there & for these many years this toleration & liberty has been known & continued in the Government of that Province.

Those Persons of the Church of England there who at any time have encouraged any Ministers to come over into that Province have had several sent unto them as at this time there are residing there four that the Lord Baltimore knows of who have Plantations & settled beings[2] of their own and those that have not any such beings are maintained by a voluntary contribution of those of their own persuasion, as others of the Presbyterians, Independents, Anabaptists, Quakers & Romish Church are.

That in every County in the Province of Maryland there are a sufficient number of Churches and Houses called Meeting Houses for the people there and these have been built and are still kept in good repair by a free and voluntary contribution of all such as frequent the said Churches and Meeting Houses....

The greatest part of the Inhabitants of that Province (three of four at least) do consist of Presbyterians, Independents Anabaptists and Quakers, those of the Church of England as well as those of the Romish being the fewest, so that it will be a most difficult task to draw such persons to consent unto a Law, which shall compel them to maintain Ministers of a contrary persuasion to themselves, they having already an assurance by that Act for Religion that they have all freedom in point of Religion and Divine Worship and no penalties or payments imposed upon them in that particular. That in Carolina, New Jersey and Rhode Island, the Inhabitants for the people of those places have had and still have the same toleration that those in Maryland have.

---

2. Servants that they have brought into the province or taken under an indenture.

26

"A Complaint to Heaven with a Huy and Crye": Maryland Planters to the Crown, 1676*

"A Complaint" is one of the first instances in Maryland history of utilizing the "court-country" dichotomy of republican discourse to frame the conflicting interest groups: the corrupt, self-seeking oligarchy that has a lock on government against the decent, public-minded, larger society with its roots in nature's soil. The Calverts, the petitioners charge, have manipulated the system so that the court has a monopoly on power, with the country element shut out completely. Worse, by the proprietor's claims of power and authority, Baltimore dares to equate his position in Maryland with that of the king of England. His insistence on a loyalty oath to himself is an inherent contradiction of the king's sovereignty.

The letter raises the specter of the evil axis that Maryland Catholics, Indians, and the French have formed to subdue Protestants in America by any means possible, a threatening troika that will increasingly populate anti-Catholic discourse in the next century. In brief, Maryland has become a battleground between those loyal to the king and those beholden to Baltimore. On what specific grounds do they indict Calvert for his failure to provide for the general welfare of his subjects? In what ways does this petition anticipate a much more noted declaration a century later?

O Treachery plainly discovered out of ... Popish Maryland, which opened ... a Number of Grievances, which prognosticate an absolute ruin and subversion of the king's Majestys loyal subjects in Maryland, ... for which they call now Governor Baltimore to an account before our Sovereign Lord, the king and parliament in England, and do charge him—That he is guilty of the late murders in Virginia and Maryland, and a great many of the Kings Majestys subjects lives lost before, and the ruinating of their Estates. That He is guilty of the Mischief done by the Sinnico[3] Indian, that come now every year down and rob the Country.... That He raised the People in Arms for his private gain and Interest, only to oppress the king's subjects with great

*PRO, CSP, vol. 52, in *AM* 5: 134–49.
3. Susquehanna.

taxes in his and own creatures pocket.... So did he likewise in the former Indian ... War, when they took all the plunder from the poor soldiers and sent the Indian prisoners to Barbados for Negros, but forced the poor inhabitants to bear and pay all the charges....

Now when any thing in the popish chamber is hatched that must have a Country cloak, warrants issue forth to every County to choose 4 men.... But at a day afterward appointed, a writ comes but for 2 out of these 4, picked out for his purpose, viz. either papists, ones creatures and familiars or ignoramuses....

Now when these are confined in a room together, they are called the lower house and the provincial Court men in an other chamber, styles themselves the upper house, and prescribes what the lower house is to consent unto, which if any grumbles at, then persuading spirits go forth, and if any stands out or up for the common good, frowns and threatenings scares them to be quiet right or wrong: and this they call Acts of Assembly, but the Country calls them dissemblings.... These Acts must be first ... sent into England to the proprietary there.... [A]nd what He then doth not relish is of no force.... And now pray where is the liberty of the freeborn subjects of England and our privileges in Maryland; the Lord proprietary assumes and attracts more Royal Power to himself over his Tenants than our gracious King over his subjects in England....

We acknowledge Lord Baltimore our land lord proprietary and the inhabitants his Tenants in Maryland by fealty only, paying for all manner of services the yearly quit Rent.... We are no otherwise enjoined: But our sovereign Lord the King, proprietor over Maryland, and we His only Subjects and liege freeborn people of England to [him] we owe allegiance and fidelity and to no other.... Furthermore our privileges are preserved by the expression in Maryland['s] charter to the Adventurers, for we ourselves thereupon have transported ourselves and our estates into this Country, purchased the land from the Indians with loss of Estate and many hundred mens lives (yea thousands) and must defend ourselves continually without my Lord Baltimore's ability, whereby our land and possessions are become our Own, and now we have made it a country for the glory and enlargement of the dominion and imperial Crown of England Shall we and our posterity be domineered over by the Proprietary ... because we will not be Rebels and Traitors to the King and Kingdom of England and become his purgatory slaves? And for this they begin to hang and fine People.

The King's Majesty hath entrusted the Proprietary with Maryland by Charter, to be a good steward to the Realm of England with it and to manage the affairs thereof for the common good … but they have made Merchandise of the land and now it is past almost [beyond] remedy.… so it is carried along and all Arts and devises used, to persuade and create fit turncoats to bring their purpose step by step to pass, from one degree to another, … [S]uch are the instruments, with which my Lord Baltimore … converts the common good to his private ends, under the cloak of Assemblies and Assent of the freemen within the Province which is utterly denied.…

Our great King and Parliament, judge now between your loyal subjects and my Lord Baltimore and his Champions and favorites in Maryland[.] [A]re we Rebels because we will not submit to their arbitrary government and entangle our innocent posterity under that tyrannical yoke of papacy? …

All [taxation] is yearly extracted out of the Country to particular uses, and the poor people left, to maintain themselves and all other public charges, so that there is little difference between them and bondslaves that work 3 days for themselves and 3 days to maintain others … thus the poor Country is robbed, … every one serving their own turn, without any true fear and worship of God.… This is the way to exasperate men's spirits, to depopulate the country in stead of increasing, and if the proprietary could give us the re-all[4] for our Estates, a great many protestants would leave the Country to him and his papists. Which is the very Needle the politic compass turns upon viz. Either to turn papists, or to be turned and banished out of the Country in time to come by degrees. Which is a miserable extremity, the poor inhabitants are and see themselves involved viz. with oppression and war from within, and Hazard of life and Estate by Indians from without, and at home.…

O great noble and prudent Parliament in England … intercede for us …

1. That our Sovereign Lord and Imperial Majesty may be pleased to take the Government of Maryland unto his gracious self: appointing protestant Governors that have or shall take first the usual Oath of Allegiance and supremacy And to swear and rule the inhabitants according to the custom of England.…

5. That Protestant Ministers and free schools and glebe lands may be erected and established in every County, notwithstanding liberty of conscience and maintained by the people: Item:[5] the free men to choose their

4. The price worth the value of the property.
5. Likewise.

delegates ... in the Assemblies; to enact for the common General good for the people and Country; without any ... compellment and persuasion or interruption.

27

"All Christian Churches ... Shall Have the Same Privileges": New York's Charter of Liberties and Privileges, 1683*

The body of fundamental rights of citizens and the limited powers of government that the charter enunciated was an effort to undergird the province with a social contract between people and rulers, in which religious bodies and ethnic groups would be on equal footing. According to the charter, what does "religious toleration" amount to in New York? How explain the assembly's enactment of this charter?

FOR The better Establishing the Government of this province of New York and that Justice and Right may be Equally done to all persons within the same

BE it Enacted by the Governour Council and Representatives now in General Assembly met and assembled....

THAT The Supreme Legislative Authority under his Majesty and Royal Highness James Duke of York Albany &c Lord proprietor of the said province shall forever be and reside in a Governour, Council, and the people met in General Assembly....

THAT According to the usage Custom and practice of the Realm of England a session of a General Assembly be held in this province once in three years at least. THAT every freeholder within this province and freeman in any Corporation Shall have his free Choice and Vote in the Electing of the Representatives without any manner of constraint or imposition. And that in all Elections the Majority of Voices shall carry it....

THAT the persons to be Elected to sit as representatives in the general Assembly from time to time for the several Cities towns Counties Shires or

*Donald S. Lutz, ed., *Colonial Origins of the American Constitution: A Documentary History* (Indianapolis: Liberty Fund, 1998), 271–76.

Divisions of this province and all places within the same shall be according to the proportion and number hereafter Expressed....

THAT All bills agreed upon by the said Representatives or the Major part of them shall be presented unto the Governour and his Council for their Approbation and Consent All and Every which Said Bills so approved or Consented to by the Governour and his Council shall be Esteemed and accounted the Lawes of the province....

THAT No freeman shall be taken and imprisoned or be disseized of his freehold or Liberty ... or be outlawed or Exiled or any other ways destroyed.... But by the Lawful judgment of his peers and by the law of this province. Justice nor Right shall be neither sold denied or deferred to any man within this province....

THAT No man of what Estate of Condition soever shall be put out of his Lands or Tenements, nor taken, nor imprisoned, nor disinherited, nor banished nor any ways destroyed without ... due Course of Law....

THAT No person or persons which profess faith in God by Jesus Christ Shall at any time be any ways molested punished disquieted or called in Question for Difference in opinion or Matter of Religious Concernment, who do not actually disturb the civil peace of the province, But that all and Every such person or persons may from time to time and at all times freely have and fully enjoy his or their judgments or Consciences in matters of Religion throughout the province, they behaving themselves peaceably and quietly and not using this Liberty to Licentiousness nor to the civil injury or outward disturbance of others....

AND WHERAS All the Respective Christian Churches now in practice within the city of New York and the other places of this province do appear to be privileged Churches and have been So Established and Confirmed by the former authority of this Government be it hereby Enacted by this General Assembly ... That all the Said Respective Christian Churches be hereby Confirmed therein And that they ... Shall from henceforth forever be held and reputed as privileged Churches and Enjoy all their former freedoms of their Religion in Divine Worship and church Discipline. And that all former contracts made and agreed upon for the maintenances of the several ministers of the Said Churches shall stand and continue in full force and virtue And ... also that all Christian Churches that Shall hereafter come and settle within this province shall have the Same privileges.

28

"The Yoke of Arbitrary Government of Tyranny and Popery": Declaration of the Protestant Association, July 1689 *

Unlike the 1681 revolt, which the militia quickly dispersed, as it had its 1676 predecessor, the revolt of the Protestant Association had two crucial advantages that the earlier uprisings had lacked: its occurrence in the immediate wake of the ousting of a Catholic king in England by a Protestant army and the public proclamation of the association's reasons for taking up arms against the proprietary government. That declaration, getting wide circulation throughout Maryland, played on the ascendant anti-Catholic prejudices that had been building for over a decade and seemed confirmed by the marvelous events that had taken place in England within the past several months. To what audience are the members of the association ultimately appealing? What do they hope to achieve by promulgating this declaration?

As ... the injustice and tyranny under which we groan, is palliated and most if not all the particulars of our grievances shrouded from the eyes of observation and the hand of redress, We thought fit for general satisfaction, and particularly to undeceive those that may have a sinister account of our proceedings to publish this Declaration of the reasons and motives inducing us thereunto. His Lordships right and title to the Government is by virtue of a Charter to his father Cecilius from King Charles the first of blessed memory[.] [H]ow his present Lordship has managed the power and authority given and granted in the same we could mourn and lament only in silence, would our duty to God, our allegiance to his Vicegerent,[6] and the care & welfare of ourselves and posterity permit us.

In the first place in the said Charter is a reservation of the faith and allegiance due to the Crown of England (the Province and Inhabitants being immediately subject thereunto) but how little that is manifested is too obvious, to all unbyasted[7] persons that ever had anything to do here[.] [T]he

---

* *AM* 8:101–7.
6. The English monarch.
7. Unbiased.

very name and owning of that Sovereign power is some times crime enough to incur the frowns of our superiors and to render our persons obnoxious and suspected to be ill-affected to the government[.] The ill usage of and affronts to the Kings Officers belonging to the customs here, were a sufficient argument of this. We need but instance the business of Mr. Badcock and Mr. Rousby, … The latter was barbarously murdered upon the execution of his office by one that was an Irish papist and our Chief Governor.[8] Allegiance here by those persons under whom we suffer is little talked of, other than what they would have done and sworn to, to his Lordship the Lord Proprietary, for it was very lately owned by the president himself,[9] openly enough in the Upper House of Assembly, that fidelity to his Lordship was allegiance and that the denying of the One was the same thing with the refusal or denial of the other. In that very Oath of Fidelity, that was then imposed under the penalty of banishment there, is not so much as the least word or intimation of any duty, faith or allegiance to be reserved to our Sovereign Lord the King of England.

How the jus regale[10] is improved here, and made the prerogative of his Lordship, is so sensibly felt by us all in that absolute authority exercised over us, and by the greatest part of the Inhabitants in the service of their persons, forfeiture and loss of their goods, chattels, freeholds and inheritances. In the next place churches and Chapels, which by the said Charter should be built and consecrated according to the Ecclesiastical laws of the Kingdom of England, to our great regret and discouragement of our religion, are erected and converted to the use of popish Idolatry and superstition, Jesuits and seminary priests are the only incumbents; (for which there is a supply provided by sending our popish youth to be educated at St Omers)[11] as also the Chief Advisers and Councilors in affaires of Government, and the richest and most fertile land set apart for their use and maintenance, while other lands that are piously intended, and given for the maintenance of the Prot-

8. In 1684 George Talbot, a cousin of Charles Calvert and a member of his council, had fatally stabbed Christopher Rousby, a customs collector for the crown, in the heat of an argument the two were having aboard a ship anchored in the Patuxent River. The captain of the boat subsequently had taken Talbot in irons to Virginia, where the governor refused to return him to Maryland until he had further orders from London. Two years later a Virginia jury found Talbot guilty of murdering Rousby and sentenced him to hang, but Talbot escaped the noose, thanks to a pardon from the Catholic King James.

9. Governor William Joseph.

10. Royal sovereignty.

11. The Jesuit school in Flanders founded in 1590 for English Catholic males.

estant Ministry, become escheats,[12] and are taken as forfeit, the ministers themselves discouraged, and no care taken for their subsistence.

The power to enact Laws is another branch of his Lordship's authority, but how well that has been executed … is too notorious.… [T]he question in our Courts of Judicature, in any point that relates to many of our Laws, is not so much the relation it has to the said Laws, but whether the Laws themselves be agreeable to the pleasure and approbation of his Lordship. Whereby our liberty and property is become uncertain and under the arbitrary disposition of the Judge and Commissioners of our Courts of Justice.

How fatal and of what pernicious consequence that unlimited and arbitrary pretended authority may be to the Inhabitants, is too apparent, but by considering that by the same reason all the use of the laws whereby our liberties and properties subsist are subject to the same arbitrary disposition, and if timely remedy be not had must stand or fall according to his Lordships good will and pleasure.

Nor is this nullifying and suspending power the only grievance that doth perplex and burthen us in relation to Laws, but these laws that are of a certain and unquestioned acceptation[13] are executed and countenanced, as they are more or less agreeable to the good liking of our Governor in particular, one very good law provides that orphan children should be disposed of to persons of the same religion with that of their dead parents. In direct opposition to which several children of protestants have been committed to the tutelage of papists, and brought up in the Romish Superstition.… [O]n the contrary those laws that enhance the grandeur and income of his said Lordship are severely imposed and executed especially one that is against all sense, equity, reason and law punishes all speeches, practices, and attempts relating to his Lordship and Government that shall be thought mutinous and seditious by the Judge of the provincial Court, with either whipping, branding, boring through the Tongue, fines, imprisonments, banishment or death, all or either of the said punishments at the discretion of the said Judges, who have given a very recent and remarkable proof of their authority in each particular punishment aforesaid, upon several the good people of this Province, while the rest are in the same danger to have their words and actions liable to the construction & punishment of the said Judges, and their lives and fortunes to the mercy of their arbitrary fancies, opinions and sentences.

12. Titles that revert to the lord or proprietor.
13. Acceptance.

To these Grievances are added

Excessive Officers Fees, and that too under Execution directly against the Law made & provided to redress the same....

The frequent pressing of men, horses, boats, provisions and other necessaries in time of peace and often to gratify private designs and occasions, to the great burthen and regret of the Inhabitants contrary to Law and several Acts of Assembly....

The ... apprehending of Protestants in their houses with armed force consisting of Papists and that in time of peace, thence hurrying them away to Prisons without Warrant or cause of commitment these kept and confined with popish guards a long time without trial.

Not only private but public outrages, & murders committed and done by papists upon Protestants without redress, but rather connived at and tolerated by the chief in authority, and indeed it were in vain to desire or expect any help or other measures from them being papists and guided by the ... instigation of the Jesuits, either in these or any other grievances or oppressions....

And now at length for as much it hath pleased Almighty God, by means of the great prudence and conduct of the best of Princes our most gracious King William to put a check to that great inundation of Slavery and Popery, that had like to overwhelm their Majesty's Protestant Subjects in all their territories and Dominions (of which none have suffered more or are in greater danger than ourselves) We hoped and expected ... a proportionable show in so great a blessing.

But our greatest grief and consternation, upon the first news of the great overture and happy change in England, we found ourselves surrounded with strong and violent endeavours from our Governors here ... to defeat us of the same. We still find all the means used by these very persons and their Agents, Jesuits, Priests, and lay papists that their malice can suggest to devise the obedience and loyalty of the inhabitants from their most sacred Majestys to that height of impudence that solemn masses and prayers are used ... in their Chapels and Oratories for the prosperous success of the popish forces in Ireland, and the French designs against England, whereby they would involve us, in the same crime of disloyalty with themselves ....

We are every day threatened with the loss of our lives, liberties and Estates of which we have great reason to think ourselves in eminent danger by the practices and machinations that are on foot to betray us to the French, Northern and other Indians ... to assist in our destruction .... But above all with due and mature deliberation ... considering and looking upon ourselves, discharged, dissolved and free from all manner of duty, obligation or fidelity to the Deputy Governor or Chief Magistrate here as such they having departed from their Allegiance ... we do ... take up Arms to preserve, vindicate and assert the sovereign Dominion and right of King William and Queen Mary to this Province; to defend the Protestant Religion among us, and to protect and shelter the Inhabitants from all manner of violence, oppression and destruction, that is plotted and designed against them....

For the more effectual Accomplishment of which, we will take due care that a full and free Assembly be called and convened with all possible expedition by whom we may likewise have our condition circumstances, and our most dutiful address represented and tendered to their Majesties, from whose great wisdom, justice and special care of the protestant religion we may reasonably and comfortably hope to be delivered from our present calamity and for the future be secured under a just and legal administration from being ever more subjected to the yoke of arbitrary government of tyranny and popery....

And we do lastly invite and require all manner of persons whatsoever residing or Inhabiting in this Province, as they tender their Allegiance, the Protestant Religion, their Lives, fortunes and Families, to aid and assist us in this our undertaking....

John Coode [and seven other signers]

29

"The Strange Rebellion of Your Ungrateful People": Catholic Views on the Revolution, 1689[*]

Among Charles Calvert's informants were three Catholics who had held office under him, including two of the highest posts. The Irish-born Charles Carroll had been in the province less than ten months as Calvert's attorney general before the revolution drove him out of

[*] *AM* 8:124–26.

office. Henry Darnall, a wealthy planter, was related by marriage to Lord Baltimore and his chancellor at the time of the revolt. Peter Sayer, a builder and former colonel of the militia, was one of the most prominent Catholics on the Eastern Shore. These confidants felt they had every reason to be optimistic about the proprietor's regaining his colony. After all, the Calverts had survived two previous coups. They still held, in the charter, the ultimate legal claim to the colony. If the radical Cromwell had, in the end, honored that, surely a conservative king and queen would. What do the three briefs have in common? How do they differ? According to Sayer's account, did the revolution play out differently on the Eastern Shore than it did on the Western?

Charles Carroll to Lord Baltimore, September 25, 1689

I believe your Lordship has ere now had some intelligence either by Captain Burnham or Johnson of the strange rebellion your ungrateful people of this your Lordship's Province have involved themselves in, moved by the wicked instigations of Coode,[14] Jowles,[15] Blackston,[16] Cheseldyn,[17] Parson Thurling[18] and several others to that degree that they have quite unhinged your Lordship's Government and (as if there were no justice to be had but such as they please to distribute, or as if the whole body of the Laws were to be annulled by their wild fancies) have taken upon themselves to declare your Lordship's charter forfeited as your Lordship may see by their malicious declaration (which the Bearer will show your Lordship). They have further taken upon themselves to give Commissions to Sheriffs and Justices of their own stamp and constitute other Officers both civil and military utterly excluding not only all Roman Catholics from bearing any office whatsoever (contrary to an express act of Assembly) but also all Protestants that refuse

14. John Coode had immigrated to Maryland in 1672. Although an Anglican, Coode in his early years in the colony was the recipient of substantial proprietary patronage. When that support was suddenly cut off for unknown reasons, Coode became one of the Calverts's fiercest and most persistent critics. He was behind the aborted uprising in 1681, but his only punishment was expulsion from the assembly. Seven years later he had been reelected to the assembly and seized the opportunity to oust the Calverts when England forced its Catholic ruler to flee.

15. Henry Jowles, planter of Calvert County, who had been second in command of the provincial militia. When the armed members of the association, including Jowles, were marching toward the capital, the Provincial Council attempted to lure him back to the proprietor's ranks by offering him command of the militia. Jowles initially agreed to make the switch but in the end chose to stay with the marchers.

16. Nehemiah Blakistone, planter of St. Mary's County.

17. Kenylm Cheseldyne, planter of St. Mary's County.

18. John Thurling, Anglican minister.

to join with them in their irregularities, imprisoning such of them as declare against their illegal proceedings, and arbitrarily threatening to hang any man that takes upon him to justify your Lordship's right. They have assumed the power of calling an Assembly the Election of which was in most Counties awed by their soldiers, ... in fine they have packed up an Assembly after the most irregular manner that ever was known, wherein they have laid down the methods of their future conduct, but is as yet kept private, ... so it is that neither Catholic nor honest Protestant can well call his life or estate his own and if your Lordship ... by a speedy application and true representation to His Majesty of these most inhuman actions do not procure some orders whereby to allay their fury a little all your friends here will be reduced to a miserable condition, for daily their cattle are killed, their horses pressed and all the injury imaginable done to them, and to no other, certainly your Lordship's charter is not such a trifle as to be annulled by the bare allegations of such profligate wretches and men of scandalous lives, as Code, Thurling, Jowles and such fools as they have poisoned by the most absurd lies that ever were invented.... [Neither] the King [n]or Parliament ... will ... approve of such unheard of actions as were committed against your Lordship & Government by these evil spirits without Commission or order from any superior power, whereby they have not only rebelled against your Lordship but also committed high Treason in taking up arms as they have done without warrant from His Majesty or your Lordship....

I believe an Act of indemnity with a few exceptions of the most notorious transgressors would prove a great means to reduce the people to their obedience: tho' the heads of them are so arrogant as to declare that in case the King should send orders, not to their liking, they would not obey them.

The Narrative of Coll. Henry Darnall Late One of the Council of the Right Honorable the Lord Proprietary of the Province of Maryland, December 31, 1689 *

On March 25 last Col. Jowles sent word to the Council (then at St. Marys) that three thousand Indians were coming down on the Inhabitants, and were at the head of Putuxent River and required Arms and Ammunition for the people to go against the said Indians, all which was with all expedition

* PRO, CSP, in *AM* 8:155–57.

sent him by Col. Digges, the next morning I went up myself to Coll. Jowles, where I found them all in arms, and they told me they heard there was three Thousand Indians at Mattapany (from whence I then came) I assured the people it was a false report, & offered myself to go in person, if they could advise me where any Enemies were, Indians or others, whereat they seemed very well satisfied. I began to suspect this was only a contrivance of some ill minded men who under this pretence would raise the Country, as by what happened afterwards we had reason to believe upon the most diligent search and enquiry into this whole matter, no Indians anywhere appeared, and whenever any Messenger was sent to the place where it was said the Indians were come, there the Inhabitants would tell them they heard they were landed at such a place, but after long search from place to place and no sign of any Indians, the people were pretty well pacified, and Col. Jowles himself wrote a Remonstrance (the Copy whereof is here enclosed) which he'd signed; as did several others who had the Examination of this matter, the which was published in order to quiet the People, who in a few days seemed to be freed from their apprehensions. From this time until July 16 following the Country was all quiet and no appearance of any Enemy to disturb them Indians or else. On the said July 16 a Messenger came to me at Mattapany in the night time to acquaint me that John Coode was raising men up Potomac, whereupon I informed the Council thereof, who immediately dispatched a person to know the truth, but the said person was taken by Coode as a spy and by him kept, so the Council had no notice until two days of anything, when they were assured that Coode had raised men up Potomac and … were all marching down toward St. Marys, and in their way were joined with Major Campbell and his men. Col. Digges having notice thereof got together about an hundred men and went into the State House of St. Marys,[19] which Coode and his party came to attack, and which Col. Digges (his men not being willing to fight) was forced to surrender, wherein were the records of the whole Province, which Coode and his party seized. In this while Major Sewall and myself went up Putuxent River to raise men to oppose said Coode and his party,[20] where we found most of the Officers ready to come in to us, but their men were possessed with the belief that Coode rose only to preserve the Country from the Indians and Papists and

19. William Digges (1651–97), the Protestant son-in-law of Charles Calvert, a member of the Provincial Council, and head of the proprietary militia.
20. Nicholas Sewall, deputy governor of the province.

to proclaim the King and Queen and would do them no harm, and therefore would not stir to run themselves into danger, so that all the men we could get amounted not to one hundred and sixty, but by this time Coode's party were increased to seven hundred. The Council seeing how the people were led away by false reports and shams, in order to quiet them and give them all imaginable assurance they were clear and innocent of inviting the Indians down as was laid to their charge offered to make Coll. Jowles (who was the chief of their party next to Coode) General of all the Forces in the Province, and sent such an offer to him, who returned a very civil answer that having communicated what he wrote to his own men he had with him, they were extremely satisfied therewith, and gave us hopes he would come down to us, but to the contrary he went and joined Coode at St. Marys, to whom and to all, then in Arms there, the Council sent a Proclamation of pardon upon condition they would lay down their arms and repair to their respective Habitations, the which Coode (as we were credibly informed) instead of reading to the People what was therein contained, read a defiance from Us, whereby to enrage and not to pacify them. Coode and his party having thus made themselves masters of the State House and the Records at St. Marys, borrowed some great guns of one Captain Burnham Master of a ship belonging to London, and came to attack Mattapany House, the which when he came before he sent a trumpeter and demanded a surrender, we desired a parley and personal Treaty in the hearing of the People, which Coode would never consent to, we knew if we could but obtain that in the hearing of the People, we should be able to disabuse them, and clear ourselves of what they were made [to] believe against us, but this we could never get at their hands, but to the contrary they used all possible means to keep the people ignorant of what we proposed or offered, and made use of such artifices as the following to exasperate them. They caused a man to come riding Post with a Letter wherein was contained that our neighbour Indians had cut up their Corn and were gone from their Towns, and that there was an Englishman found with his belly ripped open, which in truth was no such thing as they themselves owned after Mattapany House was surrendered. We being in this condition and no hope left of quieting or repelling the People thus enraged, to prevent effusion of blood, capitulated and surrendered. After the surrender of the said House his Lordship's Council endeavoured to send an Account of these transactions, by one Johnson master of a Ship bound for London to his Lordship the which the said Johnson delivered to Coode.

When we found we could send no Letters Major Sewall and myself, desired of Johnson we might have a passage in him for England to give his Lordship Account of matters by word of mouth, which the said Johnson refused upon pretended Orders to the contrary from Coode. Whereupon Major Sewall and myself went to Pennsylvania to endeavour to get a passage there, upon which Coode and his party took occasion to give out, we were gone to bring in the Northern Indians, but we missing of a passage there came back and stayed in Ann Arundel County (who never had joined with Coode nor his party) until September 26 when Major Sewall then being sick I myself got a passage hither.

Peter Sayer to Lord Baltimore, December 31, 1689[*]

Since my last to your Lordship ... there has not been a more tragic comedy of rebellion acted, since the royal bounty of King James and King Charles of blessed memory bestowed upon your Ancestors the Charter of this Province of Maryland....

As soon as the noise came into our County, that one Masinella Coode had got at the head of five or six hundred men, Griff Jones sends a note to Clayland[21] (then preaching) that he and his auditory[22] must come away presently to the Court house which they did; where this villainous rascal persuaded the poor silly mobile[23] that if they did not sign to that paper (a copy of which your Lordship hath) they should all certainly lose their estates: Upon this our County (who were before as quiet as lambs) got to such a head, and crying that all their throats should be cut by the Papists, that if Coode's order for disbanding of everybody then in arms had not come to Will: Combes, our timorous Magistrates could never have quieted 'em. With this order came up his declaration, which was read at our Court house the fourth day following which was August 15, all people being warned to come and hear it by the clerk of our County Nicholas Lowe; Colonel Coursey[24]

* PRO, CSP, in *AM* 8:158–62.
21. James Clayland, pastor of St. Michael's Anglican Church of Talbot County.
22. Congregation.
23. Mob.
24. Henry Coursey, of Talbot County, a Protestant who had held several offices under the Calverts, including service on the Provincial Council and commanding the militia of Cecil and Kent counties on the Eastern Shore. He had been a key negotiator for the proprietary government with the regional Indian tribes.

being likewise invited for his advice by Mr. Robotham[25] who accordingly came, and advised them to let no papers be read that came from any of the rebels, except they would permit him, or that Mr. Robotham himself would paraphrase, and let the people know what damn'd falsities were contained in 'em; but Mr. Robotham reply'd, that if any body should contradict anything, in that humor the people were in, they should have all their brains knocked out; says Colonel Coursey, what did you send for me for, if you won't take my advice; would you have me hear a company of lies told against My Lord Baltimore, to whom I have sworn fidelity, and so have you; if your conscience will, mine won't permit me to do it. After a great many arguments the Court was call'd, but no Col: would appear with 'em; In short, my Lord, the declaration was read, with Coode's other orders by Nick Lowe, after which Mr. Robotham (without mentioning the goodness or badness of the things read) asks them how they would dispose of the County Arms, and who should be their Officers, never mentioning the duty or faithfulness they owed to your Lordship, and your substitutes (which I believe was forgetfulness, but hoped that none of 'em by what they heard read) would act anything against your Lordship, or your Country, and to be quiet and peaceable & in a small time all would be well. Two or three days after came up Coode's circular letters commanding every county to choose four delegates, who were to be ready at St. Marys on August 26. The 24th they sent for my arms and ammunition & Madam Lloyd's; betwixt thirty and forty men headed by Sweatnam,[26] who had a warrant (in their Majesty's names) … to take what arms, and ammunition they could find for the country's use; for that our Indians (having fled from the town, and cut up their corn) had reported, that they only staid till the two great men came from the North, meaning Colonel Darnall and Major Sewall, who the day before parted from my house. I was resolved to find out who was the Inventor of those falsities, and rid down to Oxford … where I met a great Company of people, who asked me whether I knew not of Colonel Darnall and Major Sewalls being at our Indian town: No, said I; but I know they were last night at Col: Lowe's, and are now gone home. Upon this I desired … to send some people to the Indians, to know the cause why they deserted the Town, …; they said, it was a folly to go, for the Indians would not come out except Col: Coursey

25. George Robotham, who became a delegate from Talbot County in the post-Calvert assembly.
26. Edward Sweatnam, sheriff of Kent County.

came.... At last they picked out four or five men (who knew best where the Indians were) ...; they went, and brought the answer which your Lordship has a Copy of. This was the Tuesday.... On Thursday night I came home. The Wednesday following came a Justice of peace and three or four more, who ... asked me where I was last Saturday where, says I, here: Lord Jesus! Said they, what lies goes abroad? why, what's the matter? said I; Begod, said the Justice, Dick Sweatnam had much ado to keep Captain Hatfield and his Company from coming to take you; take me, said I; for what? Why, says he, there's two men at old Watts' will swear that last Saturday they see you over against the Indian town, where you shot off two pistols, and three or four canoes full of Indians came over to you, to whom you told that within ten days you would be with 'em at the head of a thousand other Indians. I asked the fellows names; & they told me, and that they lived by the Indian Towne, and desired me withal to make haste to Major Combes, for that Sweatnam was gone to tell him the story. The next day I went to Combes's, where meeting his wife at the door, she immediately cried out; O Lord! Col: I was always glad to see you, but now am ten times gladder than ever I was; why? says I, why, says she there's a parcel of lying devils would persuade the people that you were at the Indian Town last Saturday, butt that I told 'em you were a Thursday at our house, they would all come to your house. My husband's gone to the Indian Town to know the certainty. Well, says I, I'll stay till he comes back, and he sha'nt be hanged for your sake; ... I stay'd till they came back, and told me that the fellows said they were told so by an Indian, and the Indian being questioned said, he heard it from two of the Nanticoke Indians, and so it was put off from one to t'other till it was lost, and they all say now (being deceived so many times by these sham reports) that if I should really deal with the Indians against the Protestants they would never believe it, yet those damned malicious stories was in a fair way to pull my house down about my ears; and which has really turned your Lordship's Government out of the Province; for they do not pretend to meddle with your Lordship's title to it....

Last Saturday Jack Llewellyn came up to my house, and gives me this brief account of the Assembly. The first thing they did (after they voted themselves a full house, tho' there were ten of the forty two absent.... They fixed upon the State house Door a prohibition that no Papist should come into the city during the Assembly.... Only I must tell your Lordship that the Committee of Secrecy appointed for the discovery of Colonel Darnalls and Major Sewall's dealing with the Northern Indians is kept on foot still.... Upon their report to the House ... a vote passed that letters should be sent to each neighbouring Government, as far as new England, that the house had found by several substantial evidences that your Lordship's deputies have been tampering with the Northern Indians to come in and cut off the Protestants, and therefore desires all of 'em to hold a strict correspondence with this Government and to take up all persons of this Colony that shall seem any way suspicious; This is the purport, but I've promised a copy of the letter itself.... Those that have got Estates under your Lordship, are as ready to serve Jack Coode as your Lordship, but there are some ... I'm sure will never comply with it. People in debt think it the bravest time that ever was. No Courts open, nor no law proceedings, which they pray may continue, as long as they live. I asked why Coode & his Council divested themselves of that supreme power which they usurped at first; and t'was told me that Coode proposed to the House to have a standing Committee to receive all appeals, and be as the Grand Council of the Country; but the house would be all alike in power; that the Officers civil & military of each respective County should give definitive sentences in all matters whatsoever, till further Orders out of England so that Coode & his adherents now have no more power out of their County than we cashiered Officers. They have drawn many impeachments against several, which are not sent home, and which they keep until the King sends or orders Commissioners.... [M]y Lord, this comfort remains still, that the best men & best Protestants such as Colonel Coursey, Colonel Codd,[27] Colonel Wells,[28] and a great many others (men of the best Estates, & real professors of the Protestant Religion) stand stiffly up for your Lordship's interests.[29]

27. St. Leger Codd of Cecil County, who had served as a commissioner in Charles Calvert's government.

28. George Wells of Baltimore County.

29. Both Codd and Wells wrote petitions to King William that he restore Charles Calvert as proprietor of Maryland; see *AM* 8:135–36.

30

"They Might Make Great Disturbances, If Not a Rebellion": Francis Nicholson to the Board of Trade and Plantations, August 20, 1698*

By the end of his fourth year in office Governor Nicholson had seen enough to conclude that his Catholic subjects, along with their former allies, the Quakers, yearned for the old order in which they had enjoyed virtually unlimited freedom and privileges. That yearning made them worthy of little or no trust as loyal subjects. That the Catholic population seemed to be growing at a dangerous rate, mainly through the importing of Irish servants, only deepened his concern about this dissenting community. Why is Nicholson particularly alarmed by the rapid Irish increase within the province? What disturbing possibilities does he detect from the province's broader demographic trends?

The Reasons why I have not given particular Commissions [to become officers of the militia], are because I can not find men enough, that are qualified for their Loyalty, Courage, and Diligence, to be made Officers. And those who are obliged by Law, to be either, Horse, Foot, or Dragoons, and to have Arms, Ammunition &c. of their own; can not amongst them all, fully equip a twentieth part.... And with humble Submission to your Lordships I don't think it for his Majestys Service at present, to alter the method that I have taken concerning the Militia; for fear that if they have particular Commissions under my hand & seal, they may make use of that power to his Majesty's prejudice. For I think some have endeavoured to raise a Rebellion; or at least, have made very great disturbances.... Some are of Opinion that my Lord Baltimore will have his Government again: and others hope so. From the first account we had of the likelihood of a Peace,[30] especially when the

---

* Letter of Gov. Nicholson to Board of Trade, August 20, 1698, PRO, BT, Maryland Papers, Bundle C, in *AM* 23:488–502.

30. The war with Catholic France that had begun in 1689, the first of several conflicts between the two archetypal religious empires that would engulf both Europe and America in warfare for most of the next seven decades. This phase was known in Europe as the War of the League of Augsburg; in America, as King William's War.

happy News thereof came, these things have happened here. For some were very willing that his Majesty should deliver them from Popery and slavery, and protect them in time of War: because they were not then able to preserve them selves. But now it hath pleased God, by his Majesty's inimitable Valour & Conduct, and indefatigable pains, that these troubles and fears are ceased; they are not satisfied with his Majestys Government; because it curbs them in their former atheistical, loose, and vicious way of living; and debars them of their Darling, illegal trade. The Papists join with them ... and I suppose, some of the Quakers too. If my Lord Baltimore should have this Government again, they hope (as formerly) these things would be suffered. For I suppose my Lord must comply with the Jesuits in the point of Religion; who, no doubt, will take more vigorous Resolutions, and put them in Action for the promotion of their damnable tenets. And I believe his Lordship will consider that the best, if not the only way to promote his temporal Interest here, will be not to disturb them in their illegal trade, or other ill practices: for fear that if they can not enjoy them under his Lordships Government, they may assume it to them selves: which will be no very difficult thing for them to do: except his Majesty will be pleased to protect his Lordship but whether that be advisable for his Majesty so to do, or no, your Lordships are very proper Judges.... I fancy that these dissatisfied People here, design to have a trial of skill, whether they can by their own, and their accomplices, ways, and means, get my Lord his Government again. And I think they would either be Governors them selves, or have such an one as they might rule.... I am almost morally assured, that when it pleaseth God, there shall come an Account that his Majesty will keep the Government; there will be an end of all these Disturbances....

There hath been imported this summer about four hundred and seventy odd Negros, vizt 396 in one ship directly from Guinea. 50 from Virginia, which came thither in a ship from Guinea. 20 from Pennsylvania, which came thither from Barbados: a few others from other places. And by the middle of the next month, I hope to have the certain Number of Servants imported; which by such an other Computation, may be about 6 or 700. whereof most part are Irish. Now, if please God, there should every year, or within 2 or 3 years die the like Number of Inhabitants; and there should be imported as many Irish and negroes, especially of the first, who are most, if not all, Papists; it may be of very dangerous consequence to this his Majestys Province; as also to that of Virginia; being I hear they are under all the same Circumstances. And they might make great disturbances, if not a Rebellion: because these are very open Countries, and they may have easy Communication with one an other near the Falls of Potomac; And in each Province they can do it much easier: for the common practice is on Saturday nights, and Sundays, and on 2 or 3 days in Christmas, Easter, & Whitsuntide, they go and see one an other, tho' at 30 or 40 miles distant. I have several times both in Virginia and here met Negroes both single, and 6 or 7 in Company in the night time. The major part of the Negroes speak English: and most people have some of them as their domestic servants: & the better sort may have 6 or 7 in those circumstances: and may be not above one English. And they send the Negro men and Boys about the Country, when they have Business.... So that by these means they know not only the public, but private Roads of the Country, & Circumstances thereof. And as for the Irish servants, they have more privileges: and I don't know but they may confederate with the Negroes; and in the summer time they may keep out in the Woods about the Frontiers, which are very thinly inhabited. But a great many of the people's Stocks of Cattel & Hogs run there, which may supply them with Victuals: In which parts there are a great many Swamps that they may fortify; and it will be very difficult and dangerous to come at, & force them out.

And if it please God these things should happen, even the subduing of them would be a very great charge and loss to the country in general and to their Masters in particular[.] I have put the House of Delegates in mind of these things, and shall again at their meeting October 20 next, remind them of them in order to have some Law made for the restraining of servants and Negroes going and rambling so abroad.

Sources

Balmer, Randall H. *A Perfect Babel of Confusion: Dutch Religion and English Culture in the Middle Colonies.* New York: Oxford University Press, 1989.

———. "Traitors and Papists: The Religious Dimensions of Leisler's Rebellion." *New York History* (October 1989): 341–72.

Bergmann, Mathias D. "Being the Other: Catholicism, Anglicanism and Constructs of Britishness in Colonial Maryland, 1689–1763." Ph.D. diss., University of Washington State, 2004.

Carr, Lois Green, and David William Jordan. *Maryland's Revolution of Government, 1689–1692.* Ithaca: Cornell University Press, 1974.

Duncan, Jason K. *Citizens or Papists? The Politics of Anti-Catholicism in New York, 1685–1821.* New York: Fordham University Press, 2005.

Gleissner, Richard A. "Religious Causes of the Glorious Revolution in Maryland." *MHM* 64 (Winter 1969): 327–41.

Graham, Michael. "Popish Plots: Protestant Fears in Early Colonial Maryland, 1676–1689." *CHR* 79 (April 1993): 197–216.

Hardy, Beatriz Betancourt. "Roman Catholics, Not Papists: Catholic Identity in Maryland, 1689–1776." *MHM* 92 (Summer 1997): 138–61.

Hoffman, Ronald. *Princes of Ireland, Planters of Maryland: A Carroll Saga, 1500–1782.* Chapel Hill: University of North Carolina Press, 2000.

Krugler, John D., and Timothy B. Riordan. "'Scandalous and Offensive to the Government': The 'Popish Chappel' at St. Mary's City, Maryland and the Society of Jesus, 1634 to 1705." *Mid-America* (October 1991): 187–208.

Lutz, Donald S., ed. *Colonial Origins of the American Constitution: A Documentary History.* Indianapolis: Liberty Fund, 1998.

Murrin, John. "English Rights as Ethnic Aggression: The English Conquest, the Charter of Liberties of 1683, and Leisler's Rebellion in New York." In *Authority and Resistance in Early New York,* edited by William Pencak and Conrad Edick Wrights, 56–94. New York: New York Historical Society, 1988.

Peterman, Thomas Joseph. *Catholics in Colonial Delmarva.* Devon, Pa.: Cooke, 1996.

Pyne, Tricia T. "A Plea for Maryland Catholics Reconsidered." *MHM* 92 (Summer 1997): 162–81.

Stanwood, Owen Charles. "Creating the Common Enemy: Catholics. Indians, and the Politics of Fear in Imperial North America, 1678–1700." Ph.D. diss., Northwestern University, 2005.

Sutto, Antoinette. *Loyal Protestants and Dangerous Catholics: Maryland and the Politics of Religion in the English Atlantic, 1630–1690.* Charlottesville: University of Virginia Press, 2015.

Part 7

Internal Outcasts

1704–1774

*B*EFORE NICHOLSON could take any further steps to legally rein in the Catholic community, London recalled him. His successor, Nathaniel Blakiston, was a Maryland native whose irenic bent extended even to Catholics. So, under the Blakiston administration, the position of Catholics remained largely unchanged.

With King William's death in 1702, the days were numbered for the laissez-faire policy that the crown had adopted toward Maryland's Catholic community when it took over the colony. A new military governor, John Seymour, brought with him a charge not to honor the religious liberty that Catholics had continued to enjoy for more than a decade under royal rule, but to put an end to it. Seymour, who made no effort to conceal his antipathy for Catholics, was all too prepared to put in place the new Catholic policy, including the application of the English penal laws to Maryland. When he discovered during his first year in office that the Catholic community was continuing to grow at an alarming rate, largely because of the continuing tide of Irish immigrants, despite the duties imposed on servant importation, putting the policy into effect became all the more imperative.

To maximize its promulgation, Seymour seized upon the dramatic medium of a subpoena to summon the two most prominent Jesuits in the province, William Hunter and Robert Brooke, before the provincial council for some public instruction on how Catholics needed to conduct themselves in a royal colony (see "To Grow Insolent upon Civility").

Despite Governor Seymour's intent to apply the English penal laws in Maryland, whether or not those laws had efficacy in a colony remained an unsettled question. To ensure that the English corpus of penal legislation applied as fully to Maryland as it did at home, Seymour apparently was the main hand in steering through the legislature a statute that would capture the core of England's penal laws. The act was the first one based on the assumption that Catholics represented a group outside the mainstream of Maryland's free population—a group not qualified to enjoy the traditional rights and liberties that English citizens had come to prize (see "Whatsoever Popish … Priest or Jesuit … Shall Endeavour to Persuade Any of Her Majestys Liege People").

When the House of Delegates next convened, ten weeks after the passage of the anti-popery bill, they found a petition from "the Roman Catholics of Maryland" contending that the act constituted a violation of the intent of the province's charter as well as that of the Toleration Act of 1649. They professed to have reason to believe that Queen Anne had not intended such a sweeping suppression of Catholicism, but merely a redress of certain "irregularities." They urged the legislature to suspend the law until Maryland officials could consult Whitehall to ascertain the queen's mind (see "The Covenant Ought to Continue to Posterity").

Moved by the Catholic elite's appeal, the Maryland legislature suspended the Act for Preventing the Growth of Popery until the queen made known her sentiments regarding the practice of Catholicism in Maryland. Acting for the queen, the Council of Trade and Plantations, largely out of fear that the act would cause a mass exodus of Catholics, both planters and servants, from Maryland, upheld the suspension. The immediate consequence for Maryland Catholics was the privatization of religious practice. The Catholic community found itself in the same position as that of English Catholics. Unlike their English cousins, however, the Americans would not submit quietly to a marginal place within society.

Seymour continued his campaign to expand the penal legislation against Catholics. For their part, the Catholic opposition used marital connections as well as their proprietary offices to influence the lower house to defeat much of his anti-Catholic program. Their power was significantly trimmed when the governor succeeded in passing a law requiring the surveyors in the land office, most of whom were Catholic, to take test oaths in order to qualify. But Seymour's sudden death in 1709 brought relief for Catholics. His successor, Edward Lloyd, was the offspring of a Catholic-Protestant marriage; his mother, Henrietta Maria Bennett Lloyd, was probably the most prominent Catholic woman in the province.

As King William's death in 1702 had brought a profound change in the religious status of Catholics in Maryland, so Queen Anne's death a dozen years later touched off a series of events that led to the completion of the removal of Catholics from the body politic. With Anne's Hanoverian cousin, George I, on the throne, Charles Calvert, still the proprietor but no longer the ruler of Maryland, died in 1715. Less than two years before his death, his oldest son, Benedict, had renounced his Catholicism, which cost him his £450 annual stipend from his father, but this loss was more than offset by the crown's promise to restore Maryland to the Calvert family once Benedict became Lord Baltimore. Maryland's Catholic leaders were actually buoyed by this development, assuming that Benedict's conversion was nothing more than his calculation that Maryland was worth a test oath. Surely they anticipated, once the province was restored to him, that the new Lord Baltimore would maintain the family tradition of safeguarding Catholic interests in Maryland. No one was more certain of this prospect than Charles Carroll, who, called to London as Charles Calvert's executor, carried a petition on behalf of a prominent group of Catholics, probably including most of those who had petitioned the assembly a decade earlier. The petition requested that Calvert allow Catholics to regain the political position they had held before 1689—"an equal share in all the public offices of this Province."

Carroll arrived in London to discover that Benedict had died, less than two months after his father. He presented the petition to Lord Francis Guilford, who, as the legal guardian of the sixteen-year-old Charles Calvert, was effectively the acting proprietor. Guilford would not consider intervening in Maryland's government, but did award Carroll some additional responsibilities (and perquisites) as Calvert's chief agent.

When the governor of Maryland, John Hart, learned that Carroll had indeed formally presented the petition to Guilford, despite Carroll's promise (according to the governor) not to do so, it confirmed for him his worst suspicions about Catholics. Hart, like former governor Seymour, brought with him to Annapolis a profound uneasiness about the Catholic minority. He was convinced the majority of them were supporters of the pretender to the English throne, James Edward Stuart, whose adherents had seized the occasion of a newly crowned king, George I, to coordinate revolts in England and Scotland. James himself had returned to Scotland from France in December 1715, planning his own coronation as James III. So when John Hart heard that the wife of one of his council members had, by chance, come into possession of a letter written by a Jesuit known for his polemical skills and political interests, which made vague allusions suggesting a conspiracy to extend the Jacobite uprising to Maryland, he commandeered the epistle from the wife and ordered her, the Jesuit author Peter Attwood, and the prominent Catholic James Carroll (Charles Carroll's nephew) to be deposed. The letter and testimony about it became the major issue of the meeting of the Governor's Council in late January 1716 (see "Many Evil Persons, in This Province, Such as Papists").

If Governor Hart figured that his surveillance and oath-taking or prison campaign would intimidate the Catholic community, he soon discovered otherwise. At dawn of a June day in 1716 the cannon on Courthouse Hill boomed. It was the birthday of the Catholic pretender James Edward Stuart. This in-your-face salute was apparently the work of Charles Carroll. The two individuals who had been responsible for the firing of the cannon both had connections to the former attorney general. When John Hart, the governor, jailed the culprits, Carroll, testing the limits of his commission from the proprietor, claimed the right to collect the considerable fine money (£140). Infuriated by the agent's aggressive ploy, Hart insisted that Carroll take the oaths now required of all provincial officeholders. Carroll replied that conscience did not allow him to do so. Still he persisted on fulfilling his commission, requesting that Hart hereafter forward to him all revenue received from fines. When the governor refused to do so, Carroll closed the Land Office, which immediately created chaos in the real estate market. Hart finally appealed to Lord Guilford, who subsequently stripped Carroll of all the commissions he held as the proprietor's chief agent.

Carroll's abandonment by the proprietary family occurred during a string of setbacks that the Catholic community suffered in 1717–18 as Hart pushed his penal legislation through an increasingly supportive assembly:

raising the tax on imported Irish servants to a prohibitive four pounds currency, requiring oaths of all officeholders, whether provincial or proprietary, disfranchising Catholics, and repealing the anti-popery bill of 1704 as unnecessary, since Parliament's penal laws were now understood to apply to Maryland. Not only was this legislation passed, it was enforced, as were other penal laws that previously had merely gathered dust in the statute book. Still, the Catholics refused to believe that the proprietary family would not ultimately rescue them from their deteriorating condition and continued their lobbying. Hart, exasperated by this recalcitrance, while addressing the assembly in the fall of 1719, challenged Catholics to cite even one instance of persecution "for Conscience Sake" that they had suffered at the hands of his government. The following April the upper house invited thirteen prominent Catholics to address the assembly to make their case. Among the invitees was Peter Attwood, by now the superior of the Jesuit mission. The council apparently included Attwood because of a paper he was known to have prepared justifying the grievances that the Catholic bloc had against the provincial government (see Peter Attwood, "Liberty & Property or The Beautys of Maryland Displayed").

Attwood's paper was never read or sent to Maryland officials, and the baker's dozen of Catholics never took up the council's invitation. The Catholic bloc, including Attwood, evidently had concluded that there was no longer a need to state their case. The recent news that John Hart was being recalled to London seemed to them a turn in the tide of suppression that had been so devastating over the past several years. At last, Carroll and other Catholics concluded, the proprietor was doing right by them. Carroll died shortly afterward, no doubt still thinking a new era was upon them. When the proprietor finally addressed his Maryland subjects in late 1720, he called for peace between the religious factions, with the Catholics agreeing to accept their current position. The legislature, in turn, made it known that so long as Catholics created no stir, the penal laws would go unenforced. Thus began a long period of benign neglect. But the special relationship between the proprietor and the Catholic community did not revive, nor did the Carrolls regain their benefices from the Calverts or Catholics the franchise or the opportunity to worship publicly. Catholics painfully remained political and religious outcasts in Maryland society.

Pennsylvania became the second British colony on the mainland to have a significant Catholic presence. Under the Quaker proprietor, William Penn, who offered land, self-rule, and religious liberty to those who would immigrate there, Pennsylvania replaced Maryland as the colony offering the best economic and religious advantages. Although he had a low opinion of Roman Catholicism, Penn thought Catholics should have the same basic rights as others (although he stopped short of officeholding) so long as they lived in peace with their neighbors. Catholics responded with their feet. Over the last fifteen years of the seventeenth century, they began to move into the commonwealth from Maryland, New York, and abroad (Germany and Ireland). The Catholic incursion into Penn's colony led Jesuits in Maryland to include Pennsylvania sites in their circuits. In 1729, in recognition of the rapid increase in the Catholic population, the Society of Jesus established a dependent mission centered at Philadelphia. That city experienced such extraordinary growth that by mid-century it was the largest in British America.

The immigration from German states that was a major reason for Pennsylvania's rapid development included a significant minority of Catholics. Indeed German Catholics, settling in Philadelphia as well as the towns and rural areas of southeastern Pennsylvania, were, by the 1750s, the largest ethnic group within the Catholic community. That demographic induced the Jesuit superior in Maryland to petition Rome for some German Jesuits to minister to the German-speaking Catholics in Pennsylvania. Supported by two endowments from English Catholic benefactors, two German Jesuits, Theodore Schneider and William Wappeler, arrived in 1741, the first of nine German Jesuits to work in Penn's colony in the late colonial period (see "We Have … All Liberty Imaginable in the Exercise of Our Business").

The Catholic community in Maryland, while fighting to regain the full citizenship they had known before the Glorious Revolution, adapted a modified manorial Catholicism in coping with the penal laws. As the population, including Catholics, spread north and eastward in the province, the homes of the gentry, as in England, became the center of the Catholic community in those parts of Maryland. For the clergy, itinerant ministry continued to be their daily lot, increasingly by horse rather than boat. Nowhere was this kind of peripatetic ministry more the norm for the mid-century Catholic community than on the Eastern Shore, where Joseph Mosley ministered and evangelized for over a quarter of a century (see "In the Desert Parts of America").

"To Grow Insolent upon Civility": Governor John Seymour's Rebuke of the Jesuits William Hunter and Robert Brooke, 1704*

Hunter was the superior of the mission, Brooke the scion of one of the first families of Maryland and the first Maryland Catholic to become a priest. Summoned before the Provincial Council on charges of saying Mass publicly and consecrating a chapel, the two Jesuits explained that Hunter could hardly have consecrated a church or chapel inasmuch as he was not a bishop, who alone had the power to do so; as for a public Mass, Brooke pointed out that he was merely doing in the great chapel in St. Mary's City what his fellow priests had been doing there and throughout the province for decades without incurring any penalty or accusation. In the political theater the provincial government was staging, their statements mattered not at all. On cue the council determined that, this being their first offense, their punishment would be a public reprimand from the governor. Seymour proceeded to carry out his part in the performance by making it brutally clear to the Jesuits and their fellow Catholics what their position in Maryland now was. Or so he thought. But what did it mean to be told to conduct oneself in a "civil and modest manner"? Why does Seymour deem the Catholic chapel in St. Mary's City "Scandalous and offensive to the Government?" What, if anything, of religious liberty remained for Catholics under the new policy?

Minutes of the Council, September 9, 1704

The said Mr. William Hunter and Mr. Robert Brooke appeared and are told on what occasion they were called before his Excellency[.] Mr. William Hunter ... says he is very sorry for any annoyance in his Conduct as to his consecrating the Chapel he did not Consecrate it for that is an Episcopal Function and that no body was present but himself in his common Priests vestments ... but if any such thing was done it was above fourteen months

---

*Assembly Proceedings, September 5–October 3, 1704, Council Minutes, September 9, 1704, in *AM* 26:44–46.

ago, and long before his Excellencys arrival Mr. Brook says he did say mass in the Court Time at the Chapel of St. Marys but found that others had formerly done so.

Advised that this being the first Complaint the said Mr. Hunter & Mr. Brooke be severely reprimanded and told that they must not Expect any Favor but the utmost Severity of the Law upon any misdemeanour by them committed and being called in his Excellency was pleased to give them the following Reprimand Viz.

Gentlemen

It is the unhappy temper of you and all your Tribe to grow insolent upon Civility and never know how to use it and yet of all People you have the least reason for considering that if the necessary Laws that are made were let loose they are Sufficient to crush you and which (if your arrogant Principles have not blinded you) you must need to dread. You might methinks be Content to live quietly as you may and let the Exercise of Your Superstitious Vanities be confined to yourselves without proclaiming them at public times and in public places unless you expect by your gaudy shows and Serpentine Policy to amuse the multitude and beguile the unthinking weakest part of them an Act of Deceit well known to be amongst you.

I am willing upon the earnest Solicitations of some Gentlemen to make one trial (and it shall be but this one) of your temper.

In plain and few words Gentlemen if you intend to live here let me hear no more of these things for if I do and they are made good against you be assured I'll chastize you.... Therefore ... I ... advise you to be civil and Modest for there is no other way for you to live quietly here.

You are the first that have given any disturbance to my Government and if it were not for the hopes of your better demeanour you should now be the first that should feel the Effects of so doing....

After which they were discharged.

The members of this Board taking under their Considering that such use of the Popish Chapel of the City of St. Marys in St. Marys County where there is a protestant church and the said County Court is kept is both Scandalous and offensive to the Government do advise and desire his Excellency the Governour to give immediate orders for the Shutting up the said Popish Chapel and that no Person presume to make use thereof under any pretence whatsoever.

Whereupon it was ordered by his Excellency the governour that the present Sheriff of St. Marys County lock up the said Chapel and keep the Key thereof.

32

"Whatsoever Popish … Priest or Jesuit … Shall Endeavour to Persuade Any of Her Majestys Liege People": A Bill for Restraining the Growth of Popery, 1704[*]

Within weeks Catholics learned a great deal more about the government's plan for controlling the practice of their faith when the legislature enacted a bill that Governor Seymour promptly signed into law. Beginning as a simple ban on Catholic proselytizing, it metastasized into a comprehensive outlawing of priestly ministry and Catholic education, as well as a renewal of a punitive duty on Irish servants brought into Maryland. The result was the 1704 "Act to Prevent the Growth of Popery within This Province," an act that closely followed (in title and substance) one passed by the English Parliament four years earlier. What strategy are province officials utilizing in order to combat Roman Catholicism in Maryland? Is the bill aimed at the containment of Catholicism or something more?

An Act to Prevent the Growth of Popery within This Province, September 30, 1704

Be it Enacted by the Queens most Excellent Majesty by and with the Advice and Consent of her Majestys Governour Council and Assembly of this Province and the Authority of the same that whatsoever Popish Bishop Priest or Jesuit shall baptize any Child or Children other than such who have Popish Parents or shall say Mass or exercise the function of a Popish Bishop or Priest within this Province or shall endeavour to persuade any of

[*] *AM* 26:340–41.

her Majestys Liege People[1] of this Province to embrace and be reconciled to the Church of Rome ... shall forfeit the sum of fifty pounds Sterling for every such Offence ... and shall also Suffer six Months imprisonment of his or their body or bodies without bail or Mainprize.[2]

And be it further Enacted by and with the Advice Consent and Authority aforesaid that if any Popish Bishop Priest or Jesuit after such Conviction aforesaid shall say Mass or Exercise any other part of the Office or function of a Popish Bishop or Priest within this Province or if any Papist or Person making profession of the Popish Religion shall keep School or take upon themselves the Education Government or Boarding of Youth in any place within this Province such person or persons being thereof lawfully convicted that then every such Person shall upon such Conviction be transported out of this Province to the Kingdom of England together with his Conviction in order to his Suffering such pains and penalties as are provided by the Statute made in the Eleventh and Twelfth year of the reign of his late Majesty King William the third Entitled An Act for the further preventing the Growth of Popery.[3] And to the end that the Protestant Children of Popish Parents may not in the life time of such their parents for want of fitting Maintenance be Necessitated in Compliance with their parents to embrace the Popish Religion contrary to their own Inclination[:]

Be it Enacted by the Authority aforesaid ... if any such parent in order to the Compelling such his or her Protestant Child to Change his or her Religion shall refuse to allow such Child a fitting Maintenance Suitable to the degree and Ability of such parent and to the Age and Education of Such Child then upon Complaint thereof made to the Governour of this Province or the Keeper of the Great Seale it shall be lawful for the said Governour or Keeper of the Seale to make such order therein as shall be agreeable to the Intent of this Act.

---

1. "Liege People": a not-so-subtle coupling of the Protestant and "loyal" segments of Maryland's free-born population.

2. Surety, bail.

3. The act, passed by Parliament in 1700, established the penalty of life imprisonment for priests convicted of saying Mass or carrying out any other priestly ministry.

33

"The Covenant Ought to Continue to Posterity": Remonstrance of the Roman Catholics of Maryland to the House of Delegates, December 21, 1704[*]

Although we do not know the persons behind the petition, it is a safe presumption that they constituted the Catholic economic elite: major Catholic merchant-planters, such as Henry Darnall, his son-in-law Charles Carroll, and Richard Bennett. It proved to be the first public manifesto of a group of citizens consciously identifying themselves as Catholics and appealing to their colony's origins and history to claim their rights and liberties. It was the opening shot of a very long campaign to regain political and social equality for Maryland Catholics. What does this "remonstrance" reveal about the Catholic elite that composed it? What satisfaction, if any, would they have gotten from the government's response?

Remonstrance of the Roman Catholics of Maryland to the House of Delegates. The said Roman Catholics are much surprised to find themselves by an Act passed the last sessions deprived of that liberty in point of religious worship which they and their ancestors have without interruption constantly enjoyed from the first seating of this Province together with the rest of their fellow-subjects of different persuasions, and that not only by the public conditions proposed by the proprietor to all persons for encouragement of seating here, but also by a law heretofore passed by the whole representative body of the Province and assented to by the proprietor, which has for a long time been found by evident experience to have contributed very much to the people of the country, and the firm settlement of a friendly and sincere union between all the people towards carrying on the common interest of the Crown of England and their own. It is no small addition to their surprise herein when they consider that in this Assembly are several persons who cannot be ignorant that the said Roman Catholics or their ancestors have always been as active and forward in hazarding their lives and fortunes for the common interest and reduction of the country to the English subjection and suppression of the Hea-

[*] PRO, CSP, America and West Indies, 1704–5, no. 1530 (December 21, 1704): 735–36.

then as any other proportionable number of the people, and that in the several attempts therein a great many of them lost their lives as well by the hands of the infidel enemy as by the hardships which the seating of such a desert as this was must of necessity render people liable to, and that now they think it the greatest of hardships, when they and their posterities are in a fair way of reaping some advantage of their past labours and expence in conjunction with the rest of their fellow subjects to be deprived of that liberty and freedom upon the encouragement whereof they or forefathers chiefly transported themselves hither. The Charter which laid the foundation of this Province being granted by a Protestant Prince to a Peer known to be a roman Catholic, it cannot in reason be conceived but that it was given for granted by that Prince [that] the said Peer and successors should allow a toleration and freedom of conscience as well to such of his own persuasion as should transport themselves from their native country to contribute towards the peopling a Desert at so great a distance, as to others, and if so in the beginning of the settlement, it is humbly conceived that in all justice and conscience the covenant ought to continue to posterity. The said Roman Catholics ... most humbly pray that ... directions may be given that such moderate methods may be taken therein ... that thereby the said Roman Catholics (who no longer wish for freedom of conscience in this Her Majestys Province than they behave themselves as becomes dutiful and loyal subjects) may be left in the same circumstances they have hitherto been, till Her Majestys pleasure in relation to them be known.

34

"Many Evil Persons, in This Province, Such as Papists": Peter Attwood and the Catholic Threat, 1716*

The Hart administration felt confident that, with the Catholic treason apparently revealed in the requisitioned Attwood letter, it had finally secured, if only by chance, hard evidence of the conspiracy the leaders of the Catholic opposition had been a part of since 1689. When

---

* Proceedings of the Council of Maryland, January 1716, in *AM* 25:326–36.

the head of the Jesuit mission, Peter Attwood, and the planter-merchant James Carroll both made convincing explanations of the basic innocence of the letter's seemingly incriminating language, the council had no choice but to accept their word. The whole business seemed at an end. As Attwood, Carroll, and the Catholic community were all too soon made aware, it was more like the beginning of a new phase of the war against Catholics, Quakers, and other undesirables in Maryland. What is new about the action taken by the council immediately following Attwood and Carroll's appearance before them?

By his Excellency's order, [the following letter] was opened at the Board ... and read....Reverendus in. Christo Pater

What you mentioned of Mr. James Carroll's Liberality, was News to me. I do not see why we may not Strike, while the Iron is hot. Why can we not enter thereon, tho' with some difficulty? all beginnings are hard, but why may not we rub through as well as Our forefathers? Wou'd not two or three Hands Suffice for a beginning? & this I shou'd think might be procured: I acknowledge myself unfit for such an undertaking but shou'd be very willing to do my Endeavours, to struggle with it were it Committed to my Charge, and why don't we admit the Offer, since a new Supply[4] is expected with the Major? I am much of the Italian's mind, that no Occasion is to be Passed by[.] I suppose what you mentioned, was Secret, and shall therefore do my Endeavour, to take away difficulty, and forward the main concern.... Mr Darnall is always so extremely obliging to me, that I am ashamed to Come to the Wood Yard, ...

> 1obr 21, 1712
> Your obliged humble Servant,
> P. Attwood, SJ

As for News ... the Pretender is still in France, the Dutch and Spaniard are not agreed, and constantly make Prizes of each other, hence the Dutch dare not sail in the Mediterranean, and are forced to Employ the English in those Parts, the D: Daumon is the French Ambassador but will soon be Succeeded by another, many of Our Soldiers are disbanded, Six or eight thousand are sent for Ireland....

I think to make my Exercise and recollection next Monday, so hope to see You towards the latter end thereof: Mr. Hall left two of my Books at

---

4. Their covert history in England had made aliases and coded language in correspondence second nature to the English Jesuits. We get a glimpse here of the latter device. Jesuits tended to use commercial terms to describe their ministries and activities. So "supply" here means additional Jesuits, "factory" refers to the Mission itself, and so forth.

Mr. Hills, Pray desire him to send them hither, by the first Occasion, or to deliver them to You.

Mr. William Digges supposes Mr. Rosier carried my powder flask away with him, if so desire him to make restitution, for it belongs to Mr. James Carroll, who has bought my Gun for 50£ Sterling.... Pray burn the Letter for I believe its all nonsense....

P. Attwood, SJ

On Saturday the twenty eighth day of January ... [1716]

Appeared before the Honorable Samuel Young Esquire one of the Members of the Council of State ... Mrs. Mary Hemsley the Wife of Mr. Philemon Hemsley, of this City, and being ... Examined upon her Corporal Oath ... concerning, a certain letter, dated December 21, 1712, Subscribed P. Attwood SJ and directed to Mr. William Kittuck, at the Wood yard.... She ... Sayeth that about 12 months ago, she lent to Mr. William Hunter, a Popish Priest at Port Tobacco a Book of the Practice of Physic, which he returned her, about eight months ago, amongst the Leaves of which Book she found the said Letter open, and finding in the said letter, some Latin and dark expressions, which she was Curious to know the meaning of, show'd it to some of her friends. That His Excellency the Governor John Hart Esquire having got some ... information of the said Letter, ... required and commanded [her], to send it him, which she did by the said Clerk of the Council.

The Examination of Mr. Peter Attwood, before his Excellency John Hart Esqr and the honorable Lt Col. Samuel Young.... On January 28 [1716] [Attwood] acknowledges the said Letter, to be by Him wrote, ... As to the second Paragraph where mention is made of Mr. James Carroll's liberality, the Deponent meant an offer made by the said James Carroll ... of a Tract of about three hundred acres in Baltimore County, to him or any other Priest of the Romish Communion, that would go Settle and live thereon.

And that by the Expression, why should we not Strike while the iron is hot, He meant he did not know how long the said Mr. Carroll, might be of that opinion, or they have the like Offer from him or any body else. As to the Words why cannot we enter thereon, tho' with some difficulty, all Beginnings are hard, but why mayn't we rub through as well as Our Forefathers, they are meant Concerning the Settling, the said Tract of Land, as some others had been formerly done by some other Priests of their Society....[5]

5. The Jesuits, who had to self-fund their ministries in Maryland, had been employing labor to work their lands since the first decade of the province's founding. Initially, this plantation work

As to the Words Why do not we admit the offer, since a New Supply is expected by the Major

He the Deponent meant, why might not they accept the said Mr. James Carrolls Offer, since another Priest might be expected with Major Sewell from England.

As to the Expression of, I suppose what You mentioned was Secret, and shall therefore do my Endeavours, to take away Difficulty, and forward the main Concern, the Deponent meant thereby, that he Supposed Mr. James Carrolls Settlement was to be kept Private, & promised to endeavour, to remove any difficulty's thereabout, and forward it.

Peter Attwood

Mr James Carroll, appearing at the Board, … and being … asked … if he ever heard or knew of any Rebellion, or disturbance, intended to be made by any Roman Catholics in this Province, about the Year 1712 or at any time since. The said Mr. Carroll answers he never did.

Being asked if ever he made an Offer of a Tract of Land, in Baltimore County—he says that he did, about three Years ago, offer some Land there, as a Charity….[6]

His Excellency put the Question to the Board whether there be any Sufficient Grounds, in the said Letter, to prosecute the Persons writing it, or the Person it is written to, or Mr. James Carroll, who is Mentioned therein.

Upon Which they unanimously answer they don't think there is any matter, of Moment in the said Letter, worthy his Excellencys further notice.

His Excellency acquaints the council, he has had some intimation, that Sundry Roman Catholics, and other disaffected Persons to his Majestys Person of Government especially in Prince Georges County, have spoke disrespectively of the Government & Showed their disaffection, to his Majesty, by Spreading sundry false Rumours, … whether it may not be fit, to Caution the magistrates and Sheriffs, of the respective Counties, … carefully to observe the Demeanour of such Persons, & … to tender them the Oaths &c.…

---

had been done by indentured servants. By the late seventeenth century, the Jesuits, along with Maryland planters in general, had turned to African slaves as their chief labor pool. Increasingly, as the eighteenth century wore on, slave labor became a larger and larger portion of the workforce on the Jesuit plantations on the Eastern and Western Shores.

6. Thirteen years later James Carroll died. In his will he bequeathed his major plantation, White Marsh in Prince Georges County, approximately ten times the size of the tract he was offering in Baltimore County, to the Society of Jesus.

To which all the Members of this Board, do unanimously answer, that they think such Caution, and Directions, from his Excellency to the several Magistrates, and Sheriffs, is very advisable, to be done by Proclamation.

And the said Proclamation being prepared, & read as follows, was forthwith Issued. [February 14, 1716]

Whereas it is rumoured, that many evil Persons, in this Province, such as Papists, Non Jurors, & others disaffected to the most Sacred Person, & happy Government of our Gracious Sovereign King George of Great Britain &c upon Notice of the late Insurrection & Rebellion, in Great Britain, adhering to the open & avow'd enemies of his Majesty's Crown, and the British Constitution, have industriously spread about divers malicious false and untrue Reports ... of his Majestys Troops being over powered by those of the Rebels in Great Britain, & by drinking the Health, & otherwise favouring the false & traitorous Claim, of a Popish Pretender against his Majesty's most lawful & rightful Title, to the Kingdoms he so Gloriously Possesses, and auspiciously governs.

In order to restrain such unaccountable, Traitorous & disloyal Actions, ... in this Province I have thought fit ... to Issue this my Proclamation ... strictly charging & requiring, all Sheriffs & Magistrates ... carefully to observe the demeanour, of such Persons in their respective counties, and upon any Notice or Suspicion, they shall have of any such Traitorous disloyal, or other unwarrantable Proceedings of any such Papists, Non Jurors, or other suspected Persons, forthwith to Cause them to be apprehended & brought before the said Magistrates, who are to tender unto them, the Oaths appointed by Act of Parliament instead of the Oaths of Allegiance & Supremacy also the Oath appointed by the Act, of ... the late Queen, Entitled an Act, for ... the Succession to the Crown of Great Britain in the Protestant Line which they are to require them to take, ... [on the] refusal whereof, the said Magistrates, are hereby commanded & enjoined, to oblige them, to find and give good Security, for their Behaviour, & Appearance at the next County Courts, on Default whereof they are to Commit them to the County Goal.

35

[Peter Attwood,] "Liberty & Property or The Beautys of Maryland Displayed. Being a Brief & Candid Inquiry into Her Charter Fundamental Laws & Constitution. By a Lover of His Country," 1720 *

Like Charles Carroll, Attwood had not been cowed by the governor's harsh policies toward Catholics. In the following document, Attwood makes the case for Catholic rights from Maryland's past. The ultimate test for the validity of any legislative act is its congruence with the province's Constitution, or fundamental body of laws, foremost of which is that establishing liberty of conscience. Parliament may be the supreme lawmaker in the empire, Attwood argues, but, short of allowing Maryland appropriate representation in its ranks, it lacks both the knowledge and interest to enact legislation that will promote the public good of the citizens of Maryland. Only the local legislature has the wherewithal to do that. Which is why, from the colony's very beginnings, its legislature had enjoyed limited autonomy. Only Marylanders can legislate for Maryland, by being true, in their legislation, to the province's Constitution and history, which guaranteed to Catholics all the rights and liberties enjoyed by their fellow citizens. How does Attwood use the English crown's actions regarding Maryland's Catholics to confirm his contention that the different circumstances surrounding mother country and colony respectively dictate different laws? In this treatise is Attwood breaking new ground in his defense of Catholic rights in the province?

Maryland being first granted to Sir George Calvert upon the change of his Religion, & afterwards [confirmed] to his son the Lord Cecilius a professed Roman Catholic, it is no [leap] to suppose that the Crown designed that they who were to be hereditary Proprietors of Maryland [have] the free use of their Religion & other privileges ... enjoy[.]

Cecilius ... soon publishes a Declaration thro' out all England & other the Kings Dominions, that whosoever of his Majestys Subjects would go and Settle in Maryland Should not only have a considerable Tract of Land grant-

*University Archives, GULBFCSC.

ed unto him Gratis, but should there enjoy all Rights & Privileges equally & without Distinction: & it was upon this prevailing Encouragement that many English, Scotch & Irish of all Religions, Churchmen, Dissenters & Roman Catholics transported themselves & Families: tho' *the chief Adventurers Were Papists ... of good Families, who expected full Liberty, under a Proprietor of their own Religion,* especially since by the above said Declaration he had promised an equal enjoyment of all Rights & privileges unto all.

Now ... we find that these Adventurers were no sooner settled but they began to consider how they should [safeguard those rights and privileges], not only unto themselves but to their later offspring, ... & ... we behold the whole Country voting for & the Lord Cecilius consenting unto a *fundamental Law whereby Liberty of Conscience is allowed to all, that profess to believe in Jesus Christ....*[7]

So were they firmly resolved to use their utmost Endeavours to [enact] ... a fundamental & Stable Law to Confirm & secure this Liberty to all Christians, & that forever, as the chiefest of our Privileges & the material Branch of our Constitution....

The Law of Liberty of Conscience is so far from being inconsistent with our Constitution ... that it is rather the most fundamental part of our Constitution....

That the happy fruit of this Fundamental Law of Liberty of Conscience were not only the Peopling of this Province in so short a space, but that Happy Union & agreement of its Inhabitants, who, altho' differing in their Judgments as to matters of Religion, lived nevertheless *together in the greatest Peace Order & Concord Imaginable.*

Such a Law ... never met with any countermand, check or opposition from the Crown or Government of England, not even in the days of Oliver Cromwell, who altho' he used his utmost Endeavours to extirpate Both the Church of England & Popery out of the whole Kingdom, did nevertheless permit both to enjoy their ancient Privileges, here in Maryland....

A Body Politick, as well as natural, is best preserved by the continued influence of those means to which it owes its existence & production; & consequently Since this Law of Religion was our first, our chief, our fundamental Law, & the dearest branch of our Constitution, by which we live, grow up to, flourish, to strike hereat, would be to unhinge the Government, destroy

---

7. As becomes clearer in later references to the Act Concerning Religion, Attwood appears to be conflating the 1638/39 legislation concerning religion and the Toleration Act a decade later.

our Foundation, & reduce this flourishing Colony to ruin & Confusion; besides the great injustice would be done to those whose Forefathers were prevailed upon to become Residents in this Province by this fundamental Law, which, like the Conditions of their Plantations, was to be inviolable & unalterable....

Lastly as this Law & the enjoyment thereof has peopled our Province, & made it the most happy & most flourishing of all the British Colonies, so the cessation or annulling thereof would be, not only Injurious to our late Posterity, but would render us a Divided & unhappy People, & *tend much to depopulate this his majestys so profitable Colony*....

Under the Protection of this Fundamental Law, ... for 50 years & upwards ... all Christians enjoyed not only the free use of their Religion, but an equal share, in all other Rights, Places, & Privileges: So that whenever Counsellor, or Burgess, a Judge or Justice, was to be chosen, or appointed; his Religion was neither a Help nor a Hindrance, & nothing came under Consideration, but his Integrity, Parts & Capacity, were he Churchman or Presbyterian, Quaker or Papist & hence it is to be presumed that the Country was never better Served nor could it be, than in those halcyon Days, when neither his Lordship nor the People were debarred, he from appointing, or they from choosing, the most knowing & proper Persons, be their Persuasion what it would. Nor was this equal enjoyment of Privileges confined to Religion & officers only; no, there was also an entire Liberty & full enjoyment of all other Rights, Privileges & immunities for all Subjects of Great Britain.... & that the Penal Laws of England extend not hither, was for 70 years & more the opinion of all in Maryland in Court & out of Court. Tho' Some of late to Secure, what may be justly deemed an Englishman's Birthright, the enjoyment of all Beneficial Laws, or Laws of Privilege, which were made in England before our first Settlement, have unwarily advanced too much, in claiming all the Laws of Great Britain: for should we examine into the necessary Consequences thereof so extensive a Claim might be found to be not beneficial, but highly prejudicial to, if not destructive of our Constitution.

Since the Parliament is neither knowing of nor interested in our Affairs! & whether it be better for us who are so highly concerned in improving this colony, & so feelingly Sensible of our own Interest to make our own Laws or to leave them to be made by such who are strangers to our Constitution, & not only ignorant of but perchance unconcerned for our Advantage, is so easy for an unprejudiced Person to determine, that I believe most will join with me, in advising Such as will Still insist for all the Laws, to Supercede[8] this claim, till they have obtained two things of the Crown; the first is that our Prince may be freed from the unnecessary Trouble & Expense, of having Assemblies; for if all the Laws of England Should extend hither, & we are not allowed to contradict the Same, or to make Laws contrary to them, … to have Assemblies, would be an unnecessary Charge & a Superfluous Trouble. The 2d is to obtain Leave that our freeholdings may choose sufficient Number of Delegates from among themselves that may be our Representatives, & both sit & vote in the British Parliament for what can be more reasonable, than that we ourselves should have a vote in those Laws that are to bind us: & yet whether either of these would be granted by the Crown, or, if granted, would be beneficial to this Province, I leave the disinterested & impartial to be Judges.

It may be asked whence comes it, then, that at present, there is not that entire union & Harmony among our Inhabitants, nor that equal Share of all privileges enjoyed either by the Quakers or the Roman Catholics: to such a Question I give our Saviours Answer, *Ab initio non erat sic* from the beginning it was not so; its true. Both the Quaker & the Roman Catholic, be they otherwise never so well qualified, … are nevertheless excluded from all offices; but *from the beginning it was not so* & what is still harder neither Quaker nor Roman Catholic are allowed to have a vote in the making of any Law, tho' they & their late Posterity might be bound by the same, but *from the beginning it was not so.* & what is yet more Severe, the poor Papist … can neither vote in nor out of the House neither be, nor send a Representative; but *from the beginning it was not so!* …

3d That Maryland Should deem a Papist unworthy to be a petty drayman or Constable, whilst the Crown thought a Papist sufficiently deserving to be both her Proprietary & hereditary Governor is most Surprising! That Maryland Should be worse than her Promise, & deny the enjoyment of her Fundamental Law to any of her People, whose Fathers were allured by the same to become her Inhabitants, is more wonderful as well as more deplorable….

For 60 years our Proprietor was our Governor, … Thus we enjoyed both Peace & Plenty during the civil wars in England, & amidst all its unhappy changes, we alone were unchangeable & still the same, until the Revolution,

8. Suspend.

in which our unhappy Country could not escape the common Deluge, &
what was done here in opposition to our lawful Government could not fail
of an approbation at Home in that unhappy circumstance: … From this ep-
och we may date our changes, not only in Government but in manners Love
& union to & with each other: … such was the will Such the pleasure of
our new Governors sent in by the Crown; Governors that were Strangers to
our Constitution, & unconcerned for our Prosperity: Governors that came
to fleece & not to feed, to raise their own Fortunes, not to advance ours:
Governors who instead of healing our wounds, widen'd our Breaches, fo-
mented our Divisions, & when no other Crime could be objected made the
Religion of Some high Treason, or at least a mark of Disgrace, & a hindrance
not only to Promotion, but to the equal common & undoubted Rights &
Privileges of a Marylandian! Hence they impose & require Such oaths &
conditions to Qualify for Offices, that the Quakers & Roman Catholics are
excluded from Places: tho' for 60 year Fidelity to his Lordship was the only
requisite: this was the first & open Breach of our Constitution, … When
Governor Seymour … resolved … to ruin all: hence he puts his engine to
work & at length brings forth an Act entitled *An Act against the Growth of
Popery* which might have more justly [been] Styled *An Act to extirpate Popery Root & Branch* [and the subsequent suspending acts] From which Acts
I infer first that neither Governor Seymour nor our Assembly were of opinion that the Penal Laws of England extended hither, for to what end should
they trouble themselves, or risk such a severe check, as they had from the
Crown by making a Law for that, for which the Laws of England had more
severely provided, had they dreamed they had Laws ready made in force &
more Severe. 2dly that the general voice of the whole Country is, that no
one should be debarr'd of use, or be oppressed for or in respect of their Religion … [;] the Lords Commissioners of Trade & Plantations were highly offended thereat & weighing the injustice as well as its consequences thereof
… & then … Addressed the Crown … that this Law would deprive the Roman Catholics even of the Private use of their Religion, *& that the Rigorous
Execution of the Said Act would in a great measure tend to depopulate … her
Majestys profitable Colony.*…

The Queen & Council, as well as the Lords Commissioners & Bishop of
London, thought there was a wide disparity between England & Maryland;
so that what might [be] Treason there, might be both Innocent & Lawful
here; …

I conclude, that as Liberty of Religion with an equal Share in all Privileges laid the first Foundation of this Province, & brought it to perfection, So I hope that all [devoted?] to this Province will contribute all they can to continue & preserve the same, Since all things are best preserved by the same means by which they were first produced!

36

"We Have ... All Liberty Imaginable in the Exercise of Our Business": Growth of the Catholic Community in Penn's Colony, 1741

Henry Neale (1702–48), from one of the oldest Catholic families of Maryland, had been among the gentry children sent abroad for a Catholic education in the Lowlands. Like scores of other Maryland transplants, Neale entered the Society of Jesus. In 1740 he was assigned to the Pennsylvania portion of the Maryland Mission. Philadelphia represented a new phase of the English Jesuits' mission in America: the beginning of an urban ministry. In the following letter written to his provincial superior in England, how does Neale find this urban environment affecting his particular mission? What else is distinctive about the Pennsylvania segment of the Maryland Mission?

Letter of Henry Neale, SJ, to Henry Shire, SJ, April 25, 1741*

Since my arrival, I've made it my business to inform myself of the situation of affairs in these parts as far as may be worthy your attention.

I am sorry to find things otherwise than represented in England; I mean as to what regards a competent maintenance of one in my station. For an annuity of £20 only will not absolutely suffice. I was told this by our gentlemen in Maryland, and find it so in effect. Most necessaries of life are here as dear, and several dearer, than at London itself. The gentleman who proposed £20

---

* Hughes, *History*, Documents, vol. 1, part 1 (New York: Longmans, Green, 1908), 342–44.

as a tolerable sufficiency says he meant it in regard of a German who, he supposed, would spend the greatest part of his time among his countrymen, and meet with assistance from them, being to be but now and then in town. But for one who is to have his abode in town, as I must, he himself declares it will no wise suffice. Among other expenses I must of necessity keep a horse, in order to assist poor people up and down the country, some twenty miles, some sixty, some farther off. For, at present, [Father Greaton][9] is sufficient for the service of the town (tho' 'tis a growing congregation, and will in all likelihood soon require both more hands and a larger house). Now, traveling expenses in my regard will be considerable, since little or nothing can be expected from the country Catholics, who, tho' very numerous, are most of them servants or poor tradesmen, and more in need oftentimes of charity themselves, than capable of assisting others. To be short, Sir, I wish I could make £30 do. Tho' every body I advise with assures me £40 annuity is as little as I can reasonable propose to live and act with. The gentleman [Greaton] who lives here, tho' he has made a thousand shifts to assist this poor congregation, has never made things meet under thirty pounds sterling a year, including the charities he was obliged to; tho' he never was at the expenses of keeping a horse. The rising of our country currency, which is now within a trifle of 33½ per cent. from sterling, contributes not a little to render a sterling annuity less valuable.

I have spent no little pains in considering myself and consulting friends, about the most advantageous methods of making a settlement according to your proposals. And, as things are at present, a purchase of land seems evidently the best and securest establishment that can be made, both for present and future views. Several tracts of land have been lately sold for double the price they were bought for a few years ago. And a valuable tract may now be purchased for eight hundred or a thousand pounds, yet in a few years will in all probability be held at two or three thousand. Nor is there any difficulty of our purchasing now, tho' there may be perhaps afterward. If this proposal of a land establishment seems suitable to your inclination, I shall make it my business, with the advice of friends, to seek out a place that may be answerable to the end you propose; and beg you'll acquaint me your sentiments hereupon as soon as possible; as also what sum you think proper to

9. Joseph Greaton, who had opened the mission in Philadelphia in 1729 and was responsible for the early development of Catholicism in the colony, including the recruiting of German Jesuits.

advance, and on whom we may draw for the same, in case we should light upon a place to advantage.

We have at present all liberty imaginable in the exercise of our business, and are not only esteemed but reverenced, as I may say, by the better sort of people....

The German gentlemen [Schneider and Wappeler] are not yet arrived. Their presence is very much wanted. My heart has yearned when I've met with some poor Germans desirous of performing their duties, but whom I have not been able to assist for want of language. I hope in a short time I shall be able to give you a more ample account of many particulars, being as yet almost stranger in these parts.

37

"In the Desert Parts of America": Joseph Mosley's Correspondence with His Family in England, 1758–1773[*]

Joseph Mosley (1731–87) was from an old Catholic family in Lincolnshire, a traditional re-cusant stronghold in Northern England. In 1742 as an eleven-year-old, Mosley acquired an alias (Joseph Frambeck), a common practice for those sent across the channel for a Catholic education. He was at St. Omers for six years before entering the Jesuit novitiate at Watten in 1748. Less than a decade later he volunteered for the Maryland Mission. He spent the rest of his life as a missionary in Maryland, first for seven years in the Catholic heartland of Charles and St. Mary's counties, then on its frontier on the Eastern Shore for nearly a quar-ter century. He discovered a Maryland that was far from the "best poor man's country" that George Alsop had extolled a century earlier in urging the young of all classes to seek their fortunes in Lord Baltimore's colony. Mosley himself saw at close hand the miserable lot that indentured servitude had become by the mid-eighteenth century: the slave-like conditions that marked their term of servitude and the absence of any prospects once they were le-gally freed.

If life as a circuit rider in backwater Southern Maryland was harsh enough for Mosley,

* Mosley Papers, GULBFCSC; Hughes, *History*, vol. 1, part 1, 328–30.

the primitive Eastern Shore took an even worse toll on both soul and body of an itinerant clergyman. Still he endured, overcoming lack of means and companions as well as chronic kidney stones to give Catholicism an institutional footprint in the Shore's lower portion when he opened St. Joseph's Mission in Talbot County near the Wye River in 1765. For the next two decades, Joseph Mosley was the face of Catholicism through most of the region. During the quarter century plus that Mosley labored in Maryland, he maintained, as best he could, a correspondence with his siblings, his brother Michael, a priest in England, and his married sister, Helen Dunn, in Northumberland, whom he had last seen when he left home for St. Omers in 1741. What changes, if any, in his opinions about Maryland, its people, and his own calling does his family correspondence over the years reveal?

Joseph Mosley to Helen Dunn, London, February 25, 1758

I've arrived safe to London at last. Again I am come to see my own country, from whence I've been, as I may say, banished now above 16 years. I really have not time to descend as far as the North to see you. So I write you this parting Letter according to my promise. I set off for America the 10th of next month; not to be banished from my own country for only 16 years, but for Love of God and the conversion of souls, to abandon it and you for always: nothing but what I've mentioned should ever have brought me to it, for if I consider things according to the Law of Nature, what can indulge it more than to live at home amongst our own friends and relations: but if we examine for what we were born, it was not to give way to the whole Law of Nature, but according to every one's call let the Law of Nature be ruled and governed by the Law of Grace. This I write that you may not condemn my undertaking, which was entirely my own choice. For if I consider the call of my state of life with which God has blessed me, I am not in all things to follow what is even innocently delightful, but to seek what tends more to the honour and glory of God.... [F]or my part, I think that seeing one another is of little satisfaction, unless our lives are such that we may see one another in a happy eternity: when there we meet, we meet for ever. In this life nothing is certain, but that we must sooner or later separate: So, now let it be Adieu, Sister—when we meet again, it will be never to have the pain of separating again....

Joseph Mosley to Helen Dunn, Newtown, September 8, 1758

I arrived safe and sound to Maryland on June 19, after a long and tedious voyage of ten weeks. I find here business enough on my hands in my Way of Trade,—I've care of above fifteen hundred souls: we stand in need here of Labourers, if more only had zeal enough to come to our assistance: for myself, I can say, that I preferred this place to any I knew, and I hope to spend my life and whole strength, I think it the happiest place in the world, and I also find it so, for one of our calling. No Prince in his Court can have more satisfaction and enjoy himself more, than I do in instructing those that are under my charge. I am daily on horseback, visiting the sick, comforting the infirm, strengthening the pusillanimous, &c And I enjoy my health as yet as well. As if I were breathing my own native air.

Joseph Mosley to Helen Dunn, Newtown, September 1, 1759

You desire a short account of this part of America. The climate is very hot and sultry in summer to a great excess nay several West-Indians that lay under the very sun tell me, that they find it warmer here than there: the winter is not so cold as in England: the changes of weather is a prodigious sudden— ... The country is the best laid out for trade of any in the world. The Rivers are spacious & wide.... Ships by those rivers can sail above 200 miles up into the country. Our greatest commodity, you know, is tobacco.... The people seem to me to be very poor, and not to be compared in Riches to the rest of our colonies....

Our horses are almost all natural pacers, they will easily go ... a whole day without food, at the rate of 7, 8, 9 miles an hour, in a constant pace: which is a great comfort to us in our way of life. The buildings in this country are very poor and insignificant, all only one story, commonly all the buildings made of wood plastered within,—a brick chimney in the better houses. You may find a brick house here and there: our Body[10] commonly has them. The poorer people have nothing but a few boards nailed together, without plastering, or any brick about it. Very few houses have glass windows.

Now I look upon myself out of the world in the desert parts of America, yet don't think that I am tired of my situation. I am here as content as a King, and never shall desire a change if I can keep my health and be of service; I

10. The Society of Jesus in Maryland.

allow our fatigues are very great, our journeys very long, our rides constant and extensive. We have many to attend, and few to attend them. I often ride about 300 miles a week, and never a week but I ride 150, or 200: and in our way of living, we ride almost as much by night as by day, in all weathers, in heats, cold, rain, frost or snow. Several may think the colds, rains, &c, to be the worst to ride in, but, I think to ride in the heats far surpasses all, both for man and horse.

Joseph Mosley to Helen Dunn, Newtown, October 5, 1760

I received the Favour of yours last Night, as I returned Home from a long Ride of three Days.... I can't say that my health is at present so good as it has been; for a ride of 52 miles in the rain, and another of the same length in a warm day all in the sun, cast me into violent fevers attended with constant vomitings: but, thanks be to God, I am upon the recovering hand....

This year has gone very hard with us; the rains have caused a great many diseases, and to us a great many rides. Our Hands are few, weak, and in great decay. Our rides are often twice a day: yet, I've often in a week rid between 50 & 60 miles a day. It's true, our horses in this country go so easy that a ride of 50 miles, perhaps, won't tire a man so much as 20 or 30 with your horses in England; yet, they are so frequent, that it is enough to break the strongest constitution....

I recommend myself to all your good prayers in this Life I lead, banished into the remotest corner of the world, amongst Indians, Negroes and Slaves, and separated by the Atlantic from my dearest friend: yet, notwithstanding all this, perhaps the happiest man that breathes: for, if true happiness consists in a contented mind, never did it reign more true than in this Blessed country.

Joseph Mosley to Michael Mosley, Portobacco, July 30, 1764

The method of our lives seems to give you some uneasiness for us.[11] I think you may be easy, as you reckon our deaths will be precious in the sight of God.... I am sure that our multitude of fatigues and oppressive labours, as you are pleased to style them, will be abundantly rewarded. You hope, I'll be a better steward of a life, not at my disposal: but it is at God's, and he is

11. Michael Mosley, also a Jesuit, was a private chaplain to the Acton family in Shropshire.

welcome to it, to spend it in the service of my fellow-creatures, or Brethren in Christ. My crown won't be the less for having labored the longer, it's true, if you and I can agree about the word *labour*. *Consummatus in brevi* will sooner have your approbation than *Puer centum annorum*, or *Longam vitam injusti*.[12] I know you have good sense, and are a great Master of Divinity, and *argue well by means* of both in favour of prudence and discretion: yet, to my comfort, He who came to destroy and confound the prudence of the prudent, and the wisdom of the wise, labored but three years amidst indefatigable hardships and insupportable miseries and wants for our example, and died, "a folly to the Gentiles": and the great Xaverius,[13] the glory of our Society, trod in his footsteps, in an immense field, where he was yet much needed, died after ten years labour and fatigue: Fr. Campion[14] was cut off in the very first year of his great undertakings. To be numbered amongst this glorious Company is beyond all my pretension, *et non tali me dignor honore*:[15] if I could follow them, although *non passibus aequis*[16] would be the very summit of all my zeal and ambition. As to the circumstance of long fasting (which you can't well comprehend in the details of our labours), I am afraid you never will understand by any explication I can give: Theory will never do; experience may convince you, to your cost, of all I said. "Have our people we visit neither eatables nor drinkables?" "Do they live on the air?" So much I know, as to the first demand, that I've asked, when I've been almost fainting, for a mouthful of bread, or a glass of milk, and I could not get it. As for bread, few or none ever use it in this country: what they eat with their meat is a sort of hasty-pudding made of Indian corn, which they term *Mush*.... This Indian corn they turn into different shapes, to supply the place of bread: but, in none, does it agree with an English constitution. As to the second demand, of living on the air. I know not, let them answer for themselves.... I've often taken with me, as you suggest in yours, a crust of English bread, as we term it here, to support foreseen wants.... As for saddlebags, it's true we have them, but they are too cumbersome to be troubled with them, in our frequent long rides, and too apt to heat our horses, whose ease we chiefly consult, even more than our own. Here, perhaps, you'll object *prudence*: but, while I favour my horse, I think I consult my own ad-

---

12. Mosley is suggesting, in a brotherly way, that Michael, when all is said and done, would much prefer him to accomplish much in a brief time than to be an eternal adolescent or old scoundrel.

13. Francis Xavier.   14. Edmund Campion.
15. "I am not worthy of such an honor."   16. "Not at the same pace."

vantage, for one night in the woods under our treacherous air, would be of worse consequence with us, than twenty without supper.... You advise me to change my clothes on those occasions when wet, or to have a Fire to dry them.... [O]ur Chapels ... are in great Forests some miles from any House of Hospitality: As for Fire, the Weather in Summer is far too warm to come nigh one, or to ask for one in that season, would be like a man in a warm oven, asking for a Fire to be at the mouth of it, to dry his clothes, ...

As for our present labours, they are more or less the same as I've acquainted you, and the accidents of life as various. Swamps, runs, miry holes, lost in the night, as yet, and ever will in this country attend us: thank God.... Between 3 or 400 mile was my last Mass fare, on one horse.... I am just leaving Portobacco[17] to go to Bohemia, where they tell me I am wanted. The Congregations are fewer, but the rides much longer. On the 1st Sunday, 50 mile, where I pass the whole week in that neighborhood, in close business with the ignorant. On the 2nd, I go down to Chesapeake Bay, 40 mile farther, which makes me 90 mile from home: the other two Sundays are easier. The Mission has picked me out to settle a place between these two, if I can, to make it an easier Miss[io]n. Pray that I may succeed; I shall have at Bohemia a fair plantation to manage, the best, I believe, we have, and nigh Philadelphia, which is a vast advantage.

Joseph Mosley to Helen Dunn, Tuckahoe, Talbot County, October 14, 1766

I was deputed in August, 1764, to settle a new place in the midst of this Mission: accordingly I set off for those parts of the country; I examined the situation of every Congregation within 60 mile of it: and, before the end of that year, I came across the very spot, as Providence would have it, with land to be sold, nigh the centre of the whole that was to be tended. I purchased the land, and took possession, in March following. On the land there were three buildings, a miserable dwelling-house, a much worse for some negroes, and a house to cure tobacco in. My dwelling-house was nothing but a few boards riven from oak trees, not sawed plank, and these nailed together to keep out the coldest air: not one brick or stone about it, no plastering, and no chimney, but a little hole in the roof to let out the smoke. In this I lived till the winter, when I got it plastered to keep off the cold, and built a brick chimney;

17. The Jesuit plantation, St. Thomas Manor, in Charles County, Maryland.

the bricks I was obliged to buy and cart above five mile.... I have now my cows, my sheep, hogs, turkeys, geese, and other dunghill fowl: I've my own grain, and make my own bread. In fine, I had a thousand other difficulties to go through, which at present I can't call to mind and which then took up all my time and thoughts, exclusive of all the hardships and fatigues of a very laborious mission: but, thank God, I have had and have at present my health as well as ever I had it in my life, and I think this inland situation suits my constitution better than the waterside, and if it was not for a few gray hairs on my head, you would never know by my present health, the long fasts, fatiguing rides and restless nights, that I've already undergone. My brother Mick tells you, that we need not expose ourselves to the dangers and hardships we do.... His advice is good, when it can be followed: but, in the circumstances we are in, what part of our labours can we cut off, without neglecting our duty.... It's fine talking over the fireside: but, it's what I can't practice, when the circumstances occur.

Joseph Mosley to Helen Dunn, Tuckahoe, June 5, 1772

I received your favour of Febry 28, 1771, on March 23, 1772, after it had wandered thro' the world for better, than a year.... It grieves me, Dr. Sister, to hear of the loss, you've had in Mr. Dunn....

I once saw the cousin of ours ... about 3 years ago.... He had been with you at the Devine Service & Prayers on the Sunday, & that's all I could find that he had ever practiced in our Religion. Such ignorant youths appear with Disgrace abroad. He was sold to a Protestant who gave him to his daughter in marriage, to be her Hair-dresser. Wm Heath, his 2d Master by Marriage, is a fallen Catholic, & as severe as ever he would have met with. It was under this master that I saw him, who soon had taught him to repent of his Folly in leaving England.... Dear Sister, I must give you an insight of the Nature of an imported Servant, indented here to be sold, 1st an indented Servant must be publicly sold, for a Slave, for the term of years signed in his Indenture, which brings him for that Term of Years on a footing with our Negro Slaves, 2dly, they have no choice of Master, but the highest Bidder at public Sale, carries them off, to be used at his Mercy, without any Redress at law, 3dly These Masters ... are in general cruel, barbarous, & unmerciful, some worse than others, 4thly the Servants labour is chiefly in the field, with an ox, plow, or Hoe, with an overseer by them, armed with a cudgel, to drive them on with their Work, 5ly Their diet is mean & poor, chiefly some composition of our Indian corn, which at best is very strong & ill savour'd to an European Taste, & I think more fit for Horses & Hogs, than Xtians altho' in my Missions, I've made many a heartily meal of it. Lastly, & what is the worst of all, for Roman Catholics; by the law of Maryland every indented Servant must take the Oath on Landing, & the Captains of ships pay 5£ for each servant. A Law invented to hinder the Importation of Catholic Servants. The Captains of ships, before landing use the utmost Rigour with them to bring them to it.[18] Many have told me that they have, for trifling faults, been severely whipt to bring them to that one Point. Most are brought to it by threats & promises before they come to anchor. I beg of you, to use all your Interest, to hinder any of your acquaintance, especially of our Persuasion, from shipping themselves to America; they will bitterly repent it, when it is too late. Masters of ships may sing them fine Canterbury Stories of this wild Country, but as a Friend they may believe me, as being an Eye-witness of what I say, & advance. It has been a fine poor man's country, but now it is well peopled, the lands are all secured, & the Harvest for such is now all over. The Lands are mostly worked by the Land-Lord's Negroes, & of consequence white servants after their term of Bondage is out, are strolling about the Country without Bread....

I am as yet on my new settlement of Tuckahoe ... tending the most laborious Mission we have (more by Reason of the length of the Rides in a dispersed Flock, than the Number of them) has at last entailed on me an ailment that I shall never get clear of. I mean violent Paroxysms or Fits of the Gravel and Stone ... riding whole Days in excessive Heats, the use of bad Water, salt meats (the standing meats of this hot climate), bad accommodations, violent colds, poor open lodgings, often out whole Nights in the woods, & Dew, has engendered the tormenting complaints, I am now subject to.... I am loath to give up & quit, yet two or three more such Fits as I've had, will either force me to it, or finish me. Last June, I was desired to attend at Philadelphia with all speed. Philadelphia, from my house, is 110 miles. On a Sunday, after prayers to my Congregation, I set off after one o'clock, P.M, taking at my house a light refreshment of a few dishes of tea. The day was excessive hot, and I arrived that evening at Bohemia, 50 miles.... The next day, we went to Philadelphia, 60 miles, a very sultry day, where after some necessary excursions into the country, I returned home again in two days,

18. Taking the oath.

the weather being very warm. On my return, after a constant ride in June and July in the heats of the year of about 430 miles, I was seized with a violent fit of the gravel:[19] I've had several small fits since, but none so violent. That particular fit held me ten days, without any respite, ease or sleep, night or day. If all the caution I now use prove unsuccessful, I must quit, and see my native country once more, which I never intended. God's will be done. If I can't ride, I should be here an unprofitable servant. Horsemen are little needed in Flanders or in England.

Joseph Mosley to Helen Dunn, Tuckahoe, July 5, 1773

I've had as yet no violent return of the gravel, or as the physicians call it, a paroxysm of it. I am forever troubled with a heaviness about my loins and kidneys: if it is a stone, I've reason to dread the next paroxysm or motion of it. I am in all other respects as well as I ever was in my life; some few precautions I take have been of great service to me in that complaint, as well as in my health in general. Long rides, night and day, I can't avoid, to comply with my calls and duty. I know they hurt me, but God's will be done. This last winter, I was riding the whole night to the sick, three or four times, as I remember. One night in particular, in a ride of sixty-four miles, raining from the first jump of my own door till I returned, to a sick person that is as yet alive and little wanted me. It was the third ride I've had to that same man, three successive winters. He lives in a little hovel of his own. How I fared for any comforts there, you may well guess. I returned through the rain, next day, with no sleep, victuals or drink, except bad water.... I could tell you of a thousand other uncomfortable accidents of this kind, that happen often to us, which would make you pity us.... I can't as yet hear of quitting my stand; he is a cowardly soldier that quits it. He that puts his hand to the plough and looks back is not the man for Christ's service. When I am unfit, and a burden, I'll listen then to an invalid's berth; a berth that I can never wish for.

Joseph Mosley to Helen Dunn, November 5, 1773

The gravel ... has growled much this Fall, yet, thank God, it has not come to a set Fit of it, or a Paroxysm, as Doctors call it. It has made me very stiff in the small of the Back, with sharp Pains there when I move, stoop or bend,

19. Kidney stone.

if I sit for a while, it takes me some time before I can get straight, it's with great Pain I buckle my Shoes. Dear Sister God's Blessed Will be done. In this my broken State, I'll acquaint you what I can still do. I tend 8 Congregations, one at home & seven abroad. It takes two months to go there.... These Rides with the frequent calls to the Sick into these Congregations, & often beyond our Places of Meeting on Sunday, are sufficient for an able man, I can & do perform them, therefore I am yet an able Man. I am like an old Woman, grumble much & do much.

Sources

Burnard, Trevor. *Creole Gentlemen: The Maryland Elite, 1691–1776.* New York: Routledge, 2002.

Hardy, Beatriz Betancourt. "Women and the Catholic Church in Maryland, 1689–1776." *MHM* 94 (Winter 1999): 397–418.

Heinz, Helen. "'We Are All as One Fish in the Sea': Catholicism in Protestant Pennsylvania, 1730–1790." Ph.D. diss., Temple University, 2008.

Hughes, Thomas. *History.* Documents. Vol. 1, part 1. New York: Longmans, Green, 1908.

Linck, Joseph C. *Fully Instructed and Vehemently Influenced: Catholic Preaching in Anglo-Colonial America.* Philadelphia: St. Joseph's University Press, 2002.

Pyne, Tricia T. "Ritual and Practice in the Maryland Catholic Community, 1634–1776." *USCH* 26 (Spring 2008): 17–46.

Schwartz, Sally. "A Mixed Multitude: The Struggle for Toleration in Colonial Pennsylvania." Ph.D. diss., New York University, 1987.

Part 8

Clash of Families and Empires

1739–1766

*T*HE ANTI-CATHOLICISM that John Hart had epitomized died down in Maryland with his departure. Yet throughout America, the anti-Catholic virus persisted, if below the surface in many places, including Maryland. It persisted largely because it had become an important factor for English identity. To be English was to be anti-Catholic or, put positively, Protestant. That equation applied on both sides of the Atlantic. Protestantism was as much an integral part of the American character as it was of the English. To maintain the purity of that character, interested observers began to urge the application of England's penal laws regarding Catholics to her American colonies. The law itself would establish Protestants as the only true citizens within British domains (see "Absolutely Necessary to Restrain Roman Catholics by Law").

Ironically, a reverse pattern developed in Maryland, where the majority of the Catholic population in British America lived. Following the departure in 1720 of Governor-General John Hart and the death of his arch-antagonist

Charles Carroll the Settler, a détente was implicitly struck between the Maryland Catholic minority and the dominant Protestant majority. So long as the Catholics accepted their lower status in provincial society—that is, no political participation and private practice of their religion—Protestant authorities would not enforce the penal laws against them. For three decades this odd bargain was observed. Then in the spring of 1751, the religious peace was shattered. A committee of the lower house of the assembly reported on the disturbing institutional growth of the Catholic Church in Maryland, driven by the ever increasing wave of German and Irish Catholic immigrants and made more ominous by the encroachment of other Catholic forces—the French and their Indian allies—on the province's backcountry. All these trends pointed to the Catholic community in Maryland becoming "a dangerous intestine enemy" … "manifestly prejudicial to the Protestant Interest." It was imperative, the committee concluded, that the colony, for its own self-preservation, had to put new penal laws on the statute books as well as to enforce the ones already there.[1]

A family dispute was at the root of this peace breaker. Charles Carroll of Annapolis and his surgeon cousin of the same name had become co-executors of the estate of another cousin, James Carroll, who had died in 1729. Part of the estate was to go to two Irish nephews, both of whom in the interim had become Catholic priests. For two decades the legacies to the nephews remained unsettled. Dr. Carroll, who controlled them, had been using the funds as if they were his own. At the same time the ambitious Dr. Carroll had renounced his Catholic faith and rapidly made his way up the political establishment of the province. When Charles Carroll of Annapolis pressed his cousin to make good, not only on the legacy but on the interest that had accrued over the past twenty-plus years, the doctor utilized his considerable political connections to have the Committee on Grievances reopen the topic of the threat that the "growth of popery" represented to the province. It was a desperate but quite effective defense.

Having put in motion the penal machinery of the province, Dr. Carroll proceeded to declare that he was powerless to award James Carroll's legacy to two individuals who as Roman Catholic priests were barred by Maryland law from receiving any inheritance. His cousin was not about to allow this self-serving maneuver to stand. Charles Carroll of Annapolis posted a notice on the front door of the statehouse, the most public place possible, in a

1. *AM* 46:549–50.

manifesto that accused Dr. Carroll of orchestrating the pending penal legislation in order to conceal his embezzlement of the greater part of his nephews' legacy. The House of Delegates promptly ordered the Catholic Carroll confined to his home in Annapolis to prevent any further demonstrations. The lower body of the assembly passed the desired legislation and sent the governor, Samuel Ogle, along with the bill, a request that, in the future, he appoint "none but faithful Protestant Subjects" to any government post ("places of Trust and profit").[2] That produced two petitions from prominent Catholics, including Carroll, reminding the executive of the informal agreement that Maryland Catholics and provincial rulers had struck in 1720; the act the lower house had passed was a direct violation of that understanding. The petitions carried the day with the governor and his council. The bill died in the upper chamber.

Three years later there was a new governor, Horatio Sharpe, and, with the French and Indian seizure of Fort Necessity just above Maryland's northwestern border, an undeclared war. The House of Delegates took up a measure that not only extended much of England's corpus of penal legislation to Maryland, but added a ban on landowning by priests (see "The Insolence and Disaffection of Papists within This Province").

The new act "to prevent the growth of Popery" did not satisfy the anti-Catholic forces in Maryland, particularly as war with Catholic France seemed increasingly inevitable. No Jesuit manors or properties were seized for the simple reason that no Jesuit held legal title to any land in the province. Eight years earlier, the Jesuit superior had put all of the Society's property in Maryland into the trust of a layman, in order to prevent any such happening. Even though the bill authorized the appropriation of Jesuit property held in trust, implementing it proved a more challenging matter. Still many were more than willing to show how it could be done (see "[Catholics] Can Never Be Faithful Subjects").

As Great Britain and France maneuvered in the mid-1750s toward renewing what, since the 1690s, had become virtually a permanent state of war between the two powers in both Europe and North America, Nova Scotia was perhaps the greatest flashpoint for violence in the latter theater. This strategic territory, since 1713, had been split between the two empires, with the French controlling Île Royale (Cape Breton Island) and the British the main peninsula. Most of the inhabitants on that peninsula were Acadians,

2. AM 46:594.

descendants of French settlers and indigenous people. From the time they assumed jurisdiction over Nova Scotia, the British had made periodic attempts to relocate the French-speaking Acadians, but few responded to the offers to leave. Nor would they take the unconditional oath of loyalty that the British insisted all permanent residents take.

When the French seized Fort Necessity in western Virginia from a British colonial force in the summer of 1754, the British retaliated by attacking a French fort that guarded the entrance to the Canadian mainland from Nova Scotia. When the stronghold surrendered to the British expeditionary force in June of 1755, some of the French defenders turned out to be Acadians. They were allowed to return to their homes, but had to give up their arms, as were all Acadians in the territory ordered to do. Then came news of the disastrous defeat of General Edward Braddock's army in Pennsylvania. That shock seemed to tip the scales against the Acadians, whom the British already regarded as their greatest internal security threat in North America. The British governor on Nova Scotia ordered the Acadians to be expelled from their homeland (see "One of the Greatest Things That Ever the English Did in America").

By ruse and/or force some 7,000 were put on ships to be distributed willy-nilly among the colonies to the south. Three years later, after the French fortress on Cape Breton fell, an additional 3,000 Acadians were removed, this time to France. The several thousand who managed to escape the dragnets found themselves stripped of all they possessed: homes burned, animals seized or destroyed, lands taken over by New Englanders or Scots. By the end, an estimated 10,000 Acadians had died, victims of disease, starvation, or their own futile resistance to this "greatest" undertaking of the British in North America.

The undeclared war that France and Great Britain had been waging became a formal one in 1756. The Seven Years' War brought to a climax the anti-Catholic agitation that had been surging in Maryland for the past five years. All the suspicions about the loyalty of the Catholic community became much more plausible in a war where the foe was a Catholic imperial power whose soldiers and their Indian allies were on the province's frontier. The lower house of the Maryland Assembly passed several laws that imposed prohibitive fines upon Catholic clergy for proselytizing or (for foreign-born priests) merely preaching. All priests had to post a £500 bond, which they would forfeit by any actions that raised questions about their loyalty. The upper chamber failed to support any of these measures, but the delegates found a clever way to penalize Catholics by making the measure part of an act funding the war. To help the province provide its share for the prosecution of the war, the delegates voted to double-tax the property of Catholics on the dubious ground that since Catholics did not serve in the militia, they needed to provide due support for the war by bearing more of its financial burden (as though Catholics were not serving in the military out of choice).

This kind of economic warfare was nothing new with the lower house. Previous attempts to employ this kind of punitive legislation had always foundered in the upper chamber of Maryland's assembly, which had become the Catholics' protector in government. To ensure the continuation of that pattern a group of Catholic leaders submitted a formal petition to the council listing all the reasons they should not approve such a bill. The upper body shocked the Catholic community by supporting the double-tax provision and passing it on to Governor Sharpe for his signature.

The Catholics turned their appeal to the governor (see "They Did Not Fly from Penal Laws"). Besides presenting the petition, four Catholic leaders, including Charles Carroll, secured a meeting with Governor Sharpe, who assured them he had no such bill on his desk. It was a lie, as the Catholics shortly found out once he signed the measure into law.

The Catholic leadership had not played its last card. The proprietor himself had continued to show an openness to the Catholic community, even after Benedict Calvert had made his opportunistic conversion to the Church of England in 1713. They would make their ultimate appeal to him. For that task they turned to a Jesuit, as had another group of Catholic leaders thirty-five years earlier. George Hunter, like Peter Attwood before him, was the superior of the Maryland Mission. Like his predecessor, Hunter had a command of the province's history, in particular the fundamental rights that the proprietor and the assembly had enacted by law for all settlers, including Catholics, and an understanding of how Maryland thrived economically and socially under that dispensation. Hunter became the spokesman for restoring Catholics to their rightful place in the province and made the trip across the Atlantic to make, on behalf of the Catholic community, a personal plea to the proprietor. In it Hunter stressed the persistent loyalty that Maryland Catholics had displayed over the past half century, despite all the discriminatory laws and treatment during that time. Even during the present conflict with France, Catholics, although barred from bearing arms themselves, had contributed to the war effort "prodigiously beyond their proportion" of the province's population.[3]

Despite the well-organized Catholic lobbying, Lord Baltimore, like his governor, fearful of his veto igniting a populist, war-inspired backlash, signed the double-tax bill. For Charles Carroll of Annapolis, the proprietor's cowardly compliance was an alienating reprise of the shameful treatment his father had endured from an earlier Calvert. It led him to consider what George Hunter had warned the proprietor about: Catholics deserting Maryland because of the persecution the state was legally waging against them. For Carroll that meant moving to the French colony of Louisiana, with its much more promising prospects for Catholics trapped in British America. That was the advice he had for his son, Charley, still pursuing the European education his father had meticulously mapped out for him.

Beginning in the 1680s an education in English recusant schools in the low countries became a major part of the coming-of-age experience for Maryland's Catholic elite. The Carroll family's connection with St. Omers and the other institutions in this English Catholic network long antedated their settlement in Maryland. Charles Carroll, the grandson of Charles Carroll the Settler, was among the hundreds of sons and daughters of Maryland Catholic gentry who were sent across the Atlantic for their education during the period of benign neglect of the penal laws from the 1720s to the 1750s. None had their formation so rigorously planned out for him as did the young Carroll by his father. Despite the vocational limits, particularly in the political realm, placed upon Catholics in Maryland, Charles Carroll of Annapolis wanted to give his son the best possible preparation for building upon the remarkable economic success that had made the elder Carroll, like his father before him, the richest man in the province. But the anti-Catholic developments in the 1750s, culminating with the proprietor's failure to protect the Catholics against the double tax, had badly shaken the senior Carroll (see "Remember the Cruel Usage of the Roman Catholics").

After peaking during the Seven Years' War, anti-Catholicism waned in the 1760s. Some elements of the anti-popery movement endured, however, particularly in places like New England, where Catholics had no significant presence. There anti-Catholicism became a means toward reaching a greater

3. MPA, Box 3, folder 12, GULBFCSC, printed in *WL* 10 (1881): 14–21.

end. Pope's Night, which had originated in British America in the seven-teenth century as Guy Fawkes Day, an occasional celebration of the thwart-ing of the notorious Gunpowder Plot in November 1605, by the eighteenth century had become an annual occasion of unity building within New Eng-land and New York by the ritual parading and execution in effigy of their common enemies (see "Brave Youths, Drag on Your Pope").

38

"Absolutely Necessary to Restrain Roman Catholics by Law": *Some Thoughts Upon America and Upon the Danger from Roman Catholics There*, London, 1739[*]

The following broadside well illustrates the nexus between religion and national identity that Protestants were increasingly invoking. Promoting Protestant immigration to the American colonies and minimizing any Catholic influx, the author proclaims, is the key to the development of a secure and prosperous America. On what ground(s) does the author base his as-sertion that Catholics ultimately cannot be permitted to have an equal place in either English or American society? How best to assure that that equilibrium will never occur?

As I am, in every sense, *an* Englishman, and fixed in this Kingdom, I cannot help wishing, that our Plantations may be made as secure, and as serviceable and beneficial, as possible, to their Mother-Country....

It is now felt, that our Colonies would deal with us much further, and would take off vastly more of our Manufactures, which they stand in absolute necessity of, had they but wherewithal to make Returns, and pay for the same.

In hopes, therefore, that we shall, now in these our Days, see the things which belong to our true Interest, it has given me great Pleasure to see a Bill brought into Parliament, for naturalizing Foreign *Protestants, who have or* shall settle in our Colonies in *America*: A Scheme so well adapted to in-crease the Wealth and Strength of our Colonies, (and consequently of this

[*] Broadsides Collection, GULBFCSC.

Nation) that I think it cannot fail of producing those good Ends; since it is most undoubtedly true, that the Lenity of *Our Government*, the Purity of our Religion, the benefit of our Laws, the Advantages of our Trade, and the Security of our Property, left no *Other* Inducement wanting, *but that*, to invite vast Numbers of Foreigners to flock to our Colonies; and whoever lives a few Years, may reasonably hope to see an extraordinary Concourse of Foreigners to our Plantations, as the Consequence of that good and salutary Bill.

I BEFORE told you that I was, in every sense an Englishman, and I will add thereto, if it be necessary, that I am a *Protestant*, and, as such, was extremely glad to see, that the Great Privilege proposed to be given *by that Bill*, was confined to *Protestants* only.

BUT I carefully observed, that no *Roman Catholic* in our Colonies can claim the particular Privilege *thereby* allowed to others; and, indeed, no surer Ground-work could be laid for the Loss and Destruction of our Colonies, than to encourage the Resort of *Roman Catholics* thither.

MUCH do I fear, that the *other* Advantages recited in that Bill, (which *Roman Catholics*, as well as all others, are already entitled to in our Colonies) may have already been, and may continue to be ... powerful Motives and Inducements to many *Roman Catholics to resort* thither, which might be of the utmost Danger to our Settlements in *America*, as there are great Numbers of *French Roman Catholics on the back of all our colonies*.

I UTTERLY detest *Persecution*, on account of *Private Sentiments* in Religion; but there is a wide Difference between *that* and nursing up a Set of People who are infatuated till they believe it their *Duty* to cut our Throats, in return, and that 'tis meritorious, and even doing Honour and Service to the All-merciful God, for them so to do. ...

Considering the Number of our separate Provinces in *America*, each distinct from, and independent of, the others, (and which very thing, in other respects, may be of great benefit to this Kingdom) 'tis scarcely to be expected that any one, regular System, with regard to the *Roman Catholics*, should be established or observed *throughout all* those distinct Provinces, unless the restrictive Laws, made in *Great Britain* with respect to *Roman Catholics*, were by one short and general Law to be passed here, extended to all our Colonies and Plantations in *America*, which always were intended to be, and in such fundamental Points always ought to be, just upon the same Footing.

THIS Nation has found it *absolutely necessary* to restrain *Roman Catholics by Law*.

"The Insolence and Disaffection of Papists within This Province": An Act for the Security of His Majesty's Dominion, and to Prevent the Growth of Popery within This Province, May 30, 1754 *

The new governor of the colony, Horatio Sharpe, had brought with him a reputation of being sympathetic to Catholics. Whatever instincts he had for vetoing the legislation that the lower house presented him in May of 1754 were more than offset by his fear of offending the Protestant public, which clearly favored the bill. He signed, and the bill went into effect. Why would the government focus its anti-Catholic legislation on the banning of property-owning by priests? How does that address the ominous trends the legislators purport to see regarding Catholics in Maryland?

Whereas the Right Honourable the Earl of Holderness, one of his Majesty's Principal Secretaries of State, … hath signified the March of a large Body of French, to commit Hostilities on his Majesty's Dominions here, and directing him to keep a Correspondence with the other Governors of his Majesty's Territories on this Continent, in Order to concert the needful Means for preventing any evil Consequences therefrom; and, since which, the Indians and French have, not only dispossessed his Majesty's Subjects of Settlements, which they had in the Territory of Virginia, within the King's Dominions, but committed barbarous Murders, and made Prisoners of several Traders, and taken their Effects, and are now actually fortifying themselves in those very Places, from whence they have dispossessed his Majesty's Subjects.

And whereas the Insolence and Disaffection of Papists within this Province, to his Majesty's sacred Person and Government, has been too often manifested by many of them; and as many Popish Priests, and Jesuits, hold sundry large Tracts of Land, Manors, and other Tenements, within the

---

* *AM* 50:514–19.

Province, and on them, or some of them, have Dwellings, where they live and cohabit, as in a collegiate Manner, having public Mass-Houses, where they celebrate their Religious Functions, in the most public Manner, perverting many of his Majesty's dutiful Protestant Subjects to Popery, as also many Servants and Slaves belonging to his Majesty's Protestant Subjects, which from their known Principles, in Church and State, must prove of most dangerous Consequence to his Majesty's Dominion and his Protestant Subjects here, as well as from the vicinity of the French, and their allied Indian Nations, and the manifest Encroachments, making by them, on his Majesty's Territories adjoining to this Province, and the Danger of their being joined and assisted by these our domestic Enemies: To prevent, therefore, such Evils, and the further Growth of Popery, within this Province, it is humbly prayed that it may be enacted, … That all Manors, Lands, Tenements, and Hereditaments, which were vested in any Popish Priest or Jesuit, or Popish Priests, or Jesuits, or reputed Popish Priest or Jesuit, on the first Day of October, in the Year, One Thousand Seven Hundred and Fifty One, or which were held in Trust for such Popish Priest of Jesuit, or reputed Popish Priest or Jesuit, or which were occupied by such Popish Priest or Jesuit, or Popish Priests or Jesuits, or reputed Popish Priests or Jesuits, or by him or them rented out, or by any other Trust for him or them rented out, to under Tenants, on the said first Day of October, One Thousand Seven Hundred and Fifty One, shall and is hereby vested in … Commissioners appointed for that Purpose, and their Successors: …

And it is hereby further Enacted, … That the said Commissioners, … shall and may … from Time to Time … take Depositions of any Person or Persons to the Purposes of this Act, in Order to make the best and fullest Discovery of all Lands and Tenements belonging to Popish Priests or Jesuits within this Province. . . .

And it is hereby further Declared and Enacted, That so soon as may be, after the First Day of October, One Thousand Seven Hundred and Fifty-four, all the said lands and Premises, which did belong to any Popish Priest or Jesuit, or Popish Priests or Jesuits, or were held in Trust for them or him, within the Province … shall be sold by Public Sale to the highest Bidder … and to continue the same full six Weeks. . . .

And the said Commissioners, or the major Part of them, or their Successors … are hereby empowered and directed to tender, to all such Popish Priests or Jesuits, or reputed Popish Priests or Jesuits, the Oaths of Allegiance, Abhorrence and Abjuration, and to require him or them to repeat and subscribe the Test, and ... upon ... Refusal or Non-Appearance of such Popish Priest or Jesuit, when summoned, the same shall be taken as full and conclusive Evidence to prove such Popish Priest or Jesuit, a Popish Recusant Convict, and shall forfeit all his or their Lands, Tenements, and Hereditaments, to the Uses mentioned in this Act.

And it is hereby Declared and Enacted, That it shall not be lawful for any Popish Priest or Jesuit, or any reputed Popish Priest or Jesuit, to hold any Lands or Tenements, either in his own, or their Right, or in Trust for him or them, within this Province, or to keep on such Lands public Mass-Houses, or cohabit in Societies.

40

"[Catholics] Can Never Be Faithful Subjects": A Letter to the Editor of the *Maryland Gazette*, October 17, 1754

Since Jonas Green had acquired the Annapolis weekly in 1745, the *Maryland Gazette* had been waging an on-again, off-again campaign against Maryland's Catholics. With the revival of anti-Catholic legislation in 1754, the editions of the *Gazette* were once again filled with letters and articles expressing concern about the Catholic menace. One such letter follows. The writer is most likely Alexander Malcolm (1685–1763), an accomplished musician and mathematician whose publications in both fields had won for him scholarly prominence in Great Britain and the Continent. It is not known what led him to emigrate in 1731 or 1732 from Scotland to New York, where he opened a free school. In 1740 the Anglican missionary Society for the Propagation of the Gospel in Foreign Parts appointed Malcolm minister to the Anglican Mission in Marblehead, Massachusetts. After nearly a decade in that New England village, Malcolm accepted an invitation from the vestry of the prestigious St. Anne's Church in Annapolis to become their rector. The posting plus the much larger salary must have both been decisive attractions for Malcolm, who had finally married just the year before the offer came from Annapolis.

In Maryland's capital, Malcolm quickly found himself at the heart of the associations and enterprises that were, by mid-century, making Annapolis a benchmark of American cultural and intellectual life. Shortly after arriving in Annapolis, Malcolm had petitioned successfully to join the Tuesday Club, the most exclusive social organization in town. His musical knowledge and prowess as both a violinist and flutist made him instantly important as a member of the musical ensemble, which was a major club activity. Fellow musicians included Jonas Green, the editor of the *Maryland Gazette*, and Daniel Dulany Jr., attorney and politician. Needless to say, there were no Catholic members of this elite group. A little more than a year before this letter appeared in the *Gazette* Malcolm had led a special meeting of the Anglican clergy called to discuss the dangerous growth of "popery" in Maryland. The group of clergymen concluded that Maryland, as a Protestant colony, needed to have its government take appropriate steps to defuse the power of the Jesuits, "those great enemies to the Christian religion and to all virtue."[4]

Malcolm, seeking a less demanding post as a concession to age (he was approaching seventy) asked Governor Horatio Sharpe in the fall of 1753 to be transferred to St. Mary's Parish in Dorchester County on the Eastern Shore. He left Annapolis for his new assignment in June 1754. That Green would have solicited his views on the roiling topic of Catholicism's menacing growth seems a reasonable surmise. More certain is that Green was not disappointed by the response he received. The letter, with all its invective, not only brilliantly summed up the deepest fears about the Catholic menace, but also proffered the legal means to make it toothless. The picture that he drew of Maryland was a Jesuit-infested province awash in their vast estates where the priests, monk-like, banded together in communities to celebrate their superstitious rites and from which to go forth to preach their pernicious doctrines. The Jesuits were about nothing less than recreating in Maryland pre-Reformation monastic England. How does Malcolm propose to meet this threat head-on? Which country is his model for the plan he proposes?

Dear sir,

In Answer to your obliging Letter of September 20, wherein you desire my Sentiments on the Subject of our late Conversation; I must premise, without farther Ceremony, that, in my Opinion, there is no Maxim in Politics which more immediately gains the Assent, than "that Papists ought to be excluded from all Share in the Government of a Protestant People." But that the Test-Act hath effectually excluded them, or is likely to do so, I deny, and could mention several recent Examples among ourselves to the contrary; and if History is to be credited, that informs us that in the Year

4. Ethan Allen, *Synodalia. Records of Clergy Meetings in Maryland, 1695–1773* (Baltimore: 1864), 167, 171; quoted in James R. Heintze, "Alexander Malcolm: Musician, Clergyman, and Schoolmaster," *MHM* 73 (September 1978): 231–32.

1682, long after the Test-Act was made, several Papists, under the Disguise of Protestants, thrust themselves into Place and Employments; among a Number of other Instances, that one *Duffy* got into the Rectory of *Rail* in *Essex*, and Dr. *Goodman* obtained the See of *Gloucester*.[5] Some conscientious Papists there may be, and I hope there are; but there is too much Ground to suppose, as to [the] great Part of them, that if they have a Service to do for MOTHER CHURCH, they can swallow SACRAMENTS; not only without Scruple, but with Merit. They have Abundance of Maxims to help them over such little Difficulties, "either the End consecrates the Means, or the Nullity of the Orders and Ministration in the Church of *England*, invalidates all consecration of the Elements," and consequently prevents their *wonderful Transformation*; and then they remaining as they were, partaking of them is no more than eating a Bit of common Bread, or drinking a Sip of ordinary Wine: Or if the Scruples of a Papist Conscience requires it, Dispensation from the Pope, or his Commissioners, may be procur'd; for what will *they* not grant Dispensations for, *who* canonize Murderers for Martyrs, and celebrate for Saints the vilest Miscreants.

I own the present melancholy Situation of my Mind is greatly aggravated, when I reflect on the peculiar Circumstances of this Province. There appears so little Unanimity among us, whilst our intestine Enemies the Jesuits, and their Tools and Emissaries, are embracing every Opportunity to foment Divisions, and exercising all their Craft and Subtlety to force or deceive us into our own Destruction: And here I cannot help observing that too many who profess themselves Protestants, in order to serve some paltry views of Interest or Favour, countenance and carry on the Deceit, at the Risk of every Thing that is valuable to Freemen and Englishmen. So that, I fear, without some extraordinary Interposition of Providence, or a speedy Alteration of our Conduct, we must submit to see our most inveterate Enemies the *French*, and their allied *Indians* (who have already attacked and invaded our Neighbour Colony of *Virginia*), lording it over all the *British* Dominions in *America*.

Does Popery increase in this Province? The great Number of Popish Chapels and the Crowds that resort to them, as well as the great Number of their Youth sent this Year to foreign Popish Seminaries for Education, prove

5. Malcolm, particularly as the son of a Scottish clergymen, would have had a familiarity with British ecclesiastical history, even at the diocesan level, that few, if any Marylanders could claim.

to a Demonstration that it does; moreover, many Popish Priests and Jesuits, hold sundry large Tracts of land, Manors and Dwelling-Houses, where they live in a collegiate Manner, having public Mass-Houses, where they exercise their religious Functions, and propagate their Dangerous Doctrines, with the greatest Industry, and without controul! Good God! Is it possible we can be so stupid, so deluded, as not to perceive the pernicious Consequences of such illegal Practices to us and our Posterity? ... I shall always be against persecuting those who have the Misfortune to be brought up in the Popish Religion, yet I must think it behooves our Government, to take as much Care as possible, that his Majesty's Subjects may not be perverted to it. This they ought to do not only for religious but political Considerations; because, by the very Principles of that Religion, tho' those that profess it should be quiet,[6] they can never be faithful Subjects. As you, Sir, are so singular as to consider the true Happiness of our Constitution, I cannot but earnestly recommend it to you to declare yourself a Candidate for the next General Election for your county; then ... it will be in your Power to brighten and enforce the true Principles of Liberty to our deluded Countrymen; to show them the apparent Dangers they are exposed to by suffering a most detested Swarm of Jesuits, those Traitors and Patricides to their Country, to engross and occupy such large Possessions among us; to evince the Absurdity of allowing them, as they are known to be implacable Enemies to our happy Constitution, both in Church and State, the Enjoyment and full Benefit of those Laws, they are incessantly endeavouring to overturn: I will not say, it would be just in us to compel them to come in, but I am sure it would be prudent in us to compel them to go out; I must here be understood to mean the Jesuits only.

From what has been said we have too much Reason to conclude, that Popery is the Foundation of all our present Distractions, Divisions and Dangers; let us then take away the Cause, and the Effect will cease; let us modestly and calmly unite to refuse our Voices, at the next General Election of Representatives, to any Candidate that will not bind himself by Promise to promote some such Bill, as passed the Lower House, last May Session, by a great majority of Patriots and Friends to Liberty and the Protestant Cause; I mean, *The Bill to prevent the Growth of Popery, within this Province*; let us take away the Cause and the Effects will cease; ... I am not for Dragooning, Imprisonment, Banishment, or the Galleries; but still, I am for Self-Preservation, and

6. "Should be quiet," i.e., practice their religion strictly in a private way.

for such Laws as will put it out of the Power of the Jesuits, and their deluded Votaries, to endanger the Peace of this Province, and the Repose of all the British Colonies upon this Continent: Let us imitate the glorious Example of the Parliament of *Ireland*: to their wise Laws is owing the Tranquility of that Kingdom, and, to the due Execution of them, it is that Popery subsists among the Lower Class of their People: Let us examine their salutary Laws, and adopt such of them, as shall be found most suitable to our Circumstances.

41

"One of the Greatest Things That Ever the English Did in America": The Expulsion of the Acadians, August 1755*

On September 11, 1755, the *Maryland Gazette* carried an anonymous dispatch from Halifax. It was the first news of an unprecedented happening in North American history: a mass relocation of an ethnic group, an event whose tragic consequences would eventually spill over to most of the colonies, including Maryland. The short report not only celebrated the radical action that the British had adopted to deal with their "Acadian problem" but revealed all too clearly that security concerns were not the only motives behind the expulsion. How could such a disastrous operation be put in motion? And rationalized?

We are now upon a great and noble Scheme of sending the neutral French out of this Province, who have always been secret Enemies and have encouraged our Savages to cut our Throats. If we effect their Expulsion, it will be one of the greatest Things that ever the English did in America; for by all the Accounts, that Part of the Country they possess, is as good Land as any in the World: In Case therefore we could get some good English Farmers in their Room, this Province would abound with all Kinds of Provisions.

August 17. This Day sailed out of the Harbour, Three of his Majesty's Ships of War, in order, its thought to join Admiral Holbourn.

A few Days since, three French Men were taken up and imprisoned, on Suspicion of having poisoned some of the Wells in this Neighbourhood.

*MG, September 11, 1755.

They are not tried as yet; and 'tis imagined if they are convicted thereof, they'll have but a few Hours to live after they are once condemn'd.

With the Blessing of God, we are at present, plentifully stock'd with all Kinds of Provisions; whilst our Neighbours, the Cape-Bretoners, have felt in a most surprising Degree, the Effects of the several Prohibitions on the Continent, being now in a most deplorable Condition for want of the common Necessaries of Life, and afflicted with various Kinds of Diseases....

The Officers of the Navy, as well as those in the military Service, and every Individual in this Province, were extremely alarmed and shocked on hearing of the Defeat of General Braddock; and the Circumstances attending their unhappy and unlook'd-for Overthrow, seemingly exaggerates the whole Affair.

42

"They Did Not Fly from Penal Laws … That Their Posterity Would Be Subjected to Them Here": The Roman Catholic Petition to Governor Ogle regarding a Double Tax, 1756*

In their petition the Catholic representatives retraced the history of religious liberty in Maryland to its roots in the avowed intentions of Cecil Calvert and the subsequent legislation of 1639 and 1649 that made religious freedom a sacred right of all Maryland's Christians. What stood out in this long history, they noted, was the irony of Protestants as the ones seeking guarantees from Lord Baltimore and his representatives in the province (the large majority of whom were Catholics until 1689) that this freedom applied to them. Time and again they had received assurances that it did. Now the tables were turned. Protestants were in power, and Catholics had become the seekers. The petition bears comparison with Peter Attwood's tract more than a quarter century earlier. How do its arguments compare with the earlier text? How accurate is its summation of the early history of the province?

* MPA, Box 3, folder 11, GULBFCSC.

The Petition of Sundry Roman Catholics in behalf of themselves and others of the Same Communion residing in the Province aforesaid Humbly Showeth....

That our Ancestors had not the least ground to suspect that their Roman Catholic descendants would be deprived of the Benefit of a Law so earnestly contended for by Protestants & so often and so Solemnly confirmed at their request and so readily consented to by the Roman Catholics, for it is beyond doubt but that Cecilius Lord Baltimore and most of the Gentlemen then in power were Roman Catholics....

That when our Rom. Cath. Ancestors quitted their native Countries that they and their Posterity might enjoy Freedom and peace of Conscience here, they little dreamed that we should be troubled on the score of religion. That it is evident they did not cross the Ocean & encounter all the difficulties they underwent for a Temporary enjoyment of Liberty of Conscience to themselves only. That they did not fly from Penal Laws foreseeing that their Posterity would be subjected to them here.

That we beg your Excellency to reflect the Bulk of the first Settlers here were Roman Catholics, that they [settled here] at the expence of their fortunes & many of them at the price of their blood without recapitulating the many other hardships they underwent. According to the articles of the Charter they entered the Kings empire and Dominion and thereby have not only increased the Trade and riches of their Mother Country, but laid the foundation of the present flourishing State of this Province, from which his Lordship draws annually a noble and splendid fortune and that therefore we humbly conceive his Lordship not only in Justice but in gratitude is bound to preserve to us our Rights & liberties which the double Tax strikes at. And as his Lordship sensible of your merits has constituted you his Governor and Representative we hope you will not pass the Clause we have so just reason to complain of. That we had not the least reason to suspect this under his Majestys just and mild government [any attempt] would be made to invade these our Rights which Oliver Cromwell held Sacred and did not disturb, that oppressions and persecutions have always proved hurtful to States. That some if not all the Roman Catholics in the Province may be forced into other Provinces to the great prejudice of Maryland. That we are sensible we are charg'd with disaffection to his Majesty's Person and government, but we aver it to be a Scandalous Calumny and a charge unsupported by the least shadow of a proof. That under his Majestys long mild and happy reign his British Roman Catholic subjects have enjoy'd an uninterrupted period of quiet & peace. That his Majesty's Roman Catholic subjects in his foreign Dominions as far as we are informed equally partake of his favours and affection & in return pay him a sincere tribute of Love & duty. That your excellency is well acquainted that the Roman Catholics residing in this Province are in number very inconsiderable compared to the other Inhabitants. That your Excellency knows the Province is surrounded by Populous Protestant colonies & that therefore the Roman Catholics must be not only Fools but madmen to entertain any thoughts of disturbing the peace of the government.

That we do not charge our Enemies with being Fools or Madmen but we submit it to your Excellency to determine what Character they deserve who lay such black Charges to our doors not only without proof but even without the shadow [of] probability.

43

"Remember the Cruel Usage of the Roman Catholics": Charles Carroll of Annapolis's Correspondence to His Son, 1759–1760*

In relating to his son the sordid betrayal that the family had suffered at the hands of the Calverts, "Papa's" advice to "Charley" was that the revived anti-Catholicism had made Maryland such a toxic place for Catholics, even for aristocratic ones like the Carrolls, that he should look elsewhere than Maryland for a place to stake the family's future. His disgust and bitterness toward the Calverts and the local government notwithstanding, Carroll, as his letters to his son reveal, was as patriotic as anyone in Maryland in supporting the war against the French and looking toward an American victory over their "enemy." Are there any indications in the letters that his patriotism is perhaps being strengthened by improving relations between Charles Carroll of Annapolis and Maryland authorities? Is there any evidence of a change of attitude, on Carroll's part, toward the present Lord Baltimore in the year and a half covered by the letters?

* Box 8, Carroll Papers, MHS.

Feby 9, 1759

I still persist in my Resolution to sell my Estate here.... The disposition of our Lower House of Assembly towards us [makes one ask who] would live among men of such disposition that could live elsewhere....

Upon the whole our Campaign in America has been a glorious one, & we doubt not the Conquest of Canada next Campaign, if the Efforts of this year be equal to the last which we have no room to doubt: By our Superiority at Sea all supplies are cut off from Quebec their Entrepôt Louisbourg is in our hands the Isle of St. Jean[7] and several of their Settlements are destroy'd & the Inhabitants sent to old France; ... Things are in a quite opposite Situation with us, the pay of so many Troops, the money laid out in provisions & providing magazines &c for them circulates briskly among us, & we have plenty of Provisions for much more numerous Forces & more than enough beside to supply our West Indian Islands, so that the War which at the 1st as a new thing was terrible to us is now our Interest & desire—Besides by the Possession of Fort Duquesne the Western Frontier of Virginia Maryland & Pennsylvania is secured against the Cruelties of the Savages at the same time we see the power of our Mother Country to be such that she awes, invades & terrifies the Coasts of France, ruins her Settlements in Africa whither she has sent a Squadron to secure them to ourselves & that she has sent out a Strong Squadron & a Considerable Number of Land forces to reduce some of the Islands belonging to the French in the West Indies.

April 16, 1759

I really think it will be to your advantage Comfort & Satisfaction to sell my Estate here, however I shall keep my Estate in & nigh Annapolis two large seats of Land containing each about 3000 acres my slaves & Ironworks to the last so that you may choose, but I doubt not you will think as I do if you should ever know our people....

It is no wonder we have been so successful in America, our vast Superiority at Sea secured & will always secure our Successes ... under such a Minister as Mr. Pitt[8]— ... Here we promise ourselves no less this Campaign than the reduction of all Canada & without storms to ruin our Fleets, & Epi-

7. St. John's Isle (Prince Edward Island).
8. William Pitt, the British prime minister.

demical distempers to destroy our Armies, I do not think our hopes too sanguine.... [We] expect that unless France is very fortunate this summer on the Continent of Europe, we hope at the end of this Campaign to prescribe such a peace as we please, & such a one as she must Submit to.

October 6, 1759

Altho' I still think it will be for your Interest & Happiness to sell my Estates in Maryland, yet I would not have you either decline or Solicit an acquaintance with Lord Baltimore or his uncle Mr. Cecilius Calvert. If you should accidentally fall in their way you may when proper let them know that you are acquainted [with your grandfather's history].... That the memory of the favours conferred on your grandfather will always incline you to promote the interests of the Proprietary family where you can do it with Honour & Justice. But remember the ill treatment your Grandfather met with after so long a Series of Services remember the cruel usage of the Roman Catholics by the late and present Lords Baltimore, & let that so weigh with you as never to Sacrifice your own or your Country's Interest to promote the Interest or power of the Proprietary family. It is true they have it in their power to confer some places of Profit & Honour worth acceptance, but as you cannot hold any of them as the Laws stand, & supposing that impediment removed, as I would not wish you to hold any of them but upon Honourable terms, I cannot think it will be worth your while to pay a Court there, or show any other Respect than such a one as is due to them, as Lords of the Country where your fortune lays—

July 14, 1760

Pray how came you to dine with Mr. Sharpe? I hardly think you paid him a Visit: I conjecture our Governor wrote to him to take notice of you, if so, it was kind & Genteel in him. He & I are at present on Good terms & were a Law now to be passed to double Tax the Roman Catholics it would hardly meet with his Connivance. You say Mr. Calvert returned your Visit, this implies a previous Visit paid by you, & yet from what I wrote to you October 6, 1759 I hardly think you took that step, this shows you cannot be too full, explicit & circumstantial in your letters.... You have seen Lord Baltimore, perhaps you have since seen him, if so maybe you can give me his Character. If our house of Commons[9] could have their way, such is their Malice that they would not only deprive us of our property but our Lives—Maryland was Granted to Cecilius Lord Baltimore a Roman Catholic all persons believing in Jesus Christ were by the Charter promised the Enjoyment not only of Religious but Civil Liberty & were entitled to all the Benefits of Lucrative places &c. It was chiefly planted & peopled in the beginning by Roman Catholics; many of them were men of better families than their Proprietary, these privileges were confirmed by a Fundamental & perpetual Law past here & all sects continued in a peaceable enjoyment of these privileges until the Revolution when a mob Encouraged by the Example set them by England Rebelled against the Lord Baltimore, stript him of his Government, & his officers of their places—Then the Crown assumed the Government; the toleration Act … was Repeald & Several Acts to hinder us from a free Exercise of our Religion past.

Benedict Lord Baltimore upon conforming to the Established Church in the year 1714 was Restored to his Government & died the same year, his Son Charles Lord Baltimore the present Lords father succeeded & the people here making a handle [?] of the Rebellion in 1715[10] Enacted Laws enjoining all the oaths taken in England to be taken here & disqualified any person from voting for members to Represent them in our Assembly who would not take those Oaths & many other scandalous & oppressive Laws. To these the proprietary was not only mean enough to allow but also he deprived several Roman Catholics employed in the management of his private patrimony & revenue of their places & among the Rest your Grandfather who was his Agent & Receiver general &c & had held the former places under three Lords Baltimores, this no Act compelled him to do, & he did it to Cajole an insolent Rabble who were again aiming to deprive him of the Government. From that time to the year 1751 we were unmolested, but then the Penal Laws of England were attempted to be introduced here, & several Bills to this & of like purposes were past by our Lower House but rejected by the upper House, at last in 1756 an Act was past by all the Branches of the Legislature here to double Tax us & to this Law our present proprietary had the meanness to assent tho' he knew us innocent of the Calumnies raised against us.… From what I have said I leave you to judge whether Mary-

9. Maryland's assembly or lower house of the legislature.
10. The uprising of the supporters of the Stuart Pretender, James Edward, following the death of Queen Anne.

land can be a tolerable Residence for a Roman Catholic. It is true Nature has been almost beyond Bounds bountiful to it, the Climate is very good, & every year improving as the Country is opened; the Soil in General is very fruitful & yields with very little labour a plentiful increase of whatever is trusted to it, Cattle & Poultry of all sorts multiply surprisingly with moderate care & are Excellent in their kinds, a vast variety & succession of several sorts of grain, pulse, roots & make a famine almost impossible: our fruit are delicious and … no Country in the world is better watered.… As it is, were I younger I would certainly quit it, at my age … a change of Climate would certainly shorten my Days, but I embrace every opportunity of getting rid of my Real Property, that if you please you may the sooner & with more ease & less loss leave it; how ever my most valuable Lands & Slaves shall be kept to the last that you may choose for yourself & make yourself as happy as possible, it is my greatest Study & Concern to make you so.

44

"Brave Youths, Drag on Your Pope": Popes-Night Broadside, 1766*

Broadsides of doggerel, as the following one for Boston, would typically advertise the yearly remembrance of the generic popish iniquity that Guy Fawkes epitomized. By 1766 the "common enemy" had expanded to include the British, as Pope's Night became a vehicle to protest the Stamp Act and the other imperial legislation that set the colonies on the path to revolution. The pope and his consorts in evil became surrogates for tyrannical British officials. So important a channel of anti-British opposition had Pope's Night become by 1774 that its celebration in that year spanned the colonies, from Boston to Savannah, fueled by the Quebec Act, which most colonists interpreted as a capitulation to the Catholic Canadian province that would have very damaging consequences for the "Protestant" colonies to the south. That one year notwithstanding, Pope's Night never became part of the anti-Catholic tradition in either Maryland or Pennsylvania, where most Catholics were. How to explain that Pope's Night tended to be a prominent part of anti-Catholic culture in the very places where Catholics had a very weak presence?

* Manuscripts Division, LC.

Extraordinary VERSES ON POPE-NIGHT

OR, a COMMEMORATION OF THE *Fifth of November*, giving a History of the Attempt, made by the *Papists*, to blow up KING and PARLIAMENT, a.d. 1588. Together with some account of the POPE himself, and his Wife, *JOAN*; with several other things worthy of notice, too tedious to mention.

    1. *HUZZAH!* brave Boys, behold the *Pope,*
       Pretender[11] and *Old-Nick,*[12]
       How they together lay their Heads,
       To plot a poison Trick?

    2. To blow up KING and PARLIAMENT[13]
       To Flitters, rent and torn:
       —Oh! Blund'ring Poet, since the Plot,
       Was this Pretender born.—

    3. Yet, sure upon this famous Stage,
       He's got together *now,*
       And had he *then,* he'd been a Rogue
       As bad as t'other *two.*

    4. Come on, brave Youths, drag on your *Pope*
       Let's see his frightful Phiz:
       Let's view his Features rough and fierce,
       That Map of Ugliness!

    5. Distorted Joints, so huge and broad!
       So horribly drest up!
       'Twould puzzle Newton's Self to tell,
       The *D___l* from the *Pope.*

    6. See! How He Shakes his tot'ring Head
       And knocks his palsy Knees;
       A Proof *He* is the *Scarlet Whore,*
       And got the foul Disease.

11. James Edward Stuart, Pretender to the English Throne, whom Catholics supposedly recognized as the legitimate monarch. In the iconography of the Pope's Day celebrations, the pope, the Stuart Pretender, and Satan formed a natural axis of evil.

12. Another name for the devil.

13. A reference to the 1605 abortive plot of Guy Fawkes and some other Catholic gentry to blow up Parliament while the king was officially opening its fall session. Thereafter, every November 5, the anniversary of the exposure of the plot, a celebration culminating in an effigy burning became an extremely popular annual ritual. Initially known as Guy Fawkes Day, by the 1760s it had long since metamorphosed into Popes-Night, with an effigy of the pontiff now replacing Fawkes's on the pyre.

7. Most terrible for to behold,
   He Stinks much worse than Rum:
   Here, you behold the *Pope* and here
   Old Harry[14] in his *Rome.*

8. D'ye ask why *Satan* stands *behind?*
   Before he durst not go.
   Because his Pride won't let him Stoop,
   To kiss the *Pope's* great Toe.

9. *Old Boys,* and young, be Sure observe
   The *Fifth* Day of *November;*
   What tho' it is a Day apast?
   You still can it remember....

14. *"How dreadful do his Features show?*
    "How fearful is his Grin?
    "Made up of ev'ry Thing that's bad;
    He is the Man of Sin."

15. If that his *deeden* Self could see
    Himself so turned to Fun:
    In Rage He'd tear out His *Pope's Eyes,*
    And scratch his Rev'rend Bum.

16. He'd kick his triple Crown about,
    And wear of his Life,
    He'd *curse* the Rabble, and away
    He'd run to tell his *Wife.*

17. Some Wits begin to cavil here
    And laughing seem to query,
    "How Pope *should have a* Wife, *and yet,*
    The Clergy *never marry."*

18. Laugh if you please, yet still I'm sure
    If false I'm not alone;
    Pray *Critic*, did you never hear
    Nor read of fair *Pope Joan.*[15]

19. *"Help* Joan! *see how I'm drag'd and bounc'd,*
    "Pursu'd, surrounded,—Wife!

14. Yet another name for the devil.

15. Pope Joan. This legendary figure first appeared in the literature of the thirteenth century. Eventually Pope Joan became a staple in anti-Catholic celebrations.

> "And when I'm bang'd to Death, I shall
> "Be Barbacu'd alive." ...

22. Asham'd, enrag'd, and mad, and vex'd,
    He mutters ten Times more,
    "I'll make a Bull,[16] and my He-Cow
    "Shall bellow, grunt and rear."
    So dismal and forlorn!
    We know that thou a Cuckold art,
    For thou hast many an Horn....

26. His End so near, each Cardinal
    Quite old himself would feign:
    He tries to stoop and cough that he
    Might his Successor reign.

27. And now, their Frolick to compleat,
    They to the Mill'Dam go;
    Burn Him to Nothing first, and then
    Plunge Him the Waves into.

28. But to conclude, from what we've heard
    With Pleasure serve the King:
    Be not Pretenders, Papistes,
    Nor Pope, nor t'other Thing.

Sources

Allen, Ethan. *Synodalia: Records of Clergy Meetings in Maryland, 1695–1773*. Baltimore: 1864. Quoted in James R. Heintze, "Alexander Malcolm: Musician, Clergyman, and Schoolmaster." *MHM* 73 (September 1978): 231–32.

Anderson, Fred. *Crucible of War: The Seven Years' War and the Fate of Empire in British North America, 1754–1766*. New York: Alfred A. Knopf, 2000.

Cogliano, Francis D. *No King, No Popery: Anti-Catholicism in Revolutionary New England*. Westport, Conn.: Greenwood Press, 1995.

Farragher, John Mack. *A Great and Noble Scheme: The Tragic Story of the Expulsion of the French Canadians from their American Homeland*. New York: Norton, 2006.

Hatch, Nathan O. *The Sacred Cause of Liberty: Republican Thought and the Millennium in Revolutionary New England*. New Haven: Yale University Press, 1977.

Kidd, Thomas. *The Protestant Interest: New England after Puritanism*. New Haven: Yale University Press, 2004.

16. A pun referring to a papal declaration.

Part 9

Revolution and a Changing Landscape

1773–1781

T HE QUINTESSENCE OF popery in the British Empire was the Society of Jesus, which was widely regarded as the spearhead of Rome's effort to undo the Protestant Reformation that had remade the religious landscape in England, Scotland, and beyond. In British America (prior to 1763), as noted, the Mission of the English Jesuits was the institutional presence of Catholicism. There had been a few Franciscans working in Maryland, beginning in the late seventeenth century, but by the second quarter of the eighteenth, they had long since died or returned to Europe. Most of the scores of the Maryland gentry's sons who had entered religious life following their education at recusant schools on the Continent became Jesuits. By 1773 there were twenty-three English or British-American Jesuits working in Maryland or southeastern Pennsylvania, including Joseph Mosley on the upper Eastern Shore of Maryland. At least fifteen others were in Europe as scholastics (seminarians) or priests in various ministries, including education; one such scholastic was John Carroll at the College of Bruges in Flanders.

Decades of festering anti-Jesuit sentiment within the court circles of Catholic powers led to the expulsion of the Society from the empires of Portugal and France in 1763. Ten years later the pressure of the Catholic monarchs finally forced Pope Clement XIV to issue a brief, *Dominus ac Redemptor* (one of the more ironically titled papal pronouncements), suppressing the Society of Jesus throughout the world. The agents of the brief's implementation were the local bishops in Europe and the Americas. They seized the property of the Society, expelled the Jesuits themselves, and often imprisoned them. John Carroll and his companions at Bruges were driven out of the college at bayonet point by Austrian police. The Jesuit superior general was incarcerated in the Castel San Angelo beside the Tiber in Rome and died there. Two places escaped the execution of the order: White Russia, or Congress Poland, and the British colonies on the North American mainland below Canada. Jesuits in the former were spared confiscation of property or worse by the determination of Empress Catherine to preserve the Jesuit schools in that region of her domains. Those in British America held on to their land and freedom because of the failure to create an episcopal see in Philadelphia less than a decade earlier. In one case the secular ruler refused to allow the execution of *Dominus ac Redemptor*; in the other, there was simply no prelate in the neighborhood to carry it out. The nearest bishop in British North America was Jean-Olivier Briand in Quebec. The French bishop did forward to the priests in Maryland and Pennsylvania a form from the Holy See declaring their submission to the papal decree, which they were required to sign. But Briand had no intention of being the pope's collector of property below Canada. He had made perfectly clear in the wake of the British takeover of his diocese in 1763 that he had no interest or desire to have any jurisdiction over the other British colonies on the mainland (see "The Jesuit's Metamorphosed into I Know Not What").

Charley Carroll returned home to Annapolis in 1764, having completed the sixteen-year European course of education that his father had so meticulously charted for him. He did not, however, heed his father's advice in 1759 to plant his future somewhere other than Maryland. In the past five years the climate for Catholics had warmed considerably. Partly the change reflected the turning of the war in Britain's favor with the capture of Quebec in the fall of 1759. With the collapse of the French empire in America, anti-Catholicism fell sharply, as well. In Maryland the proprietor's instruction that officials not impose "further penalties" upon Catholics unless there was sufficient cause to do so signaled a new era of benign neglect during which the Catholic Church in Maryland experienced unprecedented growth, including the construction of public chapels that had been banned for Catholics since the first decade of the century. The colony itself enjoyed the fruits of a rebounding economy, nowhere more so than in Annapolis, where the good times provided the wherewithal for an architectural boom that would make Maryland's capital the urban gem of America. The Carrolls shared fully in the economic revival. Charley himself took over the management of several of the family's plantations on the Western Shore, as well as becoming a partner in the Baltimore Company, the sprawling (30,000 acres) ironworks that his father had cofounded. By the 1770s it had become one of the most important industries in British America. But the Carrolls, despite their economic importance, were still political and social outsiders. Law and custom continued to cut off Catholics, even the wealthiest, from those spheres. That suddenly changed in 1773.

Among the oligarchy of families that had come to dominate Maryland politics in the eighteenth century, none was more powerful than the Dulanys. Daniel Dulany the Younger (1722–97) served in the Maryland Assembly and, from 1757 to 1776, was a member of the Governor's Council, where he held the office of provincial secretary, the second most important position in the colony's government. A London-trained (Middle Temple) lawyer, Dulany, through his practice and writings, earned a reputation as the outstanding legal mind in Maryland. His 1765 pamphlet (*Considerations on the Propriety of Imposing Taxes in the British Colonies*) dismantling the justifications for the Stamp Act had a deep influence on the colonies' wide opposition, which led to the act's repeal in 1766. At the beginning of 1773, however, Dulany, now fifty-one, took up the pen, not to protest some new imperial legislation, but to defend the provincial administration of which he was such a part. At issue was the governor's prerogative to set the rate of fees that government tobacco inspectors could collect for their work in lieu of the failure of the lower house of the Maryland Assembly to reform the old fee schedule before the act authorizing it expired. Many delegates, representing what was coming to be called the "country" party, considered the current fees to be excessive, a boondoggle for the collectors, many of whom had connections with the Dulanys and the other elite families within the "court" circle. Governor Robert Eden, Lord Baltimore's brother-in-law, in November of 1770, by proclamation continued the old fee schedule, much to the dismay of many Marylanders outside the circle, who regarded fee or tax setting as a power reserved to the legislature. Over the next two years the governor and his council were gridlocked with the lower house over the issue. Finally in the fall of 1772 Eden dissolved the General Assembly and called for new elections to be held the following May.

In this context the *Maryland Gazette* over the first five months of 1773 became the principal venue for championing the "government's" or "people's" cause. Numerous "letters" were published on the fees question, some from major figures in the province, including Samuel Chase, William Paca, Thomas Johnson, and Jonathan Boucher, many under noms de plume such as "A Planter," "Independent Whig," and "True Patriot." Virtually all were one-time appeals to the minds and hearts of voters. What appeared on the second page of the first issue of the *Gazette* for 1773, however, proved to be the beginning of a debate that would be decisive in shaping not only the resolution of the fees controversy, but Maryland's political order for the next generation (see "Who Is This Man, That Calls Himself a Citizen?").

Even before Carroll and Dulany had concluded their five-month exchange in the pages of the *Gazette*, Maryland voters rendered their verdict in Carroll's favor in the May assembly elections by giving the Popular Party, for whom Carroll had become the leading spokesman, a majority in the House of Delegates. Before the new ruling party could work out some resolution of the fees issue with the governor, however, a colonies-wide crisis developed, so disruptive in nature that it led to the creation in the respective colonies, including Maryland, of shadow governments that by 1775 had become the de facto organs of government.

Resistance to the latest British legislation for raising revenue—the Tea Act of 1773—had impelled Great Britain to resort to a series of punitive measures against Massachusetts, which had become the hub of opposition to the act, most dramatically through the Boston Tea Party. "The Intolerable Acts" united the colonies from Massachusetts to Georgia as nothing else previously had. Boycotting associations, formed as one means of economic protest, quickly evolved into political conventions that coordinated the resistance movement. By the fall of 1774 the provincial assemblies had agreed to send delegates to Philadelphia for a "Continental Congress" to plan a common strategy. Even in this parapolitical order, the ban on Catholic participation in politics prevented Carroll from being selected as a delegate. It did not keep the Maryland convention from asking Carroll, clearly one of their actual leaders, to accompany the provincial delegation as an unofficial adviser. Carroll suppressed his frustration about still being an outsider and went along.

"No King, No Popery" was the slogan one veteran of the Revolution remembered being used as a recruiting tool in New Hampshire at the outbreak of the war.[1] Pope and monarch became dual symbols of oppression and tyranny, as the iconography at the recent Pope's Day celebrations had vividly depicted, and the protests over the Quebec Act had quickened ancient feelings. What the colonists in America were staging was nothing less than a second Glorious Revolution against an arbitrary ruler consorting with Rome to suppress his American subjects (see "Popery ... Equally Injurious to the Rights of Sovereigns and Mankind").

While the Continental Congress was in its first session, news reached them of the latest evidence of the conspiracy of the British government against the rights and liberties of the colonists. The Quebec Act might have been a prudent measure in dealing with an alien population of whom the British had become the rulers in the Treaty of Paris (1763), but to many Protestant Americans it confirmed the gnawing fears of a devious design to impose popery on Protestant America. By upholding the traditional place of Catholicism in the Canadian province while extending its southern border to encompass much of the territory the colonies already claimed, the British government was sending clear signals of their intention to frustrate the "Protestant Interest" of the colonists and use the French colonists and their Indian allies in the West as a barrier to their expansion. Resolutions decrying the act flew fast and thick from local and provincial assemblies from Massachusetts to South Carolina (see "To Submit to POPERY AND SLAVERY").

Exploiting the anti-Catholicism deeply implanted in American culture by tarring the British as papist flunkies was, to American leaders, enormously counterproductive. They were determined to take Rome out of the calculus for war. One good reason for this determination was the rebels' hope of attracting to their revolution other colonies, including ones whose populations were primarily Catholic, such as Quebec and Ireland. A month after hostilities broke out between the thirteen colonies and the British in April

1. Daniel Barber, *The History of My Own Times* (Washington, D.C.: 1827), cited in Francis D. Cogliano, *No King, No Popery: Anti-Catholicism in Revolutionary New England* (Westport, Conn.: Greenwood Press, 1995), 53–54.

of 1775, the Continental Congress invited "the oppressed Canadians" to join them in the "defence of common liberty" that they might better convince King George of the egregious treatment the colonies were enduring under his "licentious Ministry" (see "Uniting with Us in Defence of Our Common Liberty").

The following November George Washington underscored the new Catholic policy when he banned any observance of Pope's Day in the Continental Army. Not only were the American rebels hopeful of having the Catholic Canadians join their revolution, but they were looking to the Canadians' recent ruler, the Catholic king of France, as a war-changing ally. The last thing Washington and a growing number of American leaders wanted was a blatant display of anti-popery by American forces (see "That Ridiculous and Childish Custom"). Less than two months before his Pope's Day order, George Washington had addressed the Quebecois, appealing to them as American citizens to become part of the "indissoluble union" that the rebelling colonies were forming. The general commanding all of the colonial forces assured the Catholic Canadians that religion and ethnicity were no bars to citizenship in the emerging nation. The sole requirement was a commitment to liberty and an end of arbitrary government. This was not to be a Protestant republic.[2]

Despite the anti-papist reputation that the revolution-makers had justly acquired from their inflammatory reaction to the Quebec Act, *les habitants* initially proved remarkably receptive to the American invasion. They willingly provided arms and supplies for the Americans. Enough men joined the expeditionary force to form two new regiments (an impressive recruitment coup, considering the limited pool of Quebec's adult male population). When Montreal fell to the invaders in October, the likelihood of Quebec becoming the newest member of the American coalition seemed more than possible. The Americans pushed north to Quebec City, which they put under siege, just as the British had done in the climactic campaign against the French sixteen years earlier. For the next seven months they remained before the walls of the city. Meanwhile the Continental Congress had determined to send a delegation to Canada to lobby Canadians, both lay and clerical, to support the patriot cause. Three members of the Congress were se-

2. Proclamation of General George Washington to Canadians, September 14, 1775 (Cambridge, Mass.), reprinted in Martin I. J. Griffin, *Catholics and the American Revolution* (Ridley Park, Pa.: Martin I. J. Griffin, 1907), 1:27–29.

lected: Benjamin Franklin of Pennsylvania and two Marylanders—Samuel Chase and Charles Carroll of Carrollton. The latter had been appointed for two important reasons: his fluency in French and his religion. To strengthen the Catholic character of the mission, Charles Carroll's cousin, the ex-Jesuit John Carroll, reluctantly became the fourth member. The priest, who thought that history did not reflect well on ministers of religion caught up in political affairs, saw little hope of persuading the Canadians, particularly the clergy, to support the revolution. The mission's subsequent experience in Montreal did nothing to change the priest's thinking. The bishop of Quebec, Jean-Olivier Briand, issued orders that his clergy were to have nothing whatever to do with the delegation, including John Carroll. Carroll found out the effectiveness of the prelate's mandate when he visited a fellow ex-Jesuit, Pierre René Floquet, whom reports had identified as the chaplain of one of the recently formed Canadian regiments. All Floquet would do for Carroll was to allow him to say Mass in his chapel. Even that minimal gesture was too much for Bishop Briand, who placed an interdict on Floquet's church that amounted to a suspension of his ministerial faculties. By that time the Americans had finally abandoned their siege of Quebec, as well as their hope of adding French Canada as the fourteenth of the United Colonies (see "Was Not All This the Work of Divine Providence?").

As the makers and shakers of opinion waged, through newspapers and broadsides and pamphlets, a debate about what course the American people should pursue in their conflict with their mother country, Charles Carroll of Carrollton, suddenly a maker himself, offered his reflections in an extended essay that ran in two consecutive issues of *Dunlap's Maryland Gazette and Baltimore General Advertiser*, a weekly like its Annapolis namesake. Carroll's analysis of the political direction resistance to Great Britain should take revealed a deep knowledge of constitutional history and the lessons it conveyed for a people contemplating the creation of a republic (see "Our ... Government Seems to Be Approaching ... Its Dissolution"). In the convention called to determine what course Maryland should take in the war the colonies were waging with the mother country, Carroll, along with Samuel Chase, were the two delegates most responsible for the convention voting to declare Maryland's independence on July 3, a day before the Continental Congress in Philadelphia did so.

Although the Catholic community made up but 1 percent of the population in the United Colonies, it made a disproportionate contribution to the war effort, particularly in Maryland, both in military and government service. In the heart of Catholic Maryland, Charles and St. Mary's counties, an estimated 40 percent of the eligible males served in either the militia or the Continental Army, a figure impressive of itself, all the more so considering that Catholics for three decades had been barred from bearing arms.[3] The same proportion of Catholics took advantage of the new open society for Catholics by serving in government posts, with the Carrolls—Charles and his cousin Daniel—leading the way.[4] There were very few Tories to be found among Maryland Catholics. That was hardly the case in the two other colonies with a significant Catholic population: Pennsylvania and New York. In both colonies there were Catholic loyalist units. Pennsylvania Catholics seemed split very much in the same proportions as John Adams had estimated for the general population: one-third patriots, one-third loyalists, and one-third indifferent. The Pennsylvania Germans who made up the majority of the Catholic population in that colony almost certainly tended to be loyalists or uninvolved. Irish Catholics themselves were split over the war. But out of that group came some of the most important military leaders of the war, headed by John Barry, who earned the title "Father of the Navy," and Stephen Moylan, who could with equal justice be called "Father of the American Cavalry." All in all, the Catholic war record was one that would serve them well in the new republic.

Two months before the Continental Congress issued its formal declaration of independence at Philadelphia, the French government, seizing the opportunity that conflict between Great Britain and its American colonies offered for weakening France's traditional imperial foe, made the secret decision to provide money, supplies, and other assistance to the American rebels. Over the next year and a half it considered entering the war as an American ally, but the overall lack of patriot military success forestalled any such intervention. Then in the fall of 1777 came the startling news of the surrender of a major British force, John Burgoyne's army at Saratoga. Three months later the French and Americans signed a treaty of alliance and friendship. That proved to be the turning point of the war. In 1779 the Spanish branch of the

3. Maura Jane Farrelly, "Papist Patriots: Catholic Identity and Revolutionary Ideology in Maryland" (Ph.D. diss., Emory University, 2002), 311.

4. Beatriz Betancourt Hardy, "Papists in a Protestant Age: The Catholic Gentry and Community in Colonial Maryland, 1689–1776" (Ph.D. diss., University of Maryland, 1993), 314.

Bourbons joined the alliance, as did the Netherlands a year after that. By 1780 Great Britain found itself and its German mercenaries against this powerful alliance of traditional religious foes.

For some Americans no realpolitik justified joining military ranks with Catholic powers against the quintessential Protestant nation. Such an infamous partnership could not fail to advance popery in Europe and America. Many more, like Samuel Cooper, eventually appreciated the alliance for what it was: an association that offered the patriots their best chance for winning their independence (see "Toward the Universal Re-establishment of Popery through All Christendom"). The presupposition that the social cohesion of a country required uniformity in religious profession no longer held. The correlation between Protestantism and republican government was no longer a given. Instead of the public good demanding Protestant uniformity in religion, the common good was now the unifying goal for persons of different religious professions.

45

"The Jesuit's Metamorphosed into I Know Not What": The Suppression of the Society of Jesus and Its American Repercussions

Preserving their property was little solace to the score and three Jesuits in America who found themselves Societyless—religious orphans whose very identity had been removed by a papal order of suppression. It was a shocking experience of *anomie* that left them feeling adrift, betrayed, and with no purpose left for their lives. The following letters by John Carroll and Joseph Mosley capture well the raw feelings of bewilderment and loss that the suppression evoked. Carroll was in a Jesuit College in Flanders, having recently been a close-up observer of the intrigue that led to the pope's edict. Mosley was not only on the other side of the Atlantic, but virtually isolated at his mission on the Eastern Shore. How does this radical difference in vantage point affect their reaction to the catastrophic news?

John Carroll to Daniel Carroll,[5] Bruges, September 11, 1773[*]

The enemies of the society, and above all the unrelenting perseverance of the Spanish and Portuguese Ministries, with the passiveness of the court of Vienna, has at length obtained their ends: and our so long persecuted, and I must add, holy society is no more. God's holy will be done, and may his name be blessed forever and ever! This fatal stroke was struck on July 21, but was kept secret at Rome till August 16, and was only made known to us on September 5. I am not, and perhaps never shall be, recovered from the shock of this dreadful intelligence. The greatest blessing which in my estimation I could receive from God, would be immediate death: but if he deny me this, may his holy and adorable designs on me be wholly fulfilled. Is it possible that Divine Providence should permit to such an end, a body wholly devoted, and I will still aver, with the most disinterested charity, in procuring every comfort and advantage to their neighbors, whether by preaching, teaching, catechizing, missions, visiting hospitals, prisons, and every other function of spiritual and corporal mercy? Such I have beheld it, in every part of my travels, the first of all ecclesiastical bodies in the esteem and confidence of the faithful, and certainly the most laborious. What will become of our flourishing congregations with you, and those cultivated by the German fathers?[6] These reflections crowd so fast upon me that I almost lose my senses. But I will endeavor to suppress them for a few moments. You see that I am now my own master, and left to my own direction. In returning to Maryland I shall have the comfort of not only being with you, but of being farther out of the reach of scandal and defamation, and removed from the scenes of distress of many of my dearest friends, whom God knows, I shall not be able to relieve. I shall therefore most certainly sail for Maryland early next spring, if I possibly can.

[*]Thomas O'Brien Hanley, SJ, ed., *John Carroll Papers* (Notre Dame, Ind.: University of Notre Dame Press, 1976), 1:30–31.

5. Carroll's older brother Daniel (1730–96), a wealthy planter merchant in Prince George's County, Maryland.

6. The German immigrant communities in southeastern Pennsylvania that German Jesuits had been ministering to for the past thirty years.

Joseph Mosley to Helen Dunn, October 3, 1774[*]

Yes, Dear Sister, our Body or Factory is dissolved,[7] of which your two Brothers are members, and for myself I know I am an unworthy one, when I see so many worthy, saintly, pious, learned, laborious Missioners dead and alive been members of the same, thro' the two last ages. I know no fault that we are guilty of. I am convinced that our labors are pure, upright and sincere, for God's honour and our neighbour's good. What our Supreme Judge on earth may think of our labours is a mystery to me.[8] He has hurt his own cause, not us. It's true he has stigmatized us thro' the world with infamy, and declared us unfit for our business or his service. Our Dissolution is known thro' the world; it's in every newspaper, which makes me ashamed to show my face. Ah, I can say now, what I never before thought of: I am willing now to retire and quit my post, as I believe most of my Brethren are. A retired private life would suit me best, where I could attend only myself, after 17 years dissipation in this harvest. As we're judged unserviceable, we labour with little heart, and, what is worse, by no rule. To my great sorrow the Society is abolished; with it must die all that zeal that was founded and raised on it. Labour for our neighbor is a Jesuit's pleasure; destroy the Jesuit, and labour is painful and disagreeable.... I disregarded this unhealthy climate, and all its agues and fevers, which have really paid me to my heart's content, for the sake of my rule, the night was agreeable as the day, frost and cold as a warm fire or a soft bed, the excessive heats as welcome as a cool shade or pleasant breezes—but ... now the scene is changed: the Jesuit's metamorphosed into I know not what; he is a monster, a scarecrow in my ideas. With joy I impaired my health and broke my constitution in the care of my flock. It was the Jesuit's call, it was his whole aim and business. The Jesuit is no more.... In me, the Jesuit and the Missioner was always combined together; if one falls, the other must of consequence fall with it.

[*] Mosley Papers, GULBFCSC.

7. Members of the English Province of the Society of Jesus, operating in a country where their very presence was a capital offense, were accustomed to using code words when referring to the Society and its missions. "Body" and "Factory" were both code words for the Society itself.

8. The pope or Roman pontiff.

46

"Who Is This Man, That Calls Himself a Citizen?" Charles Carroll of Carrollton and Daniel Dulany, The Antilon–First Citizen Letters, 1773*

"You will be pleased to give a place in your Gazette to the following dialogue, which was set down by a gentleman who overheard it, after a small recollection, perfectly in substance and nearly in words, as it fell from the speakers." What followed was a clever defense, through the trope of a debate, of government officials and their allies in the business community by depicting them as promoters of the public good. There is little doubt but that Dulany, given his high self-regard, expected this to be the last word on the matter. Imagine his dismay when a month later the *Gazette* published a sequel to the dialogue, in which this second writer made clear that he knew the identity of the creator of the dialogue, someone who had been sacrificing the common good for the benefit of his family. Thus began what became perhaps the most famous political debate in American colonial history.

When Daniel Dulaney first realized that "FIRST CITIZEN was Charles Carroll of Carrollton we do not know. Whenever it was, the discovery infuriated him, if the invective that increasingly filled his later letters is any indication. The debate evolved into an exchange of letters under assumed names (Dulaney adopted "Antilon";[9] Carroll remained "First Citizen") that continued for seven months. It would have political and religious consequences of the first order. Carroll's spirited exchange with Dulaney marked the reentry of Catholics into public affairs after more than a generation. Why would Dulaney have been so outraged at discovering that Charles Carroll was his adversary? How explain the popular perception that the man of no social or political standing had bested one of the pillars of Maryland's ruling class?

---

*MG, January 7, 1773.

9. The origin and meaning of "Antilon" is unknown. Elihu S. Riley, in his *Correspondence of "First Citizen": Charles Carroll of Carrollton and "Antilon" Daniel Dulaney Jr., 1773* (Baltimore: King Brothers, 1902), concluded from his investigation that it was from the Spanish "Antillon"— meaning astringent plaster, hence someone who by applying his reason will draw out the cancerous ideas of his opponent.

Antilon's First Letter (*Maryland Gazette*, January 7, 1773):
A Dialogue between Two Citizens

1ST CIT. What, my old friend! Still deaf to the voice of Reason? ...Your Steadiness, your Integrity, your Independence made us set you down, as a sure Enemy to Government, and one too, whose force would be felt.

2ND CIT. I have impartially examined everything you suggested in our last conversation, but, cannot discover therein, the least semblance either of reason, or argument; and until you press me with some more weighty objections, I shall still continue a cordial and determined friend to Government, and, under favour, to Liberty too....

1ST CIT. You declare yourself a determined friend both to Government, and Liberty. Monstrous contradiction! ... Government has but too many, and too powerful friends already; the current sets so fatally strong that way, as to give us serious cause to dread, that we shall be overborn in all our struggles to resist it; the friends of the Constitution ... see the strongest symptoms of the sickness of their cause, even unto death; Court-influence and Corruption, rear their glittering crests.

2D CIT. Court-influence and Corruption! ... You may upbraid with the epithets of Tool, or Courtier ... the blessings of order, will still be preferred to the horrors of Anarchy; for to such must the principles of those men inevitably lead, who are fixed in their purpose, of opposing government at all adventures.... Take a liberal and impartial review of your adversaries.... Have not they as deep a stake in the safety of the Constitution as you, or your friends? What can possibly tempt them to join in the demolition of that bulwark, which alone shelters them in the enjoyment of their fortunes, and of every comfort that can plead to the reason, and interest the heart of man? ... I fancy you will hear many of my brother-mechanics raising their voices against you, who scarce know the meaning of your Court influence, and Corruption, who will stand on the side of him, whom they think, from an unprejudiced observation of his manners, the likeliest to shield them from oppression; or it may be, the increase of whose business, as it is closely connected with the prosperity of the city, bids the fairest to enlarge the sphere of action and importance, not only of every tradesman, but, of every inhabitant who lives by his labor, and the sweat of his brow.

First Citizen's First Letter (*Maryland Gazette*, February 4, 1773)

1ST CIT. There was a time, Sir, when you had not so favourable an opinion of the integrity and good intentions of government, as you now seem to have.... Your conduct on this occasion makes me suspect that formerly *some men, not measures*, were disagreeable to you.... Some of the present set (it is true) were then in power, others indeed were not yet provided for, and therefore a push was to be made to thrust them into office, that all-power might centre in *one family*. Is all your patriotism come to this?

2ND CIT. Convince me that I act wrong in supporting Government and I will alter my conduct ... does it follow, that the Court and Country interests are incompatible; that Government and Liberty are irreconcilable? Is every man, who thinks differently from you on public measures, influenced or corrupted?

1ST CIT. Your attachment to government ... proceeds, I fear, more from personal considerations, than from a persuasion of the rectitude of our Court measures; Government was instituted for the general good, but Officers entrusted with its powers, have most commonly perverted them to the selfish views of avarice and ambition; hence the Country and Court interests, which ought to be the same, have been too often opposite, as must be acknowledged and lamented by every true friend to Liberty. You ask me are Government and Liberty incompatible; ... so far from being incompatible, I think they cannot subsist independent of each other; ... a wicked minister has endeavored, and is now endeavoring in this *free government*, to set the power of the supreme magistrate above the laws; in our mother country such ministers have been punished for the attempt with infamy, death or exile; I am surprised that he who imitates *their* example; should not dread *their* fate.

2ND CIT. You talk at random of dangers threatening liberty, and of infringements of the constitution, which exist only in your imagination. Prove, I say, *our ministers* to have advised unconstitutional measures, and I am ready to abandon them and their cause....

1ST CIT. [I]t seems from your suggestions that we are to place an unlimited trust in the men ... because they are men of great wealth and have *"as deep a stake in the safety of the constitution as any of us."* Property even in *private* life, is not always a security against dishonesty, in *public*, it is much less so. The ministers, who have made the boldest attacks on liberty, have been most of them men of affluence; from whence I infer, that riches so far from insuring a minister's honesty, ought rather to make us more watchful of his conduct.

Power, Sir, power, is apt to pervert the best of natures; with too much of it, I would not trust the milkiest man on earth. . . .

2ND CIT. You seem to think the acceptance of a place [in government], as exceptionable, as duplicity of conduct. . . .

1ST CIT. There we differ then; I esteem a double dealer, and an officer equally unfit to be chosen a member of Assembly ... presuming, that men under the bias of self-interest, and under personal obligations to Government, cannot act with a freedom and independency becoming a representative of the people.

Antilon's Second Letter (*Maryland Gazette*, February 18, 1773)

The [Governor's] Proclamation was issued with the professed design of preventing extortion and oppression: but if it had not *ascertained* the fees that might be received, it would have been entirely ineffectual, as a preventive of extortion. . . .

Have they any other measure, besides the Governor's proclamation, to arraign as an attempt to set the supreme Magistrate above the Law? If they have, let them be precise in their charge, and give me another opportunity of showing them, stripped of disguise, to be *what they are*. . . . Has their malice, which all the colours of language are too feeble to express, so extinguished every spark of the little sense, "niggard nature spared them," as to beget a sanguine hope, that the free people of Maryland will become a lawless mob at their instigation, and be the dupes of their infernal rage?

First Citizen's Second Letter (*Maryland Gazette*, March 11, 1773)

His defence of [the Proclamation] ... is contrary to the spirit of *our constitution* in particular, and would, if submitted to, be productive of fatal consequences. . . .

Some proceedings in the land-office, had created a suspicion in the members of the lower house of that assembly then sitting, That the government had entertained a design, in case the several branches of the legislature should not agree in the regulation of officers' fees, to attempt establishing them by Proclamation. To guard against [that] ... they ... asserted ... that the people of this province will ever oppose the usurpation of such a right....

Notwithstanding this declaration, a few days after[wards], the Proclamation ... was issued, contrary to a seeming promise....

In a subsequent session, [the proclamation] was resolved unanimously by the lower house, "*to be illegal, arbitrary, unconstitutional and oppressive said Proclamation are enemies to the peace, welfare and happiness of this province, and to the laws and constitution thereof.*" ...

I humbly conceive that fees settled by the Governor's Proclamation ... are to all intents and purposes, a tax upon the people, flowing from an arbitrary, and discretionary power in the supreme magistrate ... they bear all the marks and characters of a tax; they are universal, unavoidable, and recoverable, if imposed by a *legal* authority, as all other debts....

One would imagine that a compromise, and a mutual departure from some points respectively contended for [between the assembly and governor on the proper fee rates] would have been the most eligible way of ending the dispute.... What was done? The authority of the supreme magistrate interposed, and took the decision of this important question, from the other branches of the legislature to itself: in a land of freedom this arbitrary exertion of prerogative will not, must not, be endured.

[F]ees can be settled in no case except by the legislature, because it requires such authority to lay a tax; ... The house of lords and the house of commons have that right derived from long usage; and from the law of parliament, which is *lex terrae*, or part ... of the law of the land. Our upper and lower houses of assembly claim most of the privileges, appertaining to the two houses of parliament....

We know, that the four principal officers in this province, most benefited by the Proclamation, are all members of the upper house; ... a regard for those gentlemen, a desire to prevent a diminution of their fees, have hitherto prevented a regulation of our staple; in a matter of this importance, which so nearly concerns the general welfare of the province, personal considerations and private friendships, shall not prevent me from speaking out my sentiments with freedom....

I have shown what, *stripped of disguise*, you are.—

"A man born to perplex, distress, and afflict this country."

Antilon's Third Letter (*Maryland Gazette*, April 8, 1773)

FEES, THE Citizen IS constrained to admit, have been *lawfully* settled by the lords *alone*, by the commons *alone*, by the upper and lower houses separately, and by the courts of law, and equity in England—that these fees have not been settled by the *legislative* authority is *therefore* clear.... Consequently the settlement of fees is *not a tax* ... he cited no instance to prove that *fees* are a *tax*....

The many instances, in which you have shown your utter disregard of truth in your assertions and of the most disingenuous prevarication in your answers, and explications, render your testimony extremely suspicious; and such is your casuistical ingenuity that *all possibility* of mean cavil and illiberal subterfuge must be absolutely precluded, before any credit will be due to *your averments*....

After all, who is this man, that calls himself a Citizen, makes his addresses to the inhabitants of Maryland, has charged the members of one of the legislative branches with insolence, because, in their intercourse with another branch of the legislature, they proposed stated salaries, and has *himself* proposed a *different* provision for officers, contradicted the most public, and explicit declarations of the governor, represented *all* the council, but *one*, to be mere fools, that he may represent *him* to be a political parricide, denounced infamy, exile, and death; expressed a regard for the *established* church of England? Who is he? He has no share in the legislature, as a member of any branch; he is incapable of being a member; he is disabled from giving a vote in the choice of representatives, by the laws and constitutions of the country, *on account* of *his principles*, which are *distrusted* by those laws. He is disabled by an express resolve from interfering in the election of members, on the *same account*. He is not a protestant.

You have *vehemently* pronounced, that the proclamation "*must not be endured*." Softly, magnanimous citizen, softly—you have already stretched the *skin* too much, and raise not your voice to so great a pitch of *dissonance*, as peradventure, may be *intolerable*.... What then are you to do? ... before you resolve upon a plan, consider seriously what you are able and what you are not able to bear.... Instead of making yourself ridiculous, perhaps, obnoxious, by endeavouring to gain the confidence of the people, who are *instructed* by the spirit of our laws, and constitution, by the disabilities you are laid under, not to place any trust in *you*, when their civil, or religious rights, may be concerned. My advice to you is to be quiet, and peaceable, and with all due application … to build baby houses, yoke mice to a go-cart, play at even or odd, (or push pin for variety) and ride upon a long cane.

First Citizen's Third Letter (*Maryland Gazette,* May 6, 1773)

The prince, who places an unlimited confidence in a bad minister, runs great hazard of having that confidence abused, his government made odious, and his people wretched: … that the unbounded influence of a wicked minister, is sure to lead his master into many difficulties, and to involve the people in much distress, the present situation of this province is a proof of both….

In vindication of his conduct, Antilon has not endeavoured to convince the minds of his readers by the force of reason, but … has attempted to render his antagonist ridiculous, contemptible, and odious; he has descended to the lowest jests on the person of the Citizen, has expressed the utmost contempt of his understanding, and a strong suspicion of his *political,* and *religious principles.* What connection, Antilon, have the latter with the proclamation? Attempts to rouse popular prejudices; and to turn the laugh against an adversary, discover the weakness of a cause, or the inabilities of the advocate, who employs ridicule, instead of argument—*The Citizen's patriotism is entirely feigned;* his reasons must not be considered, or listened to, because his *religious principles* are not to be trusted— … What my speculative notions of religion may be, this is neither the place, nor time to declare; my political principles ought only to be the question on the present occasion; surely they are constitutional, and have met, I hope, with the approbation of my countrymen…. He asks—Who is this Citizen?—A man, Antilon, of an independent fortune, one deeply interested in the prosperity of his country: a friend to liberty, a settled enemy to lawless prerogative. I am accused of folly, and falsehood; of garbling moral, and legal maxims, of a narrow, sordid, and personal enmity; … Take this as an answer, the only one I shall give, to all your obloquy and abuse— … The bad man's censures are the highest commendations.

Our constitution is founded on jealousy, and suspicion; its true spirit, and full vigour cannot be preserved without the most watchful care, and strictest vigilance of the representatives over the conduct of administration; the present measures call for our closest attention to it; … The pursuits of government in the enlargement of its powers, and its encroachments on liberty, are steady, patient, uniform, and gradual; if checked by a well concerted opposition at one time, and laid aside, they will be again renewed by some succeeding minister, at a more favourable juncture....

If the proclamation has a legal binding force, then will it undoubtedly take away a part of the people's property without their consent.... If you render property thus insecure, you destroy the very life, and soul of liberty.

Fourth Letter of Antilon, (*Maryland Gazette*, June 3, 1773)

There is *an authority to tax, warranted* by long, immemorial, and uninterrupted usage, *distinct* from the legislative, ... to have been established by the lords or commons, the upper or lower house of assembly, separately, or by the judges.... If the original settlement of any fees was a tax, it continues a tax, if it was not a tax, it can't become so from the acts of officers, and parties receiving, and paying the fees....

How has the greatest part of fees been settled ... but by the allowance of the courts ... in pursuance of the authority incident to the offices of chancellors, and judges? Every instance of a fee, so settled, contradicts the notion, that the settlement of the rates of fees is a tax, because it is not competent to any other than the legislative authority to tax....

Parliament constitutes three branches, and they must all concur to establish laws....

I have proved that justice can't be administered, nor the laws duly executive without a settlement of the rates of fees, that an authority to settle them is necessary to the protections of the people, who, if officers were not restrained, would be exposed to the hazard of very great oppression. The *conclusion*, I confess, is *not very favourable to the liberal sentiments*, and *generous* views of *those, who are adverse* to the *narrow* restrictions of *systematical certainty*, and, *if allowed to choose their ground*, would, like Archimedes, undertake to turn the world, which way they please....

The accuser was not only no party in the measure; but was entirely excluded from all knowledge of the manner, in which it was conducted....

An unhappy wretch you are, haunted by envy, and malice....

The Citizen may profess his attachment to the principles of the revolution, his regard for the established church of England, and his persuasion that it is inconsistent with the security of British liberty, a prince on the throne should be a papist, and expect its assurances (though he is a papist by profession) will be credited, because, as he informs us, "his speculative opinions, in matter of religion, have no relation to, or influence over, his political tenets"; but we are taught otherwise and put upon our guard by our laws, and constitution, which have laid him under disabilities, because he is a papist, and his religious principles are suspected to have so great influence, so as to make it unsafe to permit his interference, in any degree, when the interests of the established religion, or the civil government, may be concerned.

Fourth Letter of First Citizen (*Maryland Gazette*, July 1, 1773)

By the English constitution the power of settling *the rate* is vested in the parliament alone, and in this province in the general assembly.

Representation has long been held to be essential to that power, and is considered as its origin: ... The regulation of officers fees in Maryland has been generally made by the assemblies. The authority of the governor to settle the fees of officers, has twice only, as we know of, interposed, but not then, without meeting with opposition from the delegates, and creating a general discontent among the people, a sure proof, that it has always been deemed dangerous, and unconstitutional.... The author of the considerations once entertained the same idea, but such is the versatility of his temper, such his contempt of consistency, that he changes his opinions, and his principles, with as little ceremony as he would change his coat....

In this colony, government is almost independent of the people. It has nothing to ask but a provision for its officers: if it can settle their fees without the interposition of the legislature, administration will disdain to owe even that obligation to the people. The delegates will soon lose their importance, government will every day gain some accession of strength; we have no intermediate state to check its progress: the upper house, the shadow of an aristocracy, being composed of officers dependent on the proprietary and removable at pleasure, will, it is to be feared, be subservient to his pleasure and command....

Papists are distrusted by the laws and laid under disabilities: They cannot, I know (ignorant as I am), enjoy any place of profit, or trust, while they continue papists; but do these disabilities extend so far, as to preclude them from thinking and writing on matters merely of a political nature? Antilon would make a most excellent inquisitor, he has given some striking specimens of an arbitrary temper; the first requisite.

He will not allow me freedom of thought or speech.... To what purpose was the threat thrown out of enforcing the penal statutes by proclamation? Why am I told that my conduct is very inconsistent with the situation of one who "owes even the *toleration* he enjoys to the favour of government": If by instilling prejudices into the governor, and by every means and wicked artifice you can rouse the popular resentment against certain religionists, and thus bring on a persecution of them, it will then be known whether the toleration I enjoy, be due to the favour of government, or not. That you have talents admirably well adapted to the works of darkness, malice to attempt the blacker, and messiness to stoop to the basest is too true.

47

"Popery ... Equally Injurious to the Rights of Sovereigns and Mankind": The Quebec Act and the Colonial Reaction

As its response to the Quebec Act the Continental Congress adopted the Suffolk County (Massachusetts) Resolves that had become the model for many, if not most of the formal protests throughout the colonies. The Congress chose to issue three addresses: to the British people, those in the thirteen colonies, and the people of Quebec. In what ways do these addresses reveal the contradictory forces shaping the nascent nation's policy?

Address of the Continental Congress to the British People, October 21, 1774[*]

[W]e think the Legislature of Great Britain is not authorized by the Constitution to establish a Religion fraught with sanguinary and impious tenets, or to erect an arbitrary form of government, in any quarter of the globe. These rights, we, as well as you, deem sacred. And yet sacred as they are, they have, with many others, been repeatedly and flagrantly violated. That relating to the passage of the Quebec Act which enlarged the boundaries of that Province

---

[*] Griffin, *Catholics and the American Revolution*, 1:246–47. John Jay of New York was the principal author of this address.

and also, as the Colonies—"the Protestant Colonies" as they were declared to be believed—"established Popery in Canada" by giving the clergy the rights in the collection of tithes which they had had under the French dominion....

By another Act the dominion of Canada is to be so extended, modelled and governed, as that by being disunited from us, detached from our interests, by civil as well as religious prejudices, that by their numbers daily swelling with Catholic emigrants from Europe, and by their devotion to Administration, so friendly to their religion, they might become formidable to us and on occasion, be fit instruments in the hands of power, to reduce the ancient free Protestant Colonies to the same state of slavery with themselves.

This was evidently the object of the Act: And in this view, being extremely dangerous to our liberty and quiet, we cannot forebear complaining of it as hostile to British America. Superadded to these considerations, we cannot help deploring the unhappy condition to which it has reduced the many English settlers, who, encouraged by the royal Proclamation, promising the enjoyment of all their rights, have purchased estates in that country. They are now the subjects of an arbitrary government, deprived of trial by jury, and when imprisoned cannot claim the benefit of the habeas corpus Act, that great bulwark and palladium of English liberty. Nor can we suppress our astonishment, that a British Parliament should ever consent to establish in that country a religion that has deluged your island in blood and dispersed impiety, bigotry, persecution, murder and rebellion through every part of the world. This being a true state of facts, let us beseech you to consider to what end they lead.

May not a Ministry with the same armies enslave you? It may be said, you will cease to pay them, but remember the taxes from America, the wealth, and we may add, the men, and particularly the Roman Catholics of this vast continent will then be in the power of your enemies, nor will you have any reason to expect, that after making slaves of us, many among us should refuse to assist in reducing you to the same abject state.

Memorial of the Continental Congress to the Inhabitants of the Colonies, October 21, 1774[*]

[A]n Act was passed for changing the government of Quebec, by which Act the Roman Catholic religion, instead of being tolerated as stipulated by the

---

[*] Griffin, *Catholics and the American Revolution*, 1:250–51.

treaty of peace,[10] is established, and the people there deprived of a right to an assembly, trials by jury and the English laws in civil cases abolished, and instead thereof, the French laws established in direct violation of his Majesty's promise by his royal proclamation, under the faith of which many English subjects settled in that province and the limits of that province are extended so as to comprehend those vast regions, that lie adjoining to the northerly and westerly boundaries of these colonies.

It is clear beyond a doubt, that a resolution is formed and is now carrying into execution to extinguish the freedom of these colonies by subjecting them to a despotic government.

The people of England will soon have an opportunity of declaring their sentiments concerning our cause. In their piety, generosity and good sense, we repose high confidence, and cannot, upon a review of past events, be persuaded that they, the defenders of true religion and the asserters of the rights of mankind, will take part against their affectionate Protestant brethren in the colonies, in favor of our open and their secret enemies, whose intrigues, for several years past have been wholly exercised in sapping the foundations of civil and religious liberty.

Address of the Continental Congress to the People of the Province of Quebec, October 21, 1774 [*]

What [rights are] offered you by the late Act of Parliament ...? Liberty of Conscience in your religion? No, God gave it to you, and the temporal powers with which you have been and are connected, firmly stipulated for your enjoyment of it. If laws, divine and human, could secure it against despotic caprices of wicked men, it was secured before. Are the French laws in civil cases restored? It *seems so*. But observe the cautious kindness of the Ministers, who pretend to be your benefactors. The words of the statute are that those "laws shall be the rule, until they shall be *varied* or *altered* by any ordinances of the Governor and Council." ... Such is the precarious tenure of mere *will* by which you hold your lives and religion. The Crown and its Ministers are empowered, as far as they could be by Parliament, to establish even the Inquisition itself among you....

We are too well acquainted with the liberality of sentiment distinguishing

[*] Griffin, *Catholics and the American Revolution*, 1:17–18.
10. The Treaty of Paris of 1763, which ended the Seven Years' War.

your nation, to imagine, that differences of religion will prejudice you against a hearty amity with us. You know, that the transcendent nature of freedom elevates those who unite in her cause, above all such low-minded infirmities. The Swiss Cantons furnish a memorable proof of this truth. Their union is composed of Roman Catholic and Protestant States, living in the utmost concord and peace with one another, and thereby enabled, ever since they bravely vindicated their freedom, to defy and defeat every tyrant that has invaded them.

48

"To Submit to POPERY AND SLAVERY": Handbill Directed to the Soldiers of the British Army by the "Friends of America," 1775*

The popery/king as slavery theme was not only employed to attract colonists to the patriot cause. It could serve as well to dissuade British soldiers from being the instruments imposing slavery upon a free Protestant people, as this handbill distributed early in the war was designed to do. How effective do you think this handbill would have been with its intended audience? Is it more apt to generate a positive response from one or other of the ethnic groups that composed the British military during the Revolution?

You are about to embark for *America*, to compel your Fellow Subjects there to submit to POPERY and SLAVERY.

It is the Glory of the British Soldier, that he is the *Defender*, not the *Destroyer*, of the Civil and Religious Rights of the People. The *English* Soldiery are immortalized in History, for their Attachment to the Religion and Liberties of their Country.

When King JAMES the Second endeavoured to introduce the Roman Catholic Religion and arbitrary Power into *Great Britain*, he had an Army encamped on *Hounslow-Heath*, to terrify the People. Seven Bishops were seized upon, and sent to the Tower. But they appealed to the Laws of their

* Griffin, *Catholics and the American Revolution* 1:12.

Country, and were set at Liberty. When this News reached the Camp, the Shouts of Joy were so great, that they re-echoed in the Royal Palace. This, however, did not quite convince the King, of the Aversion of the Soldiers to be the Instruments of Oppression against their Fellow Subjects. He therefore made another trial. He ordered the Guards to be drawn up, and the Word was given, that those who did not choose to support the King's Measures, should ground their Arms. When, behold, to his utter confusion, and their eternal Honour—the whole body ground their Arms.

You, gentlemen, will soon have an Opportunity of showing equal Virtue. You will be called upon to imbrue your Hands in the Blood of your Fellow Subjects in *America* because they will not admit to be Slaves, and are alarmed at the Establishment of Popery and Arbitrary Power in One Half of their Country.

Whether you will draw those Swords which have defended them against their Enemies, to butcher them into a Resignation of their Rights, which they hold as the Sons of *Englishmen,* is in your Breasts. That you will not stain the Laurels you have gained from *France,* by dipping them in Civil Blood, is every good Man's Hope....

49

"Uniting with Us in Defence of Our Common Liberty": Address of the Continental Congress to the Oppressed Inhabitants of Canada, May 29, 1775[*]

After authorizing the address, the Congress directed that it be translated into French and one thousand copies printed, which were to be sent for distribution among the 50,000 residents of the province of Quebec. To what is "the present plan" referring? To what does the congress appeal in urging the Canadians to join their cause? In what way(s) does this appeal differ from the one the Congress directed to the Canadians eight months earlier? (See "Address of the Continental Congress to the People of the Province of Quebec, October 21, 1774.")

[*] Griffin, *Catholics and the American Revolution,* 1:182–84.

Friends and Countrymen:—Alarmed by the designs of an arbitrary Ministry to extirpate the rights and liberties of all *America*, a sense of common danger conspired with the dictates of humanity in urging us to call your attention, by our late address to this very important object.

Since the conclusion of the late war, we have been happy in considering you as fellow-subjects; and from the commencement of the present plan for subjugating the Continent, we have viewed you as fellow-sufferers with us. As we were both entitled by the bounty of an indulgent Creator to freedom, and being both devoted by the cruel edicts of a despotic Administration to common ruin, we perceived the fate of the Protestant and Catholic Colonies to be strongly linked together, and therefore invited you to join with us in resolving to be free, and in rejecting, with disdain, the fetters of slavery, however artfully polished....

When hardy attempts are made to deprive men of rights bestowed by the Almighty, when avenues are cut through the most solemn compacts for the admission of despotism, when the plighted faith of government ceases to give security to dutiful subjects, and when the insidious stratagems and maneuvers of peace become more terrible than the sanguinary operations of war, it is high time for them to assert those rights, and, with honest indignation, oppose the torrent of oppression rushing in upon them.

By the introduction of your present form of Government, or rather present form of tyranny, you and your wives and your children are made slaves. You have nothing that you can call your own, and all the fruits of your labour and industry may be taken from you whenever an avaricious Governor and a rapacious Council may incline to demand them. You are liable by their edicts to be transported into foreign Countries to fight battles in which you have no interest, and to spill your blood in conflicts from which neither honour nor emolument can be derived: nay, the enjoyment of your very Religion, on the present system, depends on a Legislature in which you have no share, and over which you have no control, and your priests are exposed to expulsion, banishment, and ruin, whenever their wealth and possessions furnish sufficient temptation. They cannot be sure that a virtuous Prince will always fill the throne and should a wicked or careless King concur with a wicked Ministry in extracting the treasure and strength of your Country, it is impossible to conceive to what variety and to what extremes of wretchedness you may, under the present establishment, be reduced.

We are informed you have already been called upon to waste your lives in a contest with us. Should you, by complying in this instance, assent to your new establishment and a war break out with *France*, your wealth and your sons may be sent to perish in expeditions against their Islands in the *West Indies*.

It cannot be presumed that these considerations will have no weight with you, or that you are so lost to all sense of honour. We can never believe that the present race of *Canadians* are so degenerated as to possess neither the spirit, the gallantry, nor the courage of their ancestors. You certainly will not permit the infamy and disgrace of such pusillanimity to rest on your own heads, and the consequences of it on your children forever....

Permit us again to repeat that we are your friends, not your enemies, and be not imposed upon by those who may endeavor to create animosities.... [Y]ou may rely on our assurances, that these Colonies will pursue no measures, whatever, but such as friendship and a regard for our mutual safety and interest may suggest.

As our concern for your welfare entitles us to your friendship we presume you will not, by doing us injury, reduce us to the disagreeable necessity of treating you as enemies.

We yet entertain hopes of your uniting with us in the defence of our common liberty, and there is yet reason to believe, that should we join in imploring the attention of our Sovereign to the unmerited and unparalleled oppression of his *American* subjects, he will at length be undeceived, and forbid a licentious Ministry any longer to riot in the ruins of the rights of mankind.

50

"That Ridiculous and Childish Custom": George Washington's Orders regarding Pope's Day, November 5, 1775*

The pope might have become a surrogate for the king by the 1770s, particularly in New England, but the commander of the American forces was not about to allow such anti-Catholic mummery in his own camp at a time when the rebels were attempting to assure Catho-

---

* Griffin, *Catholics and the American Revolution*, 1:29.

lic Canadians that the American incursion deep into Quebec Province was not an invasion, but a liberation. What are the "late happy successes" to which Washington refers? What is ironic about his reference to "the common enemy"?

As the Commander-in Chief has been apprised of a design formed for the observance of that ridiculous and childish custom of burning the effigy of the Pope, he cannot help expressing his surprise that there should be officers and soldiers in this army so void of common sense as not to see the impropriety of such a step at this juncture; at a time when we are soliciting, and have really obtained the friendship and alliance of the people of Canada, whom we ought to consider as brethren embarked on the same cause—the defence of the Liberties of America. At this juncture and under such circumstances to be insulting their religion is so monstrous as not to be suffered or excused; indeed, instead of offering the most remote insult, it is our duty to address public thanks to these our brethren, as to them we are indebted for every late happy success on the common enemy in Canada.

51

"Was Not All This the Work of Divine Providence?" Bishop Briand's Pastoral Letter to the People of Quebec, December 29, 1776[*]

On the first anniversary of the repulse of the American siege on Quebec, the French Catholic bishop of the city in his published commemoration of the crucial event could not contain his joy over its outcome. What leads the bishop to the conclusion that Providence alone accounts for the victory the British have known in driving the Americans from Canada?

What are to-day, your sentiments, Dearly beloved Brethren, on the happy and glorious event of December 31, 1775, of which the anniversary will, in three days from this date, recall the grateful and consoling memory? You looked

* Griffin, *Catholics and the American Revolution*, 1:97–98.

upon it then as a singular dispensation of Providence, to be remembered and held as a debt of gratitude to the God of armies for all time.... With the greatest consolation did we witness on the part of all the generals and faithful defenders of this town manifestations of the sentiment and see them all combine to render homage to the Supreme Being for the victory of that day.... He consummated His work, and after having amid the shades of night, rescued us by a kind of miracle, or rather by a real miracle from the hands of our enemies, and delivered them into our hands, when they deemed themselves victorious, that God of goodness, against whom neither science, nor wisdom, nor strength, nor craft, nor knavery can prevail, restored to us and not only to us but to the whole colony, the blessing of liberty.

It was God and God only, who restored to us H. E. Monsieur Carleton.[11] He it was who covered him with his shadow, who guided his footsteps, and brought him safely through the network of most vigilant sentinels specially posted at every point of vantage in order to capture him and carry him off; it was God who enabled our illustrious Governor to put courage in every heart, to tranquilize the minds of the people and to reestablish peace and union in the town. It was God himself who imparted and preserved unanimity and concord amidst a garrison consisting of men of different ranks, characters, interests and religions. It was God who inspired that brave and glorious garrison with the constancy, strength, generosity and attachment to their king and their duty, which enabled them to sustain a long and painful siege during the severity of a Canadian winter.... What more need I say? The arrival of help from Europe at a most opportune moment and but a few hours in advance of the assistance which reached the enemy; the terror manifested by the enemy on seeing His Excellency outside of the wall with a small number of men ... the precipitate flight of the enemy on the approach of our troops; the victories won on lake Champlain; was not all this the work of Divine Providence and do not these wonderful mercies call for our gratitude? ... Let us then Dear Brethren most joyfully chant a hymn of rejoicing and gratitude to our God, who has worked so many wonders in our behalf.

11. Governor-General Guy Carlton, who had commanded the Canadian forces at Quebec.

"Our ... Government Seems to Be Approaching ... Its Dissolution": Charles Carroll's Case for Independence and Government Reform, *Dunlap's Maryland Gazette and Baltimore General Advertiser*, March–April 1776

Carroll systematically undermined all the arguments for remaining as colonies in the empire. In setting independence as the logical outcome, if not the goal of the contest the colonies were waging with the British, he was staking out a position far more radical than most Marylanders were willing to take as winter gave way to spring in 1776. Is Carroll's manifesto a natural outgrowth of his reasoning in the debate with Dulany three years earlier? What else might have contributed to his shift leftward?

Dunlap's Maryland Gazette, March 26, 1776

[O]ppression must be grievous, and extensive, before the body of the people can be prevailed on to resist the established authority of the state.... Changes in the constitution ought not to be lightly made; but when corruption has long infected the legislative, and executive powers: when these pervert the public treasure to the worst of purposes, and fraudulently combine to undermine the liberties of the people; if THEY tamely submit to such misgovernment, we may fairly conclude, the bulk of that people to be ripe for slavery. In this extremity, it is not only lawful; but it becomes the duty of all honest men, to unite in defence of their liberties: to use force, if force would be requisite; to suppress such enormities, and to bring back the constitution to the purity of its original principles. If a nation, in the case put, may lawfully resist the established government, resistance surely is equally justifiable in an empire composed of several separate territories; to each of which, for securing liberty and property, legislative powers have been granted by compact, and long enjoyed by common consent: for should these powers be invaded, and attempted to be rendered nugatory and useless by the principal part of the empire, possessing a limited sovereignty over the whole; should this part relying on its superior strength and riches, reject the supplications of the injured, or treat them with contempt; and appeal from reason to the sword; then are the bands burst asunder, which held together, and united under one dominion these separate territories; a dissolution of the empire ensues; all oaths of allegiance cease to be binding, and the parts attacked are at liberty to erect what government they think best suited to the temper of the people, and exigency of affairs. The British Northern American Colonies are thus circumstanced:—they have then a right to choose a constitution for themselves, and if the choice is delayed, (should the contest continue) necessity will enforce that choice....

That the United Colonies have already exercised the real powers of government, will not be denied: Why they should not assume the forms, no good reason can be given; as the controversy must NOW be decided by the sword! ... While our people consider the King of Great-Britain as THEIR King; while they wish to be connected with, and subordinate to Great Britain; ... Confidence once betrayed ... can never be regained; the confidence of the colonies in, and their attachment to the Parent State arose from the interchange of benefits, and the conceived opinion of a sameness of interests; but now we plainly perceive that these are distinct; nay, incompatible: Why then should we consider ourselves any longer dependent on Great Britain, unless we mean to prefer slavery to liberty, or unconditional submission to independence? ... self-defence, and the preservation of all we hold dear, seem now to be necessarily connected with our independence. What is it that constitutes despotism, but the assemblage and union of the legislative, executive, and judicial functions in the same person, or persons? When they are united in one person, a monarchy is established; when in many, an aristocracy, or oligarchy, both equally inconsistent with the liberties of the people; the absolute dominion of a single person is indeed preferable to the absolute dominion of many; as one tyrant is better than twenty.... The interests of the people rightly understood, calls for the establishment of a regular and consistent government; and good policy should induce the Convention to consult the true interest of the people, by parting with the executive, and judicial powers, and placing them in different hands.

Dunlap's Maryland Gazette, April 2, 1776

OUR present government seems to be approaching fast to its dissolution; necessity during the war will introduce material changes; INDEPENDENCE, the consequence of victory, will perpetuate them.... Let the spirit of our constitution be preserved; nay, improved by correcting the errors of our old system, and strengthening its soundest and best supports.

53

"Toward the Universal Re-establishment of Popery through All Christendom": The French Alliance and Its Impact on the Status of American Catholics

The 1778 alliance forged by the American and French governments came as a shock to many colonists enculturated to view France as the bête noir of British America, an attitude the Pennsylvania *Ledger* poignantly summed up in the following editorial. For others, such as Samuel Cooper (1725–83), the alliance was a military necessity that outweighed the history of conflict between the French and British in America. Cooper, Congregational pastor of the Brattle Street Church in Boston for more than thirty-five years, had been one of the leading preachers of the anti-popery gospel. During the Seven Years' War he had given some of the most condemnatory sermons about the French as the epitome of Catholic treachery. He had been one of the earliest to apply to the persons and actions of the British the symbols and characteristics associated with the anti-Catholic tradition. Suddenly Cooper became an advocate of Catholic toleration. What was not known was that he was receiving $1,000 a year as a French agent, part of France's secret campaign to influence the war's outcome. But Cooper's conversion represented the currents of pragmatism as well. As with Cooper, so much of the nation: no longer would religious interests or concerns be the essential determinant of positions or alliances but rather economic and intellectual ones. In his sermon, what new understanding of religion does Cooper display? What connection does Cooper see between the republic they are creating and religion? What prevents the Pennsylvania *Ledger* from sharing Cooper's liberal view regarding religion?

Pennsylvania Ledger, May 13, 1778[*]

Is it possible we can *now* wish for a final separation from Britain, the ancient and chief support of the Protestant religion in the world, for the sake of upholding a little longer, at the expense of our own lives and fortunes, the arbitrary power of that Congress, who without even asking our consent, have *disposed* of us, have mortgaged us like vassals and slaves, by refusing to treat with Britain and by entering into a treaty with that ambitious and treacherous power whose religious and political maxims have so often disturbed the peace and invaded the rights of mankind? The Congress have wonderfully altered their tone of late. The time was when the bare toleration of the Roman Catholic religion in Canada, though stipulated for by the articles of capitulation,[12] was treated as a wicked attempt to establish "a sanguinary faith, which had for ages filled the world with blood and slaughter." But now the Congress are willing to make us the instruments of weakening the best friends, and of strengthening the most powerful and ambitious enemies of the Reformation to such a degree as must do more than all the world besides could do, towards the universal re-establishment of Popery through all Christendom-judge then what we have to hope or expect from such an alliance! We not only run a manifest risk of becoming slaves ourselves, under the treacherous title of independency, but we are doing everything in our power to overturn the Protestant religion, and extinguish every spark, both of civil and religious liberty in the world!

Samuel Cooper, A Sermon on the Day of the Commencement of the Constitution, 1780[†]

We want not ... a special revelation from heaven to teach us that men are born equal and free; that no man has a natural claim of dominion over his neighbours, nor one nation any such claim upon another; and that as government is only the administration of the affairs of a number of men combined for their own security and happiness, such a society have a right freely to determine by whom and in what manner their own affairs shall be ad-

---

[*] Cited in Griffin, *Catholics and the American Revolution*, 1:39.

[†] Ellis Sandoz, *Political Sermons of the American Founding Era*, vol. 1, *1730–1788*, no. 21, 2nd ed. (Indianapolis: Liberty Fund, 1998).

12. The Treaty of Paris of 1763.

ministered. These are the plain dictates of that reason and common sense with which the common parent of men has informed the human bosom. It is, however, a satisfaction to observe such everlasting maxims of equity confirmed, and impressed upon the consciences of men, by the instructions, precepts, and examples given us in the sacred oracles; one internal mark of their divine original, and that they come from him "who hath made of one blood all nations to dwell upon the face of the earth," whose authority sanctifies only those governments that instead of oppressing any part of his family, vindicate the oppressed, and restrain and punish the oppressor....

Unhappy the people who ... have not the ulterior powers of government within themselves; who depend upon the will of another state, with which they are not incorporated as a vital part, the interest of which must in many respects be opposite to their own; and who at the same time have no fixed constitutional barrier to restrain this reigning power. There is no meanness or misery to which such a people is not liable. There is not a single blessing, tho' perhaps indulged to them for a while, that they can call their own; there is nothing they have not to dread. Whether the governing power be itself free or despotic, it matters not to the poor dependent. Nations who are jealous of their own liberties often sport with those of others; nay, it has been remarked, that the dependent provinces of free states have enjoyed less freedom than those belonging to despotic powers. Such was our late dismal situation, from which heaven hath redeemed us by a signal and glorious revolution....

Upon our present independence ... we cannot deny, that when we were not searching for it, it happily found us.... It was our birth right; we ought to have valued it highly, and never to have received a mess of pottage, a small temporary supply, as an equivalent for it.... [W]e did not seek an independence; and ... Britain, though she meant to oppose it with all her power, has by a strange infatuation, taken the most direct, and perhaps the only methods that could have established it. Her oppressions, her unrelenting cruelty, have driven us out from the family of which we were once a part. This has opened our eyes to discern the inestimable blessing of a separation from her; while, like children that have been inhumanly treated and cast out by their parents, and at the same time are capable of taking care of themselves, we have found friendship and respect from the world and have formed new advantageous and honorable connections....

By this conduct of our enemies, heaven hath granted us an inestimable opportunity, and such as has been rarely if ever indulged to so great a people: An opportunity to avail ourselves of the wisdom and experience of all past ages united with that of the present, … and of choosing for ourselves, unencumbered with the pretensions of royal heirs, or lordly peers, of feudal rights, or ecclesiastical authority, that form of civil government which we judge most conducive to our own security and order, liberty and happiness: An opportunity, though surrounded with the flames of war, of deliberating and deciding upon this most interesting of all human affairs with calmness and freedom.… The origin of most nations is covered with obscurity, and veiled by fiction; the rise of our own is open as it is honourable; and the new-born state … is a "spectacle to men and angels." …

What a broad foundation for the exercise of the rights of conscience is laid in this constitution! Which declares, that "no subject shall be hurt, molested, or restrained in his person, liberty or estate, for worshipping God in the manner and season most agreeable to the dictates of his own conscience, or for his religious profession or sentiments; and that every denomination of Christians, demeaning themselves peaceably, and as, good subjects of the commonwealth, shall be equally under the protection of the law, and no subordination of any one sect or denomination to another shall be established by law." It considers indeed morality and the public worship of God as important to the happiness of society.… The citizens of this state … know [the present constitution][13] is framed upon an extent of civil and religious liberty, unexampled perhaps in any country in the world, except America.… I know there is a diversity of sentiment respecting the extent of civil power in religious matters … may I be allowed from the warmth of my heart, to recommend, where conscience is pleaded on both sides, mutual candour and love, and an happy union of all denominations in support of a government, which though human, and therefore not absolutely perfect, is yet certainly founded on the broadest basis of liberty, and affords equal protection to all.…

13. This constitution was actually the second one that Massachusetts delegates had approved in convention. The one that the 1778 convention presented for public ratification would have essentially preserved the penal status for Catholics in the state and barred them from public office and from the enjoyment of the religious freedom guaranteed to all other Christian communities. After voters rejected that constitution, they approved one that emerged from the convention held the following year—a constitution that extended full religious liberty to all Christians, including Catholics, while preserving the Congregational Church as the established religion in Massachusetts, a privileged status it would enjoy into the fourth decade of the nineteenth century.

Happy indeed, when every man shall love and serve his country, and have that share of public influence and respect, without distinction of parties, which his virtues and services may justly demand. This is the true spirit of a commonwealth, centering all hearts, and all hands in the common interest....

The treaty of alliance and friendship between *his most christian majesty* and these states,[14] is engraved on every bosom friendly to the rights and independence of America.... The interest is indeed mutual, as was openly confessed: The treaty is therefore natural, and likely to be lasting. But mutual interest doth not always banish generosity, a proof of which our illustrious ally hath given in this compact.... France, tho' a monarchy, has been the nurse and protectress of free republics....

The other great and powerful branch of the house of Bourbon, the king of Spain, tho' not at present formally allied to us, is yet evidently engaged in our cause, by the union of his arms with those of France. We cannot be wanting in the sentiments due to the amity and aide of so respectable a potentate. May God Almighty bless these princes, and their dominions, and crown their arms, and those of America, with such success as may soon restore to a bleeding world the blessings of peace....

Sources

Barber, Daniel. *The History of My Own Times*. Washington, D.C.: 1827. Cited in Francis D. Cogliano, *No King, No Popery: Anti-Catholicism in Revolutionary New England*. Westport, Conn.: Greenwood Press, 1995.

Farrelly, Maura Jane. "Papist Patriots: Catholic Identity and Revolutionary Ideology in Maryland." Ph.D. diss., Emory University, 2002.

———. *Papist Patriots: The Making of an American Catholic Identity*. New York: Oxford University Press, 2012.

Geiger, Mary Virginia. *Daniel Carroll: A Framer of the Constitution*. Washington, D.C.: The Catholic University of America Press, 1943.

Griffin, Martin I. J. *Catholics and the American Revolution*. Vol. 1. Ridley Park, Pa.: Martin I. J. Griffin, 1907.

Hanley, Thomas O'Brien, SJ, ed. *John Carroll Papers*. Vol. 1. Notre Dame: University of Notre Dame Press, 1976.

Hanson, Charles P. *Necessary Virtue: The Pragmatic Origins of Religious Liberty in New England*. Charlottesville: University of Virginia Press, 1998.

14. Louis XVI, king of France.

Hardy, Beatriz Betancourt. "Papists in a Protestant Age: The Catholic Gentry and Community in Colonial Maryland, 1689–1776." Ph.D. diss., University of Maryland, 1993.

Hoffman, Ronald. *A Spirit of Dissension: Economics, Politics, and the Revolution in Maryland*. Baltimore: Johns Hopkins University Press, 1973.

Kidd, Thomas. *God of Liberty: A Religious History of the American Revolution*. New York: Basic Books, 2010.

Lee, Jean B. *The Price of Nationhood: The American Revolution in Charles County*. New York and London: W. W. Norton, 1994.

McGreevy, John T. *Catholicism and American Freedom: A History*. New York: Norton, 2003.

Melville, Annabelle M. *John Carroll of Baltimore: Founder of the American Catholic Hierarchy*. New York: Scribner's, 1955.

Metzger, Charles H. *Catholics and the American Revolution: A Study in Religious Climate*. Chicago: Loyola University Press, 1962.

O'Shaughnessy, Andrew Jackson. *An Empire Divided: The American Revolution and the British Caribbean*. Philadelphia: University of Pennsylvania Press, 2000.

Peterman, Thomas Joseph. *Catholics in Colonial Delaware*. Devon, Pa.: Cooke, 1996.

Riley, Elihu S. *Correspondence of "First Citizen": Charles Carroll of Carrollton and "Antilon" Daniel Dulaney Jr., 1773*. Baltimore: King Brothers, 1902.

Sandoz, Ellis. *Political Sermons of the American Founding Era*. Vol. 1, *1730–1788*. No. 21. 2nd ed. Indianapolis: Liberty Fund, 1998.

Part 10

Peace and a New Order

1781–1791

THE AMERICAN-FRENCH ALLIANCE finally mustered the naval and land military power to inflict what proved to be a fatal defeat upon the British. In the fall of 1781, a joint American-French force bottled up Cornwallis's army at Yorktown in Virginia. At the same time the French fleet had gained control of the waters in the middle Atlantic around Chesapeake Bay. With no hope of securing relief by sea, Lord Cornwallis was forced to surrender his badly outnumbered army (6,000 versus more than 16,000) on October 19, 1781. "It's all over," was British prime minister Lord North's reaction to the devastating news. The Americans and French knew as much. The official peace would not come for over a year, but in all reality the war had ended. To celebrate the great event, the French minister in Philadelphia invited members of the Continental Congress and other American officials to attend a special Mass of Thanksgiving at St. Mary's Church (see "The Wonderful Work of That God Who Guards Your Liberties").

The war had proven to be a religious revolution as well as a political one. Two major consequences of the religious revolution were the establishment of the freedom to practice the religion of one's choice as a common right and the disestablishment of the Anglican Church. In the new order the state did not prescribe religious conformity, but left religious allegiance to one's free choice. The evangelical churches, with their free-will-centered conversion experience at the heart of their gospel message, seemed to a swelling number of Americans most in line with the principles that had driven the successful revolution of the colonies. The Baptists and Methodists, the evangelical off-shoots of the state-privileged Congregationalists and Anglicans respectively, emerged as the big winners, riding the democratic dynamic that the Great Awakening had launched. In this upheaval, no denomination was a bigger beneficiary than the Catholic Church, which had borne the greatest burden of legal discrimination in the colonial era. With the successful conclusion of the war, Catholics were free to compete in the marketplace of proselytizing, something Joseph Mosley, isolated as he was on the Eastern Shore of Maryland, quickly realized. That previously unknown opportunity made the lack of personnel to pursue such a potential spiritual harvest all the more frustrating (see "The Harvest Is Great, but the Labourers Are Too Few").

The priest shortage worsened the following June (1787) when Joseph Mosley died at St. Joseph's. The constant hardships of his peripatetic ministry had aged him far beyond his fifty-six years. Old and worn-out was a sad but accurate description for most of the remaining two score–plus priests in the new republic. But by the time Joseph Mosley completed the good race that he had run, the church, which at the end of the revolution had seemed an orphan, cut off from any immediate source of leadership or clergy, was one no longer, thanks to the initiatives that John Carroll took once the Peace of Paris confirmed that the United States were indeed an independent nation. In June of 1783, at a meeting at the former Jesuit plantation at Whitemarsh in central Maryland, six priests had agreed to form the Select Body of the Clergy, a group of six elected representatives charged with the administration of the property previously held by the Society of Jesus as well as with the formation of local church policy. This republican organization was the fruit of a plan that Carroll had devised from one earlier adopted by ex-Jesuits in Great Britain. Within this basic frame of government the American clergy proceeded to establish a distinct institutional church.

The Select Body moved to build a school at Georgetown that would, at least in part, serve as the first stage of education for future priests. Having made this major commitment to clerical formation, if only at Carroll's prodding, the representatives next petitioned Rome for a bishop. Consistent with the republican nation they now were part of, the Catholic clergy requested that the choice of a bishop should be by an election—by the representatives of the body of American priests. Rome acceded—for this time—to an election, and, to no one's surprise, John Carroll was the choice. He was consecrated as bishop of Baltimore in England in 1790. While in Great Britain for his consecration, the new bishop made arrangements for a group of Sulpicians to find refuge from the French Revolution by opening a seminary in Baltimore. Two years later, the Select Body was legally incorporated by the state of Maryland as the Roman Catholic Clergymen of Maryland. The Roman Catholic Church in America now had the official recognition, if not of the national government, at least of the state of the new union that had been the heart of the Catholic presence in British America (see "A Revolution More Extraordinary … Than Our Political One").

The Revolution for Carroll had been a Red Sea of liberation for American Catholics from their penal position during the colonial period. Boston, the epicenter of anti-Catholicism in British America, the colony where Catholics were the most marginalized, the most "other," the least free, had also been in the center of the forces creating a sea change in their position within American society. The June 1791 dinner celebrating the election of the Ancient and Honorable Artillery Company, the oldest military organization in New England, encapsulated the arrival of Catholics in Boston society. The dinner, with its accompanying sermon, had been an annual recognition and renewal of the region's Protestant heritage. This year there were two clergymen to deliver the blessing before the meal, one of whom was John Carroll. That Protestant and Catholic men of the cloth would have shared the ritual duties at such an iconic Protestant event would have been unthinkable fifteen years earlier. Even in New England there was a new order (see "A Country Now Become Our Own").

In the first presidential election under the new constitution, George Washington, as the man most credited with the winning of the country's independence, was the unanimous choice. On the anniversary of the president's first year in office, five prominent Catholics, including three Carrolls of Maryland—Charles, Daniel, and John—and two merchants from New York and Philadelphia, Dominick Lynch and Thomas Fitzsimmons respectively, wrote Washington to convey their best wishes on behalf of the Catholics of the new republic. At the same time, they did not hesitate to remind Washington of the crucial role that Catholics, both domestic and foreign, had played in determining the success of the revolution that created the republic he now headed. Their patriotism, displayed on the battlefield and through diplomacy and in the legislative halls, had earned them the full rights of citizenship, "rights," they pointed out, "rendered more dear to us by the remembrance of former hardships," of which they had borne far more than their share in the nation's colonial beginnings.

President Washington, for his part, showed his sensitivity to the peculiar history of Catholics in British America: their "outlaw" status for most of the colonial period and, despite that past, their extraordinary contributions to the winning of independence. The first president put an official seal on the new order of things in this young republic by observing that what qualified a person to participate fully in this civic society is one thing only: good citizenship (see "You, Sir, Have Been the Principal Instrument").

The United States had evolved into a civilization in which the members of all denominations within its borders, including Catholics, were equally entitled to enjoy the full fruits that this republican government was nurturing. There was no longer an inherent conflict between being a good Catholic and a good citizen. For the present, Catholics were no longer "intestine enemies."

54

"The Wonderful Work of That God Who Guards Your Liberties": Abbe Bandol's Sermon at the Mass of Thanksgiving for the Victory at Yorktown, November 4, 1781*

Seraphin Bandol, one of a hundred priests to accompany French forces to America as chaplains, delivered the following sermon to the distinguished congregation that had come together to celebrate and give thanks. The theme—God's strange providence—was an old one, but Abbe Bandol gave it a peculiar application that was remarkably new. What was it? What do you think the non-Catholic Americans in the pews would have found most surprising in his remarks?

*American Museum 4 (July 1788): 28–29, in Griffin, Catholics, 1:312–14.

Those miracles, which he once wrought for his chosen people, are renewed in our favour; and it would be equally ungrateful and impious not to acknowledge, that the event which lately confounded our enemies, and frustrated their designs, was the wonderful work of that God who guards your liberties.

And who but he could so combine the circumstances which led to success? We have seen our enemies push forward, amid perils almost innumerable, amid obstacles almost insurmountable, to the spot which was designed to witness their disgrace: yet they eagerly sought it, as their theatre of triumph!

Blind as they were, they bore hunger, thirst, and inclement skies, poured their blood in battle against brave republicans, and crossed immense regions to confine themselves in another Jericho, whose walls were fated to fall before another Joshua. It is he, whose voice commands the winds, the seas and seasons, who formed a junction on the same day, in the same hour, between a formidable fleet from the south, and an army rushing from the north, like an impetuous torrent. Who, but he, in whose hands are the hearts of men, could inspire the allied troops with the friendships, the confidence, the tenderness of brothers? How is it that two nations once divided, jealous, inimical, and nursed in reciprocal prejudices, are now become so closely united, as to form but one? Worldlings would say, it is the wisdom, the virtue, and moderation of their chiefs; it is a great national interest which has performed this prodigy. They will say, that to the skill of the generals, to the courage of the troops, to the activity of the whole army, we must attribute this splendid success. Ah! They are ignorant, that the combining of so many fortunate circumstances, is an emanation from the all perfect mind; that courage, that skill, that activity, bear the sacred impression of him who is divine.

For how many favours have we not to thank him during the course of the present year? Your union, which was at first supported by justice alone, has been consolidated by your courage: and the knot which ties you together, is become indissoluble, by the accession of all the states, and the unanimous voice of all the confederates. You present to the universe the noble sight of a society, which, founded in equality and justice, secures to the individuals who compose it, the utmost happiness which can be derived from human institutions. This advantage, which so many other nations have been unable to procure, even after ages of efforts and misery, is granted by divine providence to the United States; and its adorable decrees have marked the present moment for the completion of that memorable and happy revolution which has taken place in this extensive continent....

On this solemn occasion, we might renew our thanks to the God of battles, for the success he has granted to the arms of your allies, and your friends, by land and by sea, through the other parts of the globe.... Let us entreat him to maintain in each of the States that intelligence by which the United States are inspired.... And let us with one will and one voice, pour forth to the Lord that hymn of praise, by which Christians celebrate their gratitude and His glory.[1]

55

"The Harvest Is Great, but the Labourers Are Too Few": Joseph Mosley on the New Order for Catholics, 1784*

A decade had elapsed since Joseph Mosley and his sister Helen had last corresponded. When they were finally able to reconnect, they wrote as citizens of different countries. Joseph Mosley, despite his conflicted feelings and the strong loyalist sentiment on the Eastern Shore, had not only taken—at last—the oath of loyalty to the new government but even had become a force for supporting the revolution by encouraging his congregations to take the oath and to enlist in the ranks of the patriots. With the United States now independent of Great Britain, how does Mosley assess the lay of the land for organized religion? Does he see anything other than the lack of clergy preventing the Catholic Church from taking full advantage of the religious realignment that has followed the return of peace?

Our Correspondence has been long interrupted by Reason of the late, tedious, & calamitous War. Peace is returned ... we can correspond again. I am yet alive, thank God. I enjoy a middling good State of health, notwithstanding my Fatigues & long frequent Rides in my old age. I hope you are also well? I hear my Brother Michael is dead, but I've had no certain intelligence of it. I've often pray'd for him, as dead. I've heard nothing concerning you or your Family's Health since your last Letters.... I am yet on the same Farm, on which I lived, when you wrote to me last.... I've been on it

---

*Joseph Mosley to Helen Dunn, Tuckahoe, October 4, 1784, Mosley Papers, GULBFCSC.
1. The *Te Deum*.

now twenty long years. I've made it through God's Help, both agreeable & profitable to myself & to my successors; not knowing the Length of Life, my chief aim was to make it convenient, happy, & easy to my Successors, that they might with some comfort continue a flourishing Mission that I have begun; when I first settled I had not one of my own Profession[2] nigher than six or seven mile, but now, thru God's particular Blessings, I've many Families, joining, and all round me. The Toleration here granted by the Bill of Rights has put all on the same setting, & has been of great Service to us. The Methodists, who have started up chiefly since the War, have brought over to themselves, chief of the former Protestants here on the Eastern Shore of Maryland, where I live. The Protestant Ministers having [no] fixed Salary by Law, as heretofore, have abandoned their Flocks, which ... now ... [have] joined different Societies.[3] We've had some share. Since the Commencement of the War, I've built on my Farm a brick Chapel & dwelling House. It was a difficult & bold Undertaking at that Time, as every Necessary, especially Nails were very dear. I began it, trusting on Providence & I've happily finished, without any assistance either from our Gentlemen or my Congregation. The whole Building is 52 ft long & 24 ft wide, the Wall 15 ft high. Out of this length of Wall the Chapel is 36 ft long & 24 ft wide & with the Arch 20 add. ft high, no cellar under that Part. My dwelling House is 15 by 24ft, two stories high.... My Chapel will hold between 2 ... [and] 300 people. It could not contain the hearers, last Easter Sunday, when I first kept Prayers in it, & every Sunday since it has been very full, when I attend at Home, which is only once every Month. We are all growing old, we are very weak handed, few come from England to help us. I suppose they are much wanted with you; I understand that few enter into Orders of late years, since the destruction of the Society. Here, I can assure you the Harvest is great, but the Labourers are too few. Where I am situated, I attend ten counties by myself, to have it done as it ought, it would take ten able men.[4] Pray fervently, that God may bless all our undertakings. The Book of the *History of the Church* which you sent me, some years ago, has contributed much to our numbers; it is forever agoing from family to family of different persuasions.

2. Roman Catholicism.

3. Denominations.

4. Mosley's mission embraced the entire Delmarva Peninsula, excepting the counties of Cecil and Kent, from the head of the Chester River to Cape Charles.

Mosley to Sister, July 20, 1786

I received your Favour of May 25, 1785 with the Books, which you were so kind as to send me…. The Books came very safe…. They are very acceptable, … There is also a small Book of Dr. Challoner called *A Caveat against the Methodists*. As that Sect abounds in that Part of Maryland, where I live one or two copies of them would be very acceptable & beneficial to the Public. I think I begg'd in my last for another copy of *The General History of the Church, deduced from the Apocalypse*. By P. Pastorini. You sent me one, some years ago. I have it by me, but it has travelled thro' so many hands to the great Benefit of many, that it is much the worse for use. It has done great good & I hope it will do more…. I wish I could make you any satisfaction, but as these books are so beneficial to the poor Catholics, &c who are entirely unprovided of such information, which these Books give, that I sincerely beg the Almighty to reward your charity a hundredfold….

I should have answer'd yours sooner, but the bad state of Health I was in, last Fall prevented me. I've these 10 Months [been] several Times at Death's Door, with bilious Fevers & frequent Returns of the Gravel. I seem to be at present upon the recovery thro' God's Blessing, for I know not what will become of my little Flock, if I should be taken from them. It is a Mission I began about 22 years ago, where no Priest had ever settled, I found a few when I settled here, but, thank God & his divine Assistance, we can now count between 500 & 600 Communicants…. I've wrote several Times to Mr. Strickland[5] at Liege to take Pity of us & send us fresh supplies. I am yet all alone, & have but one other of my call on the Eastern Shore of Maryland, and he lives 50 Miles from me, we see one another perhaps once a Year. You may pity my Situation, I pity that, of my poor Flock, not my own. I wish I was younger & healthy to serve them as I would. My chapel or church is … full every Sunday that we keep Church or Prayers at Home.

5. William Strickland, an English ex-Jesuit, then president of the former English Jesuit Academy at Liège. Carroll was pressing him for a priest to head up the school he had been authorized to begin at Georgetown.

56

"A Revolution More Extraordinary... Than Our Political One": John Carroll's Correspondence, 1779–1787

Most of John Carroll's adult life had been spent in Europe with fellow Jesuits, mostly English. After returning home upon the suppression of the Society, Carroll stayed in touch with a number of them, none more so than Charles Plowden. Plowden (1743–1821) had been with Carroll at the English College at Bruges when the local authorities closed it and temporarily jailed many of the faculty. Whereas Carroll soon after took passage home to minister to his extended family in the Potomac Valley, Plowden remained in Flanders teaching at the English academy in Liège. A year after the Peace Treaty of Paris that officially recognized the United States as independent, Plowden became chaplain and tutor at Lulworth Castle, the home of Thomas Weld, who had been a student at the Bruges College in 1773. When John Carroll had to choose a site for his episcopal consecration in 1790, he selected Lulworth Castle. Plowden preached at the liturgy of consecration. Little wonder that Carroll and Plowden were faithful correspondents across oceans and channels for the rest of Carroll's life. To what extent, if any, do Carroll and Plowden differ in their understanding of the American Revolution? What does Carroll mean by "the fullest & largest system of toleration"? What is Carroll referring to in his assertion "a foreign temporal jurisdiction will never be tolerated here"?

Carroll to Plowden, February 28, 1779[*]

I am glad ... to inform you that the fullest & largest system of toleration is adopted in almost all the American states: public protection & encouragement are extended alike to all denominations & Roman Catholics are members of Congress, assemblies, & hold civil & military posts as well as others.[6]

*JCP, 1:53.

6. When the French Revolution forced the Liège school to relocate to Stonyhurst, England, in 1794, Plowden once again joined the faculty. Later he became the first novice master of the revived English Province and, in 1817, was appointed provincial (Henry Foley, *Records of the English Province of the Society of Jesus* [London: 1882], 7:601–3).

Carroll to Plowden, September 26, 1783[*]

Our gentlemen here continue, as when last I wrote. We are endeavouring to establish some regulations tending to perpetuate a succession of labourers in this vineyard, to preserve their morals, to prevent idleness, and to secure an equitable and frugal administration of our temporals.[7] An immense field is opened to the zeal of apostolical men. Universal toleration throughout this immense country, and innumerable Roman Catholics, going and ready to go into the new regions bordering on the Mississippi, perhaps the finest in the world, and impatiently clamourous for clergymen to attend them. The object nearest my heart is to establish a college on this continent for the education of youth, which might at the same time be a seminary for future clergymen. But at present I see no prospect of success....

Your information of the intention of the Propaganda gives me concern no farther, than to hear that men, whose institution was for the service of Religion, should bend their thoughts so much more to the grasping of power, and the commanding of wealth.[8] For they may be assured that they will never get possession of a sixpence of our property here; and, if any of our friends could be weak enough to deliver any real estate into their hands, or attempt to subject it to their authority, our civil government would be called upon to wrest it again out of their dominion. A foreign temporal jurisdiction will never be tolerated here; and even the spiritual supremacy of the Pope is the only reason, why in some of the United States the full participation of all civil rights is not granted to the Roman Catholics. They may therefore send their agents when they please; they will certainly return empty-handed. My only dread ... would be the scandal that would result from the assertion of unjust pretensions on the one hand, and of undoubted rights on the other. And these sentiments and communications you may make as public as you think proper.

[*]JCP, 1:78.

7. A reference to the Select Body of the Clergy, which had been organized the previous June.

8. Carroll had a deep antipathy to the Congregation for the Propagation of the Faith (Propaganda) because of the role they had played in carrying out the seizure of Jesuit property throughout the world.

Carroll to [?], 1784*

You are not ignorant that in these United States our religious system has undergone a revolution, if possible, more extraordinary than our political one. In all of them free toleration is allowed to Christians of every denomination; and particularly in the States of Pennsylvania, Delaware, Maryland, and Virginia, a communication of all civil rights, without distinction or diminution, is extended to those of our religion. This is a blessing and advantage which it is our duty to preserve and improve, with the utmost prudence, by demeaning ourselves on all occasions as subjects zealously attached to our government and avoiding to give any jealousies on account of any dependence on foreign jurisdiction more than that which is essential to our religion, an acknowledgment of the Pope's spiritual supremacy over the whole Christian world. You know that we of the clergy have heretofore resorted to the Vicar-Apostolic of the London District for the exercise of spiritual powers, but being well acquainted with the temper of Congress, of our assemblies and the people at large, we are firmly of opinion that we shall not be suffered to continue under such a jurisdiction whenever it becomes known to the public. You may be assured of this from the following fact. The clergy of the Church of England were heretofore subject to the Bishop of London,[9] but the umbrage taken at this dependence was so great, that notwithstanding the power and prevalence of that sect they could find no other method to allay jealousies, than by withdrawing themselves as they have lately done, from all obedience to him.

Being therefore thus circumstanced, we think it not only advisable in us, but in a manner obligatory, to solicit the Holy See to place the episcopal powers, at least such as are most essential, in the hands of one amongst us, whose virtue, knowledge, and integrity of faith, shall be certified by ourselves.

Plowden to Carroll, June 6, 1785†

I feel within myself a persuasion that the famous American revolution will tend to the propagation of catholicity & justify the ways of God who knows how to draw good from evil. You are clearly the instrument of his provi-

---

*Carroll Papers, Special, C-A-4, AAB, AASMUS. The recipient is some official within Propaganda in Rome.

† AAB 6 J7, AASMUS.

9. The Church of England in America that subsequently became the Episcopal Church of the United States after the Revolution.

dence & I trust that your zeal & prudence will at length be blessed with a complete triumph over domestic obstacles & foreign opposition. The English & American missions & indeed the whole Eng. province grew out from still smaller beginnings.

Carroll to Plowden, January 22, 1787–February 28, 1787*

We have resolved to establish an academy for the education of youth; and to solicit the appointment of a diocesan Bishop: the latter is a necessary consequence of the former: for our great view, in the establishment of an academy, is to form subjects capable of becoming useful members of the ministry; and to these a Bishop, for Ordination, will be indispensably necessary.

57

"You, Sir, Have Been the Principal Instrument to Effect So Rapid a Change in Our Political Situation": An Address from the Roman Catholics of America to George Washington, Esq., President of the United States, 1790†

The Catholic delegation had hoped to get this testament from the Catholic community to President Washington at the time of his inauguration, not near the first anniversary of it. They pled the excuse of the centripetal character of their settlement in America, with Catholics scattered throughout virtually all of the states, and beginning to fill in the territories with migrations to Kentucky, Tennessee, and beyond. Generally, what marks do they give the nation's first president in his first year of office? What are their hopes as Catholics regarding their future in the new republic?

*JCP, 1:241.
† London: J. P. Coghlan, 1790; reprinted by J. G. Shea, 1867.

The Address

We have been long impatient to testify our joy, and unbounded confidence on your being called, by an Unanimous Vote, to the first station of a country, in which that unanimity could not have been obtained, without the previous merit of unexampled services, of eminent wisdom, and unblemished virtue. Our congratulations have not reached you sooner because our scattered situation prevented our communication, and the collecting of those sentiments, which warmed every breast. But the delay has furnished us with the opportunity, not merely of presaging the happiness to be expected under your administration, but of bearing testimony to that which we experience already. It is your peculiar talent, in war and in peace, to afford security to those who commit their protection into your hands. In war you shield them from the ravages of armed hostility; in peace, you establish public tranquility, by the justice and moderation, not less than by the vigour, of your government. By example, as well as by vigilance, you extend the influence of laws on the manners of our fellow-citizens. You encourage respect for religion; and inculcate, by words and actions, that principle on which the welfare of nations so much depends, that a supertending providence governs the events of the world, and watches over the conduct of men. Your exalted maxims, and unwearied attention to the moral and physical improvement of our country, have produced already the happiest effect. Under your administration, America is animated with zeal for the attainment and encouragement of useful literature. She improves her agriculture; extends her commerce; and acquires with foreign nations a dignity unknown to her before. From these happy events, in which none can feel a warmer interest than ourselves, we derive additional pleasure, by recollecting that you, Sir, have been the principal instrument to effect so rapid a change in our political situation. This prospect of national prosperity is peculiarly pleasing to us, on another account; because, while our country preserves her freedom and independence, we shall have a well founded title to claim from her justice, the equal rights of citizenship, as the price of our blood spilt under your eyes, and of our common exertions for her defence, under your auspicious conduct—rights rendered more dear to us by the remembrance of former hardships. When we pray for the preservation of them, where they have been granted—and expect the full extension of them from the Justice of those States, which still restrict them; when we solicit the protection of

Heaven over our common country, we neither omit, nor can omit recommending your preservation to the singular care of Divine Providence; because we conceive that no human means are so available to promote the welfare of the United States, as the prolongation of your health and life, in which are included the energy of your example, the wisdom of counsels, and the persuasive eloquence of your virtue.

[signers: John Carroll, Charles Carroll, of Carrollton, Daniel Carroll, Dominick Lynch, Thomas Fitzsimmons, In behalf of the Roman Catholic Clergy and Laity.]

Answer to the Roman Catholics in the United States of America

Gentlemen,

While I now receive, with much satisfaction, your congratulations on my being called, by an unanimous Vote, to the first station in my Country— I cannot but duly notice your politeness in offering an apology for the unavoidable delay. As that delay has given you an opportunity of realizing, instead of anticipating, the benefits of the general Government,—you will do me the justice to believe, that your testimony of the increase of the public prosperity, enhances the pleasure, which I should otherwise have experienced from your affectionate Address.

I feel that my conduct, in war and in peace, has met with more general approbation, than could have reasonably been expected: and I find myself disposed to consider, that fortunate circumstance, in a great degree resulting from the able support, and extraordinary candour, of my fellow-citizens of all denominations.

The prospect of national prosperity now before us, is truly animating; and ought to excite the exertions of all good men, to establish and secure the happiness of their Country, in the permanent duration of its freedom and independence. America, under the smiles of Divine Providence—the protection of a good Government—and the cultivation of Manners, Morals, and Piety—cannot fail of attaining, an uncommon degree of Eminence, in Literature, Commerce, Agriculture, Improvements at home, and Respectability abroad.

As Mankind become more liberal, they will be more apt to allow, that all those who conduct themselves worthy members of the Community, are equally entitled to the protection of Civil Government. I hope ever to see

America among the foremost Nations in examples of Justice and Liberality. And I presume that your fellow-citizens will not forget the patriotic part, which you took in the accomplishment of their Revolution, and the establishment of their Government—or the important assistance, which they received from a Nation, in which the Roman Catholic Faith is professed.

I thank you, Gentlemen, for your kind concern for me. While my Life and Health shall continue, in whatever situation I may be, it shall be my constant endeavour to justify the favourable sentiments which you are pleased to express of my conduct. And may the Members of your Society in America, animated alone by the pure spirit of Christianity, and still conducting themselves, as the faithful subjects of our free Government, enjoy every temporal, and spiritual felicity.

58

"A Country Now Become Our Own": John Carroll Sermon, May 1791[*]

Carroll was in Boston not simply to advance the Catholic interest in a town that historically had been particularly hostile to Catholics. The small Catholic congregation at Holy Cross Church had, over the past year, been badly divided between Irish and French factions, each supporting a priest as its pastor. Carroll, now a bishop, had come to Boston from Baltimore to settle the dispute, which he managed to do by getting one of the priests to step down from his ministry there. That was the background to Carroll's preaching to the reunited Holy Cross congregation that same June. How has the long, dark history of anti-Catholic sentiment in Boston, together with the recent scandal that the Catholics' division at Holy Cross Church has occasioned, put a particular burden on the local Catholic community? What does Carroll mean by referring to freedom as both a right and a responsibility? What does Carroll see as key to preserving this double-edged sword?

God has visited you in particular by a signal instance of his mercy in removing the obstacles which heretofore cramped the free exercise of our religious functions. Our meeting together in this place to perform our public

*American Catholic Sermon Collection, GULBFCSC.

worship; that cross, the signal of our faith and monument of its triumphs over the powers of idolatry & infidelity; that altar, erected to perpetuate the great sacrifice of the law of grace, and continued oblation of Christs body & blood, as a propitiation for sin; these, Dear Brethren, are objects calculated to renew the memory of events, in which is displayed the eternal wisdom, reaching from end to end, embracing all space and ages under its comprehensive arrangements, and harmoniously disposing all things. In the events to which I allude, they, who attribute nothing in the affairs of mankind to the government of providence, will only discover the result of human counsels & passions; but they, whose enlightened faith beholds in the history of mankind the traces of a divine and overruling wisdom, will acknowledge the power of God continually exerted for the preservation of religion.

We particularly, Dear Brethren, must feel a tender sentiment of gratitude towards the bestower of every good gift for the favours we now enjoy, whenever we recall to our remembrance the vicissitudes, which have filled up the destinies of our Church since her first establishment by her head and founder Christ Jesus, down to this present day. Divine providence has so directed the course of human affairs; the Holy Ghost has so worked upon & tutored the minds of men, that now, agreeably to the dictates of our own consciences, we may sing canticles of praise to the Lord, in a country no longer foreign or unfriendly to us, but in a country now become our own, & taking us into her protection. In return for so great a blessing, your first duty was, and I trust, that you forgot it not, to render to Almighty God the tribute of thankfulness due, above all to Him; and next, to bear in your hearts gratitude, respect & veneration for them, whose benevolence was the instrument of Gods favour & mercy toward us. Let your earnest applications be addressed to the throne of grace, that every blessing, temporal & eternal, may descend on your fellow citizens, your Brethren in Jesus Christ. Be solicitous to extend, by your example and encouragement, the prevalence of Christian virtues; to recommend your religion by the innocence of your manners & the sanctity of your lives, and especially by cultivating the first of Christian duties, that, which is dearest to our Blessed and charitable Redeemer, a spirit of peacefulness, & mutual love, one for the other. Your particular circumstances call upon you for uncommon watchfulness over yourselves, and unusual exertions in all the exercises of a Christian life. The impressions made by your conduct will be lasting impressions; and the opinion, favorable or unfavourable to our holy religion, which shall result from observing your manners, will have consequences extending down to the remotest times.... May the blessed spirit be shed into your hearts, that divine spirit, which drew & held the first Christians together in the bonds of perfect unity. They buried all distinctions of birth and Country in the happy & comfortable character of disciples of Jesus. Of Medes of Parthians, of Jews & proselytes, of Elamites & the natives of Mesopotamia it was said, that their *heart was one, and their soul was one.* To this heavenly disposition of mind and affection God now calls you. Jesus Christ, the Prince of peace, solicits you by his grace to forego all jealousies and contentions; and each one to have no other views in the service of God, but the advancement of his glory, & the salvation of his own, & every one of his neighbours souls.

Sources

An Address From the Roman Catholics of America to George Washington, Esq., President of the United States. London: J. P. Coghlan, 1790.

Binzley, Ronald A. "Ganganelli's Disaffected Children: The Ex-Jesuits and the Shaping of Early American Catholicism, 1773–1790." *USCH* 26 (Spring 2008): 47–77.

Foley, Henry. *Records of the English Province of the Society of Jesus.* Vol. 7. London: 1882.

Melville, Annabelle M. *John Carroll of Baltimore: Founder of the American Catholic Hierarchy.* New York: Scribner's, 1955.

Spalding, Thomas W. "The Maryland Tradition." *USCH* 8 (Spring 1989): 51–58.

———. "The Maryland Catholic Diaspora." *USCH* 8 (Fall 1989): 163–74.

Index

Index

Index

Cheseldyne, Kenylm, 154n17

Chester River, 267n4

Chiapas, 107n2

China, 31

Church of England, 2, 4, 16, 34, 110, 211, 271

Church of England (Maryland), 2, 4, 16, 22, 34, 42, 83, 110, 136, 140–43, 183, 203, 211, 240, 242, 271

Claiborne, William: biography, 39; Calverts' overtures to, 42; as opponent of Lord Baltimore, 6, 18, 39–40, 51n21, 53

Clayland, James, 158

Clement XIV, Pope, 225, 234

Codd, St. Leger, 161

Codignola, Luca, 10

Columbus, Christopher, 105–6

Combes, William, 158, 160

Committee of Secrecy, 160

Committee on Grievances, 200

Conditions of Plantation: and Jesuits, 85–86; promulgated, 30–31; regarding towns, 45; revised, 85

Congregation for the Propagation of the Faith, 5, 10–12, 103–4, 113–16, 270

Congregational Church, 258n13, 262

Congress Poland. *See* White Russia

Connacht Province, 113n11

Connecticut River, 137

Considerations on the Propriety of Imposing Taxes in the British Colonies, 226

Continental Army, 229, 231

Continental Congress: appeals to Canada, 229; declares independence, 230–31; first session, 227; outreach to other colonies, 248–50; and Quebec Act, 228, 244–46, 248; sends mission to Canada, 229–30; at St. Mary's (Philadelphia), 261–62

Coode, John: biography, 154n14; leader of Charles County uprising, 137; and Protestant Association, 139, 149–153, 156

Cooper, Samuel, 232, 255–59

Copley, Thomas, Gen., 140

Copley, Thomas, SJ, 65n10, 69–70, 76, 84–88

Cornwall, 48n20

Cornwallis, Lord Charles, 261

Cowes, 47

Council of State, 179

Council of Trade and Plantations. *See* Board of Trade and Plantations

Coursey, Henry, 158–59, 161

Courthouse Hill, 169

Cromwell, Oliver, 126n17; as Captain-General, 105; deportation of Irish to West Indies, 130; and Fifth Monarchy, 79n15; and Lord Baltimore, 59, 154, 183, 215; as Lord Protector, 127; "Western Design," 100–101

Cuba, 94–95

Darcy, Robert (Earl of Holderness), 207

Darnall, Henry, 154–57, 159–60, 176, 178

Davis, William, 137

Declaration of the Lord Baltimore's Plantation in Maryland, 29–33

Delaware, 271

Delaware Bay, 25

Delaware River, 31, 137

Delmarva Peninsula, 22, 267n4

Devon County, 13

Digges, William, 156, 179

Dominicans, 105–6, 109, 120n15

Dongan, Thomas, 138

Dove (ship), 23–24, 47, 57, 60, 61n6

Dragon (ship), 48–49

Dudley, John, Earl of Warwick, 1

Duke of York. *See* James II

Dulaney, Daniel, Jr., 210, 226, 235–38, 240–43, 253

Dunlap's Maryland Gazette, 230, 253–55

Dunn, Helen, 184, 191–92, 195, 266

Durham, Palatine of, 26

Dutch, 127n18

Dutch America, 21, 138

Earl of Carlisle. *See* Hay, James

Earl of Holderness. *See* Darcy, Robert

Eastern Shore (Maryland), 24, 40n16, 51n21, 58, 135, 154, 158n24, 171, 189–90, 210, 217, 220, 224, 232, 262, 266–68

Eden, Robert, 226–27

Elizabeth I, 2–3, 16, 36, 104

England, 2, 5–10, 12–13, 16, 21–22, 24, 26–28,

Index

Index

Index

Sayer, Peter, 154, 158–61

Scilly Isles, 48–49

Schneider, Theodore, 171, 189

Scotland, 169, 209, 224

Searle, Daniel, Gov., 127

Select Body of the Clergy, 262, 270n7

Seven Years' War, 202, 204, 255, 246n10, 255

Seville, 31

Sewall, Nicholas, 156, 158–59, 161

Seymour, John, 166–69, 172, 174

Sharpe, Horatio, 201, 203, 207, 210, 218

Sherwill, Nicholas, 13

Sherwill, Thomas, 13

Sicily, 31

Simpson, Robert, 45

Smith, Anthony, 13

Smith, John, 30

Smith, Roger, 19

Society for the Propagation of the Gospel in Foreign Parts, 209

Society of Jesus: annual reports, 60; bequest of James Carroll to, 180n6; and Calverts, 12, 84; and Henry Neale, 187; image in British Empire, 23, 224; Institute, 93n6; in New York, 138; in Philadelphia, 171; and Select Body of the Clergy, 262; suppression of, 225, 232–34. *See also* Maryland Jesuits

Sodom, 109

Some Thoughts upon America, and upon the Danger from Roman Catholicks, 205–6

South Carolina, 228

Spain: and American Revolution, 231–32, 259; and Catholic colonization, 9; and Mary Tudor, 2; as New World competitor, 8; as object of England imperial designs, 101, 105–6, 109–10; and Thomas Gage, 105–6; in West Indies, 121, 126, 127n18

Spanish Armada, 2, 109–10

Spanish Coast, 50

Spikes Bay, 124

Stamp Act, 220, 226

Stock, Simon: as assistant to George Calvert, 4, 22; and Avalon, 12n15; and

evangelization, 11; and Newfoundland, 10; and Propaganda Fide, 5, 9–12, 113

Stonyhurst, 269

Stourton, Erasmus, 5, 12–13

Straits of Hercules, 50

Strickland, William, 268

Stritch, John, 103, 116, 118–19, 120n15, 122

Stuarts, 3, 59, 103, 135. *See also* Charles I; Charles II; James I; James II; James Edward

Suffolk County Resolves, 244

Sulpicians, 263

Susquehanna tribe, 54, 58, 73–75, 84, 144

Sweatnam, Edward, 159–60

Swedes, 38

Talbot, George, 150n8

Talbot County, 158n21, 158n24, 159n25, 190

Tayac (Kittamaquund), 65–66, 68

Tea Act, 227

Tertre, Jean Baptiste du, 120n15

Test Act, 210–11

Thames River, 52–53

Thurling, John, 154

Tiber River, 225

Tobacco in Maryland: 32, 57, 191, 194

Tobacco Inspection Act, 226

Toleration Act of *1649,* 167

Tort, 122

Tower of London, 104, 138

Treaty of Paris, 228, 246n10, 256

Trinity College, Oxford, 4

Tuckahoe, 194, 196

Tuesday Club, 210

Turks, 50

Two Brothers, The (ship), 124

Vicar-Apostolic of the London District, 271

Victory (ship), 13

Villiers, Christopher, Lord of Anglesey, 13n17

Virginia: and American Revolution, 261, 271; Bacon's rebellion, 137; Cecil Calvert argues Maryland not a threat to, 36–38; Cecil Calvert's instructions regarding, 39–44; climate in, 31; Copley and companion in, 76; death of Calvert's wife, 21; distance

Intestine Enemies: Catholics in Protestant America, 1605–1791: A Documentary History was designed and typeset in Arno by Kachergis Book Design of Pittsboro, North Carolina. It was printed on 60-pound House Natural Smooth, and bound by Sheridan Books of Chelsea, Michigan.